the best ever
20Minute
cookbook

20 the best ever Minute cookbook

200 fabulous fuss-free recipes for the busy cook, including instant indulgences, healthy snacks, family meals and last-minute entertaining, with over 750 photographs

Jenni Fleetwood

southwater

This edition is published by Southwater, an imprint of Anness Publishing Ltd, Blaby Road, Wigston, Leicestershire LE18 4SE

Email: info@anness.com

Web: www.southwaterbooks.com; www.annesspublishing.com

If you like the images in this book and would like to investigate using them for publishing, promotions or advertising, please visit our website www.practicalpictures.com for more information.

Publisher: Joanna Lorenz
Editorial Director: Helen Sudell
Project Editor: Catherine Stuart
Production Controller: Wendy Lawson
Book Design: Diane Pullen
Cover Design: Louise Clements
Contributors: Pepita Aris, Mridula Baljekar, Jane Bamforth, Alex Barker, Judy Bastyra, Georgina Campbell, Coralie Dorman, Matthew Drennan, Joanna Farrow, Maria Filippelli, Jenni Fleetwood, Christine France, Brian Glover, Juliet Harbutt, Simona Hill, Becky Johnson, Bridget Jones, Lucy Knox, Jane Milton, Suzannah Olivier, Keith Richmond, Rena Salaman, Marlena Spieler, Liz Trigg, Linda Tubby, Sunil Vijayakar, Jenny White, Biddy White-Lennon, Kate Whiteman, Rosemary Wilkinson, Jeni Wright
Photography: Karl Adamson, Edward Allwright, Caroline Barty, Steve Baxter, Martin Brigdale, Nicki Dowey, James Duncan, Michelle Garrett, John Heseltine, Amanda Heywood, Janine Hosegood, Don Last, William Lingwood, Craig Robertson and Sam Stowell

ETHICAL TRADING POLICY

Because of our ongoing ecological investment programme, you, as our customer, can have the pleasure and reassurance of knowing that a tree is being cultivated on your behalf to naturally replace the materials used to make the book you are holding. For further information about this scheme, go to www.annesspublishing.com/trees

NOTES

Bracketed terms are intended for American readers.
For all recipes, quantities are given in both metric and imperial measures and, where appropriate, measures are also given in standard cups and spoons. Follow one set of measures, but not a mixture, because they are not interchangeable.
Standard spoon and cup measures are level. 1 tsp = 5ml, 1 tbsp = 15ml, 1 cup = 250ml/8fl oz.
Australian standard tablespoons are 20ml.
Australian readers should use 3 tsp in place of 1 tbsp for measuring small quantities.
American pints are 16fl oz/2 cups. American readers should use 20fl oz/2.5 cups in place of 1 pint when measuring liquids.
Electric oven temperatures in this book are for conventional ovens. When using a fan oven, the temperature will probably need to be reduced by about 10–20°C/20–40°F. Since ovens vary, you should check with your manufacturer's instruction book for guidance.
The nutritional analysis given for each recipe is calculated per portion (i.e. serving or item), unless otherwise stated. If the recipe gives a range, such as Serves 4–6, then the nutritional analysis will be for the smaller portion size, i.e. 6 servings.
The analysis does not include optional ingredients, such as salt added to taste.
Medium eggs (US large) are used unless otherwise stated.

PUBLISHER'S NOTE

CONTENTS

GREAT FOOD FAST

Twenty minutes isn't very long. You can easily spend that amount of time puzzling over a crossword clue, or trying to telephone a company determined to leave you on hold, or waiting for a cup of coffee in a busy restaurant. So can you cook a meal in twenty minutes? Yes you can, and this is the book to tell you how to do it.

When you want great food fast, what you need in your repertoire are easy, no-fuss recipes: breakfasts you can blitz in a blender; lunches you can prepare and pack in next to no time, and suppers that raise your spirits without sapping any of the energy you have left at the end of the day. You want food that looks as good as it tastes, but doesn't require you to carve a rose out of a radish. If you are entertaining, you want to do so in style, but without missing more than a few moments of your guests' company.

You can achieve these aims – after a fashion – by frequenting the ready meal section of your favourite supermarket. Some days you'll do just that, but it is much more rewarding and nutritious to serve something you've cooked yourself. Dishing up a ready meal is rather like reading a raunchy novel; satisfying as far as it goes, but sadly lacking as a sensory experience.

AN EXPERIENCE WORTH HAVING

Food isn't just fuel and providing it need not be seen as a chore. When you prepare a meal you engage all your senses. The glowing colours of ingredients – a bunch of basil, a bowl of tomatoes, a basket of blueberries – are a delight to see. When you prepare them, your sense of touch comes into play. You cut a lemon or a lime, and immediately a lovely citrus aroma permeates the room. The pleasure continues with other satisfying smells: onions sizzling in a pan, apples and cloves simmering on the stove. With cooking smells come cooking sounds, and all help to stimulate the appetite. Before you take a single bite, you've already experienced a range of remarkable sensory experiences, and taste, the final food frontier, is still to come. Looked at that way, it isn't surprising that many of us love to cook, and would do much more of it if only we had the time.

PRESSING PRIORITIES

Time. There's the rub. We never seem to have enough of it. Whether you are a student, trying to balance study with a hectic social life, a single person trying to carve out a career or a parent with a different but equally pressing set of

Above: Ready-made dips and pâtés are always on the supermarket shopping list, but it's so easy to produce your own with just a few ingredients.

priorities, time is a precious luxury. We're all riding the rollercoaster, rushing from home to work to home to sport to parents' evening to home to sleep. Putting good food on the table should be in there somewhere, but sometimes it is difficult to achieve. That's why this book takes a pragmatic approach. Preparing your own vegetables is ideal, but if buying a bag of shake-it-out salad or some ready trimmed beans means you can eat well and still get to your night class, go for it. Look out for quick-cook versions of favourite ingredients, like polenta and rice, and don't be afraid of mixing bought items like pesto or tapenade with home-cooked pasta.

There is no longer any rule about precisely what constitutes a meal. You can have soup and a toasted sandwich one day, a stir-fry the next and a sophisticated treat like pan-fried steaks with whisky and cream on a Friday night. A simple one-pot dish like pork and pineapple coconut curry can be served solo, or with noodles that only take a minute or so to prepare. There will be some occasions when you will want to offer a vegetable side dish, and others when the dish is so complete in itself that a chunk of bread is all that is required. What matters is that you cook

Left: This melt-in-the-mouth dish of honey-glazed aubergines is just one of many innovative recipes that can be turned around in a few simple steps, and will never fail to impress.

Right: A tight time frame doesn't mean you can't experiment – a vegetarian version of this Spiced Chicken Risotto is just as easily prepared as its meaty counterpart. Many other recipes in the book offer useful tips and variations.

what you know you can cope with in the time available, and serve up something which everyone will enjoy.

THE RECIPES

The aim of this book is to provide a wide-ranging selection of recipes that can be cooked in twenty minutes or less. That's assuming the cook is reasonably experienced. If you've never chopped an onion in your life, it is likely to take you a little longer. Efficient cooking is all about organization, so do read through your chosen recipe carefully, assemble your ingredients and give some thought to strategy. If something has to go in the oven, switch it on to heat up before you do anything else; if you need to add grated cheese in Step 4, grate it straight away. Recipe methods reflect this, but you need to

Below: A sudden craving for your favourite dessert – like this glorious Baked Pineapple Alaska – can be answered in twenty minutes or less.

work within the bounds of your own ability, and the confines of your own kitchen. If a recipe calls for a slotted spoon and you need to rummage under the sink for one, you could lose valuable time, so be as well prepared as possible. If you are inexperienced, the best way to start is by choosing the shortest recipes of 10 minutes or less, or opt for something that needs no cooking at all, such as a salad. Also,

enlist aid when you can. Something as simple as having a child or partner line up ingredients can be a huge help.

Some of the recipes in this book, particularly those in the chapter entitled Easy Entertaining, require some advance preparation. The timeline at the top of the recipe will make it clear when this is required, and there'll probably be some mention of the fact in the recipe introduction, so do watch out for this. In most cases, the recipe still won't take more than 20 minutes in all, but the preparation will be in stages and not all at the same time. There are times when advance preparation is an advantage – when you want to get some dinner party cooking out of the way early, for instance.

When you have extra time on your hands, consider making stock or a few sauces that can be frozen for later use. Then, when you are in a rush, you'll have the means to make a simple speedy meal that tastes great. You'll find recipes for these, and ideas for quick and easy accompaniments, in the opening chapter. Also in this section are some suggested menus for special occasions. These show how easy it is to mix and match three or four courses and produce a meal that is stunningly simple and tastes delicious.

THE 20-MINUTE KITCHEN

Although having the right recipes gives you the best start when it comes to producing great food in the shortest possible time, there are some other criteria to consider. Every workman needs decent tools, and having a well-equipped kitchen will help you to make more efficient use of your time. This doesn't mean owning every new gadget on the market, but it is sensible to invest in good quality knives and pans, accurate measuring equipment, spoons and spatulas and a few well-chosen appliances. A food processor is just about essential these days, particularly when speed is a prime consideration, and you will also benefit from having a good hand-held electric beater. The quick cook also needs a heavy griddle pan — for cooking items like salmon, duck and Mediterranean vegetables — and a wok for the stir-fries that are central to swift cooking. It also helps to have a repertoire of simple sauces and stocks, which can be made in advance and kept in the freezer. Some of the recipes in this book suggest suitable accompaniments, but if you need more inspiration, you'll find it right here.

EQUIPMENT: PANS, CUTTING AND MEASURING

You don't need a kitchen full of equipment to be a spontaneous and versatile cook. It is quality, not quantity, that counts when you're preparing and cooking food, particularly when choosing essential pieces of equipment such as pans and knives. As long as you look after them, these items should last for many years so are well worth the investment. The following section guides you through the essential items that make cooking as simple and enjoyable as possible, and also offers suggestions on how to improvise if you don't have the right piece of equipment.

PANS AND BAKEWARE

Always choose good quality pans with a solid, heavy base because they retain heat better and are less likely to warp or buckle. Heatproof glass lids are useful because they allow you to check cooking progress without having to uncover the pan repeatedly.

Pans: small, medium and large

When cooking large quantities of food, such as pasta or rice that need to be boiled in a large amount of water, the bigger the pan the better. It does not matter whether the pan is non-stick, but it is useful to have heatproof handles and lids so that the pan can double as a large ovenproof cookpot. A medium pan is ideal for cooking sauces and similar mixtures. For these a non-stick pan is best; it will help to prevent thickened sauces sticking and burning. Washing-up will also be easier. The same guidelines apply to a small pan, which is ideal for small quantities.

Frying pan

Select a non-stick pan that is shallow enough, so that it is easy to slide a metal spatula into it. A pan with an ovenproof handle and lid can be placed in the oven as a shallow casserole dish, and under the grill (broiler).

Baking sheets

Having one or two non-stick baking sheets on hand in the kitchen is invaluable to the busy cook. They can be used for a multitude of tasks such as roasting hazelnuts, or they can be placed under full dishes in the oven to catch any drips if the mixture overflows. Choose good quality heavy baking sheets that will not buckle in the oven.

Roasting pan

As a quick cook you may only roast meat or vegetables occasionally, but when you do, a good, heavy roasting pan is essential. Choose a large pan; you will achieve better results if there is room for heat to circulate as the food cooks. Potatoes, for example, will not crisp well if they are crammed together in a small pan. Treat all pans with care to get maximum usage from them.

Below: Baking sheets are essential to the 20-minute kitchen – having more than one will mean several things can be cooked at the same time.

CUTTING AND GRINDING

Chopping, slicing, cutting, peeling and grinding are all essential aspects of food preparation so it's important to have the right tools for the job.

Chopping boards

Essential in every kitchen, these can be made of wood or plastic. Wooden boards tend to be heavier and more stable, but they must be thoroughly scrubbed in hot soapy water and properly dried. Plastic boards are easier to clean and better for cutting meat, poultry and fish.

Knives: cook's, vegetable and serrated

When buying knives, choose the best ones you can afford. They should feel comfortable in your hand, so try several different types and practise a cutting action before you buy. You will

Left: It is wise to invest in three good quality pans of different sizes.

need three different knives. A cook's knife is a good multi-purpose knife. The blade is usually about 18cm/7in long, but you may find that you prefer a slightly longer or shorter blade. A vegetable knife is a small version of the cook's knife and is used for finer cutting. A large serrated knife is essential for slicing bread and ingredients such as tomatoes, which have a hard-to-cut skin compared to the soft flesh underneath. Store knives safely and securely, out of reach of young children.

Vegetable peelers

These can have a fixed or swivel blade. Both types will make quick work of peeling vegetables and fruit, with less waste than a small knife.

Graters

These come in various shapes and sizes. Box graters have several different cutting blades and are easy to handle. Microplane graters have razor-sharp blades that retain their sharp edges. It is worth investing in several of these, with different grating surfaces.

MEASURING EQUIPMENT

Accurate measuring equipment is essential, particularly when making breads and cakes, which need very precise quantities of ingredients.

Weighing scales

These are good for measuring dry ingredients. Digital scales are the most accurate but balance scales that use weights or a sliding weight are also a good choice. Spring scales with a scoop and dial are not usually as precise.

Measuring cups

Suitable for dry or liquid ingredients, these standard measures usually come in a set of separate cups for different fractions or portions of a full cup.

Measuring jug/pitcher

This is essential for liquids. A heatproof glass jug is useful because it allows hot liquids to be measured and makes it easy to check the quantity.

Measuring spoons

Table cutlery varies in size, so a set of standard measuring spoons is extremely useful for measuring small quantities.

Left: The traditional box grater is solid, reliable and easy to handle – with several different grating blades.

Looking after knives

Although it might seem contradictory, the sharper the knife, the safer it is to use. It takes far more effort to use a blunt knife and this often results in accidents. Try to get into the habit of sharpening your knives regularly, because the blunter they become, the more difficult they are to use and the longer it will take to sharpen them. Always wash knives carefully after use and dry them thoroughly to prevent discolouring or rusting.

Below: Compact kitchen utensils such as measuring jugs and cups are vital to the art of successful quick cooking.

EQUIPMENT: BLENDING, BAKING, GRIDDLING AND WOK-FRYING

MIXING, ROLLING AND DRAINING

Bowls, spoons, whisks and strainers are vital to the 20-minute kitchen. Establish suitable places to store the following equipment, so that you always know where to find it in a hurry. Having essentials to hand is one of the golden rules of successful quick cooking.

Mixing bowls

You will need one large and one small bowl. Heatproof glass bowls are a good choice because they can be placed over a pan of simmering water to heat delicate sauces and to melt chocolate.

Wooden spoons

Inexpensive and essential for stirring and beating, every kitchen should have two or three wooden spoons.

Metal slotted spoon

This large spoon with draining holes is very useful for lifting small pieces of food out of cooking liquid.

Fish slice/metal spatula

This is invaluable for lifting delicate fish fillets and other foods out of a pan.

Rolling pin

A heavy wooden or marble rolling pin is useful for rolling out pastry. If you don't have one, use a clean, dry, tall glass bottle (such as a wine bottle) instead.

Balloon whisk

A metal balloon whisk is great for softly whipping cream and whisking sauces to a smooth consistency. Whisks are available in all shapes and sizes. Do not buy an enormous whisk that is difficult to use and will not fit into pans. Mini-whisks are not essential – you can always use a fork instead.

Sieve/Strainer

For sifting flour, icing (confectioners') sugar, cocoa and other dry ingredients, a stainless-steel sieve is essential. It can also be used for straining small quantities of cooked vegetables, pasta and rice. Wash and dry a sieve well after use to prevent it becoming heavily clogged and damp.

Colander

Choose a free-standing metal colander with feet on the base. This has the advantage of leaving both hands free to empty heavy pans, and will keep the base of the colander above the liquid that is being drained off.

ELECTRICAL APPLIANCES

Although not always essential, these can speed up preparation.

Food processor

This fabulous invention can make life a lot easier. It is perfect for processing soft and hard foods and is more versatile than a blender, which is best suited to puréeing very soft foods or liquids.

Hand-held electric whisk

A small, hand-held electric whisk or beater is very useful for making cakes, whipping cream and whisking egg whites. Choose an appliance with sturdy beaters and a powerful motor that will last.

Above: Wooden spoons and spatulas are essential for stirring, beating and lifting.

Below: A food processor is the quick cook's best friend, especially if it has a mini bowl – perfect for grinding nuts or making breadcrumbs for toppings.

Above: Cookie cutters come in all kinds of shapes and sizes.

Above: A pastry brush is useful when baking or grilling (broiling).

EXTRA EQUIPMENT

As well as the essential items, some recipes require other items such as tart tins (pans) and cookie cutters. The following are some items you may find useful, whether you are putting together a speedy snack or attempting something more elaborate.

Cookie cutters

These make quick work of cutting out pastry and cookie dough. Metal ones have a sharper cutting edge so are usually preferable to plastic ones. If you don't have cutters, you can use a glass which is much quicker.

Pastry brush

Made of bristle, with a wooden or plastic handle, this is useful for brushing food lightly with liquid – for example, brushing meat or fish with oil or marinade while grilling (broiling).

CAKE TINS/PANS

These can have loose bottoms or spring-clip sides to allow easy removal of the cake. Be sure to use the size specified in the recipe.

Tartlet tins/muffin pans

These consist of six or twelve fairly deep cups in a tray. They can be used for baking tartlets, muffins, cupcakes, buns and bread rolls.

Tart tins/pans

Available with straight or fluted sides, these are not as deep as tartlet tins (muffin pans). They come in a variety of sizes, from individual containers to very large tins. They are useful for baking all kinds of sweet and savoury tarts. Loose-bottomed tins are best because they allow you to remove the contents more easily.

Skewers

These are used for kebabs and other skewered foods. Metal skewers are reusable and practical if you cook over the barbecue frequently, or cook kebabs that need lengthy cooking. Bamboo skewers are disposable and useful for foods that cook quickly – soak them in cold water before use to stop them burning.

Palette knife/metal spatula

Use this large, flat, round-bladed, blunt knife for spreading or flipping pancakes.

Griddle pan

A good quality, heavy griddle pan is useful for cooking meat and fish. The pan should be very hot before food is placed on it and you should brush the surface of the food with a little oil to prevent it from sticking, rather than adding oil to the pan. To clean, hot soapy water can be used but make sure the pan has cooled before washing, and then rinse and dry thoroughly. Do not plunge into water for soaking.

Above: A heavy griddle pan is a boon to the quick cook.

Wok

Larger and deeper than a frying pan, often with a rounded base, a wok has high sides and a large surface area, which make it ideal for stir-frying, steaming and simmering. Clean with hot water (no soap) and wipe with kitchen paper until the paper comes away clean.

Below: Woks come with one or two handles. The two-handled variety makes a good table centrepiece when dishing up a sizzling supper from wok to plate during a dinner party or family meal.

SIMPLE WAYS TO FLAVOUR FOOD

As well as selecting the cooking method best suited to the ingredients, there are several quick and simple methods of adding flavour using herbs, spices and aromatics. Match the seasoning to the ingredient and go for simple techniques such as marinating, stuffing or coating with a dry spice rub, which will help to intensify the flavours. The longer you leave food in a marinade or with a rub, the more the flavours will penetrate, so if you want to incorporate these techniques in a quick meal, you need to do a bit of forward planning.

FLAVOURS FOR FISH

Classic aromatics used for flavouring fish and shellfish include lemon, lime, parsley, dill, fennel and bay leaves. These flavours all have a fresh, intense quality that complements the delicate taste of fish and shellfish without overpowering it. All work well added before, during or after cooking, either as a filling or a marinade.

• To flavour whole fish, such as trout or mackerel, stuff a few lemon slices and some fresh parsley or basil into the body cavity before cooking. Season with plenty of salt and freshly ground black pepper, then wrap the fish in foil or baking parchment, ensuring the packet is well sealed. Place the fish in an ovenproof dish or on a baking tray and bake until cooked through.
• To make an unusual, yet delicious, marinade for salmon, arrange the salmon fillets in a single layer in an overproof dish. Drizzle the fillets with a little light olive oil and add a split vanilla pod. Cover and chill for a couple of hours before cooking.

• To marinate chunky fillets of fish, such as cod or salmon, arrange the fish fillets in a dish in a single layer. Drizzle the fish with olive oil, then sprinkle over a little crushed garlic and grated lime rind and squeeze over lime juice. Cover the dish in clear film (plastic wrap) and leave to marinate in the refrigerator for at least 30 minutes. Grill (broil) lightly until just cooked through.

PEPPING UP MEAT AND POULTRY

Meat and poultry can take both delicate and punchy seasonings. Dry rubs, marinades and sticky glazes are all perfect ways to introduce flavour into the food. Marinating the tougher cuts, such as stewing steak, also helps to make the meat more tender. A quick way of introducing flavour to meat is to inject it with marinade using a veterinary syringe.

• To make a fragrant Cajun spice rub for pork chops, steaks and chicken, mix together 5ml/1 tsp each dried thyme, dried oregano, finely crushed black peppercorns, salt, crushed cumin seeds and hot paprika. Rub the Cajun spice mix into the raw meat or poultry, then barbecue or bake until cooked.

• To marinate red meat, such as beef, lamb or venison, prepare a mixture of two-thirds red wine to one-third olive oil in a shallow non-metallic dish. Stir in some chopped garlic and bruised fresh rosemary sprigs. Add the meat and turn to coat it in the marinade. Cover and chill for at least 2 hours or overnight before cooking.
• To make a mildly-spiced sticky mustard glaze for chicken, pork or red meat, mix 45ml/3 tbsp each Dijon mustard, clear honey and demerara (raw) sugar, 2.5ml/½ tsp chilli powder, 1.5ml/¼ tsp ground cloves, and salt and ground black pepper. Cook the poultry or meat over the barbecue or under the grill (broiler) and brush with the glaze about 10 minutes before the end of the cooking time.
• A lemon grass and ginger marinade that can be whizzed up in the food processor is quick and easy and works well with chicken or pork. Chop the lower half of two lemon grass stalks and put them in the bowl of a food processor with 30ml/2 tbsp sliced fresh root ginger, 6 chopped garlic cloves, 4 chopped shallots, ½ bunch chopped coriander (cilantro) roots, 30ml/2 tbsp each Thai fish sauce and light soy sauce, 120ml/4fl oz/½ cup coconut milk and 1 tbsp palm sugar. Process until smooth, pour over 8 chicken portions and marinate for at least 4 hours. Bake the chicken pieces in the oven or cook over a barbecue, brushing them with the marinade once or twice during cooking.

Below: Brush on sticky glazes towards the end of the cooking time; if the glaze is cooked for too long, it will burn.

Above: Adding a drizzle of sesame oil to stir-fried vegetables gives them a wonderfully rich, smoky, nutty flavour.

VIBRANT VEGETABLES

Most fresh vegetables have a subtle flavour that needs to be brought out and enhanced. When using speedy cooking methods such as steaming and stir-frying, go for light, fresh flavourings that will enhance the taste of the vegetables. When using more robust cooking methods, such as roasting, choose richer flavours such as garlic and spices.

• To make fragrant, Asian-style steamed vegetables, add a bruised stalk of lemon grass and/or a few kaffir lime leaves to the steaming water, then cook vegetables such as pak choi (bok choy) over the water until just tender. Alternatively, place the aromatics in the steamer under the vegetables and steam as before until just tender.
• To add a rich flavour to stir-fried vegetables, add a splash of sesame oil just before the end of cooking time. (Do not use more than 5ml/1 tsp because sesame oil has a very strong flavour and can be overpowering.)

• To enhance the taste of naturally sweet vegetables, such as parsnips and carrots, glaze them with honey and mustard before roasting. Mix together 30ml/2 tbsp wholegrain mustard and 45ml/3 tbsp clear honey, and season with salt and ground black pepper. Brush the glaze over the prepared vegetables to coat completely, then roast until sweet and tender. To cut the roasting time, par-boil the vegetables first.

FRAGRANT RICE AND GRAINS

Classic accompaniments, such as rice and couscous, can be enhanced by the addition of simple flavourings. Adding herbs, spices and aromatics can help to perk up the rice and grains' subtle flavour without overpowering them. Always choose flavourings that will complement the dish with which the rice or grains will be served.

• To make exotic fragrant rice to serve with Asian-style stir-fries and braised dishes, add a whole star anise or a few cardamom pods to a pan of rice before cooking. The rice will absorb the flavour during cooking. Remove the spices from the pan using a slotted spoon just before serving the rice.

• To make zesty herb rice or couscous, heat a little chopped fresh tarragon and grated lemon rind in olive oil or melted butter until warm, then drizzle the flavoured oil and herbs over freshly cooked rice or couscous.

• To make simple fresh herb rice or couscous, fork plenty of chopped fresh parsley and chives through the cooked grains and drizzle over a little oil just before serving.

• Add roasted seeds to rice for a delicious flavour. Place 50g/2oz/6 tbsp mixed pumpkin seeds and sunflower seeds in a non-stick frying pan over a medium heat. Toss until golden, cool, and mix into cooked long grain rice.

Basics: Oils, Stocks, Marinades and Dressings

Having a few ready-made basics, such as stocks, pasta sauces and flavoured oils, can really speed up everyday cooking. They can all be bought ready-made in the supermarket, but they are easy to make at home. Stocks take time to prepare, but they can be stored in the freezer for several months. Flavoured oils are straightforward and keep in the same way as ordinary oils so it's well worth having a few in the cupboard. All the basic sauces, dressings, marinades and flavoured creams on the following pages are simple to prepare and can either be made fresh or in advance.

FLAVOURED OILS

Good quality olive oil can be flavoured with herbs, spices and aromatics for drizzling, dressing and cooking.

Herb-infused oil

Half-fill a jar with washed and dried fresh herbs such as rosemary or basil. Pour over olive oil to cover, then seal the jar and place in a cool, dark place for 3 days. Strain the oil into a clean jar or bottle and discard the herbs.

Lemon oil

Finely pare the rind from one lemon, place on kitchen paper, and leave to dry for 1 day. Add the dried rind to a bottle of olive oil and leave to infuse for up to 3 days. Strain the oil into a clean bottle and discard the rind.

Chilli oil

Add several dried chillies to a bottle of olive oil and leave to infuse for about 2 weeks before using. If the flavour is

not sufficiently pronounced, leave for another week. The chillies can be left in the bottle and give a very decorative and colourful effect.

Garlic oil

Add several whole garlic cloves to a bottle of olive oil and leave to infuse for about 2 weeks before using. If the flavour is not sufficiently pronounced, leave the oil to infuse for another week, then strain the oil into a clean bottle and store in a cool, dark place.

STOCKS

When you have a little time on your hands, make stock. A supply of home-made stock in the freezer gives you the basis of dozens of quick and easy dishes, including risotto and a range of sauces. It's also a great way of using up leftover chicken, meat and fish, or a surplus of vegetables. To freeze, pour the cooled stock into 600ml/1 pint/2½ cup containers and freeze for up to 2 months.

Chicken stock

Put a 1.3kg/3lb chicken carcass into a large pan with 2 peeled and quartered onions, 2 halved carrots, 2 roughly chopped celery sticks, 1 bouquet garni, 1 peeled garlic clove and 5 black peppercorns. Pour in 1.2 litres/2 pints/5 cups cold water and bring to the boil. Reduce the heat, cover and simmer for 4–5 hours, regularly skimming off any scum from the surface and adding more water if needed. Strain the stock through a sieve (strainer) lined with kitchen paper and leave to cool.

Beef stock

Preheat the oven to 230°C/450°F/Gas 8. Put 1.8kg/4lb beef bones in a roasting pan and roast for 40 minutes, until browned, turning occasionally. Transfer the bones and vegetables to a large pan. Cover with water, add 2 chopped tomatoes and cook as for chicken stock.

Fish stock

Put 2 chopped onions, 1.3kg/3lb fish bones and heads, 300ml/½ pint/1¼ cups white wine, 5 black peppercorns and 1 bouquet garni in a large pan. Pour in 2 litres/3½ pints/9 cups water. Bring to the boil and simmer for 20 minutes, skimming often. Strain.

Vegetable stock

Put 900g/2lb chopped vegetables, including onions, leeks, tomatoes, carrots, parsnips and cabbage, in a large pan. Pour in 1.5 litres/2½ pints/6¼ cups water. Bring to the boil and simmer for 30 minutes, then strain.

MARINADES

These strong-tasting mixes are perfect for adding flavour to meat, poultry, fish and vegetables. Most ingredients should be marinated for at least 30 minutes.

Ginger and soy marinade

This is perfect for use with chicken and beef. Peel and grate a 2.5cm/1in piece of fresh root ginger and peel and finely chop a large garlic clove. In a small bowl, whisk 60ml/4 tbsp olive oil with 75ml/5 tbsp dark soy sauce. Season with ground black pepper and stir in the ginger and garlic.

Rosemary and garlic marinade

This is ideal for robust fish, lamb and chicken. Roughly chop the leaves from 3 fresh rosemary sprigs. Finely chop 2 garlic cloves and whisk with the rosemary, 75ml/5 tbsp olive oil and the juice of 1 lemon. Add the grated rind of the lemon too, if you like.

Lemon grass and lime marinade

Use this delicately-flavoured marinade with pieces of fish and chicken. Finely chop 1 lemon grass stalk. Whisk the grated rind and juice of 1 lime with 75ml/5 tbsp olive oil, salt and black pepper to taste, and the lemon grass.

Red wine and bay marinade

This easy-to-learn marinade is ideal for flavouring red meat, particularly if you want to soften the texture of tougher cuts. Whisk together 150ml/¼ pint/ ⅔ cup red wine, 1 finely chopped garlic clove, 2 torn fresh bay leaves and 45ml/3 tbsp olive oil. Season to taste with black pepper.

Below: Marinades containing red wine are particularly good for tenderizing tougher cuts of meat such as stewing steak.

DRESSINGS

Freshly made dressings are delicious drizzled over salads but are also tasty served with cooked vegetables and simply cooked fish, meat and poultry. You can make these dressings a few hours in advance and store them in a sealed container in the refrigerator until ready to use. Give them a quick whisk before drizzling over the food.

Honey and wholegrain mustard dressing

Drizzle this sweet, peppery dressing over leafy salads, fish, chicken and red meat dishes or toss with warm new potatoes. Whisk together 15ml/1 tbsp wholegrain mustard, 30ml/2 tbsp white wine vinegar, 15ml/1 tbsp honey and 75ml/5 tbsp extra virgin olive oil and season generously with salt and ground black pepper.

Orange and tarragon dressing

Serve this fresh, tangy dressing with salads and grilled (broiled) fish. In a small bowl, whisk the rind and juice of 1 large orange with 45ml/3 tbsp olive oil and 15ml/1 tbsp chopped fresh tarragon. Season with salt and plenty of ground black pepper to taste and chill before use if possible.

Toasted coriander and cumin dressing

Drizzle this warm, spicy dressing over grilled (broiled) chicken, lamb or beef. Heat a small frying pan and sprinkle in 15ml/1 tbsp each coriander and cumin seeds. Dry-fry until the seeds release their aromas and start to pop, then crush the seeds using a mortar and pestle. Add 45ml/3 tbsp olive oil, whisk to combine, then leave to infuse for 20 minutes. Season with salt and pepper to taste.

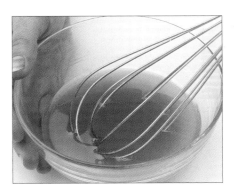

Lemon and horseradish dressing

This tangy dressing is particularly good with cooked beetroot. For a quick and easy lunch, serve it with smoked mackerel and a herb salad. There is no need to dress the salad – this delight-fully creamy relish will do very nicely sitting on the side of the plate. In a small bowl, combine 30ml/2 tbsp freshly squeezed lemon juice and 30ml/2 tbsp mirin or dry sherry. Whisk well, then add 120ml/4fl oz/½ cup olive oil, continuing to whisk the dressing until it emulsifies. Whisk in 30ml/2 tbsp creamed horseradish. Taste the dressing, and add a little salt and black pepper, if you think it needs it. The dressing should be smooth in texture.

BASICS: SAVOURY SAUCES AND DIPS

A repertoire of simple savoury sauce recipes is a must for the versatile quick cook. The following suggestions can be stirred through pasta and grains, heaped on baked potatoes, used to add interest to simple grilled (broiled) meats or fish, or served as savoury dips.

SAVOURY SAUCES

The following classic sauces can be made in a matter of minutes, and are so much nicer than their ready-bought counterparts. You'll need a blender for the pesto variations.

Easy tomato sauce

Toss with pasta, top a pizza or serve with fish and chicken. Heat 15ml/1 tbsp olive oil in a pan, add 1 chopped onion and fry for 2–3 minutes until soft. Add 1 chopped garlic clove and cook for 1 minute more. Pour in 400g/14oz chopped canned tomatoes and stir in 15ml/1 tbsp tomato purée (paste). Add 30ml/2 tbsp dried oregano and simmer for 15 minutes, until thickened. Season.

Quick satay sauce

Serve this spicy Asian-style sauce with grilled (broiled) chicken, beef or prawns (shrimp), or toss with freshly cooked egg noodles. Put 30ml/2 tbsp crunchy peanut butter in a pan and stir in 150ml/¼ pint/⅔ cup coconut milk, 45ml/3 tbsp hot water, a pinch of chilli powder and 30ml/2 tbsp light soy sauce. Heat gently, stirring until the peanut butter has melted and the mixture is well blended. Simmer for about a minute and serve immediately, while still hot.

Mustard cheese sauce

Stir this sauce through pasta, or serve with vegetables or baked white fish. Melt around 25g/1oz/2 tbsp butter in a medium pan and stir in 25g/1oz/¼ cup plain (all-purpose) flour. Remove the pan from the heat and stir in 5ml/1 tsp prepared English mustard.

Gradually add 200ml/7fl oz/scant 1 cup milk, stirring well to remove any lumps. (If the sauce becomes lumpy, whisk until smooth.) Return the pan to the heat and bring to the boil, stirring constantly. Remove from the heat and stir in 115g/4oz/1 cup grated Gruyère or Cheddar cheese. Continue to blend, away from the heat, until the cheese has melted and the texture is smooth. Season to taste.

Traditional pesto

This classic Italian sauce is made with basil, garlic, pine nuts and Parmesan cheese but there are many variations. Toss with pasta, stir into mashed potatoes or plain boiled rice, or use to flavour sauces and dressings. Put 50g/2oz fresh basil leaves in a food processor and blend to a paste with 25g/1oz/¼ cup toasted pine nuts and 2 peeled garlic cloves. With the motor still running, drizzle in 120ml/4fl oz/½ cup extra virgin olive oil until the mixture forms a paste. Spoon the pesto into a bowl and stir in 25g/1oz/⅓ cup freshly grated Parmesan cheese. Season to taste with salt and ground black pepper.

Parsley and walnut pesto

Put 50g/2oz fresh parsley leaves in a food processor and blend to a paste with 25g/1oz/¼ cup walnuts and 2 peeled garlic cloves. With the motor still running, drizzle in 120ml/4fl oz/½ cup extra virgin olive oil until the mixture forms a paste. Spoon the pesto into a bowl and stir in 25g/1oz/⅓ cup freshly grated Parmesan cheese. Season to taste with salt and ground black pepper.

Rocket pesto

Put 50g/2oz fresh rocket (arugula) leaves into a food processor and blend to a paste with 25g/1oz/¼ cup toasted pine nuts and 2 peeled garlic cloves. With the motor still running, drizzle in 120ml/4fl oz/½ cup extra virgin olive oil until the mixture forms a paste. Spoon the pesto into a bowl and stir in 25g/1oz/⅓ cup freshly grated Parmesan cheese. Season to taste with salt and ground black pepper.

Asian-style pesto

Try this Asian version of Italian pesto tossed with freshly cooked egg noodles. Put 50g/2oz fresh coriander (cilantro) leaves into a food processor and add 25g/1oz/¼ cup toasted pine nuts, 2 peeled garlic cloves and 1 seeded and roughly chopped green chilli. Blend until smooth. With the motor still running, drizzle in 120ml/4fl oz/½ cup extra virgin olive oil until the mixture forms a paste. Spoon the pesto into a bowl and season to taste with salt and ground black pepper.

Coriander and pistachio pesto

This aromatic pesto is delicious over fish or chicken. Put 50g/2oz fresh coriander (cilantro) leaves in a food processor. Add 15g/½oz fresh parsley and process until finely chopped. Add 2 seeded and chopped fresh red chillies, and 1 garlic clove. Process until finely chopped.

Add 50g/2oz/⅓ cup shelled pistachio nuts and pulse until roughly chopped. Stir in 25g/1oz/⅓ cup grated Parmesan cheese, 90ml/6 tbsp olive oil and the juice of 2 limes. Season with salt and pepper to taste.

SAVOURY DIPS

These richly flavoured dips are delicious served with tortilla chips, crudités or small savoury crackers, but can also be served as an accompaniment to grilled (broiled) or poached chicken and fish. The creamy dips also make flavourful dressings for salads; you may need to thin them slightly with a squeeze of lemon juice or a little cold water.

Blue cheese dip

This sharp, tangy mixture is best served with crudites. Put 200ml/7fl oz/scant 1 cup crème fraîche in a large bowl and add 115g/4oz/1 cup crumbled blue cheese such as Stilton. Stir well until the mixture is smooth and creamy. Season with salt and ground black pepper and fold in about 30ml/2 tbsp chopped fresh chives.

Sour cream and chive dip

This tasty dip is a classic combination and goes particularly well with crudités and savoury crackers. Put 200ml/7fl oz/scant 1 cup sour cream in a bowl and add 30ml/2 tbsp chopped fresh chives and a pinch of caster (superfine) sugar. Stir well to mix, then season with salt and ground black pepper.

Classic mayonnaise

There are some excellent makes of mayonnaise on the market and these are what you'll reach for when time is short. However, for that special-occasion meal, nothing beats home-made mayonnaise. Surprisingly, it doesn't take much longer to make than spooning the bought stuff out of the jar. Put 2 egg yolks, 10ml/2 tsp lemon juice, 5ml/1 tsp Dijon mustard and some salt and ground black pepper in a food processor. Process briefly to combine, then, with the motor running, drizzle in about 350ml/12fl oz/1½ cups olive oil. The mayonnaise will become thick and pale. Scrape the mayonnaise into a bowl, taste and add more lemon juice and salt and pepper if necessary.

Aioli

This classic French garlic mayonnaise is particularly good served with piping hot chips (French fries). Make the mayonnaise as described above, adding 2 peeled garlic cloves to the food processor with the egg yolks.

Lemon or caper mayonnaise

A tangy mayonnnaise complements cold poached fish perfectly. Make the mayonnaise as described above, adding the grated rind of 1 lemon to the food processor with the egg yolks. For caper mayonnaise, simply add 15ml/1 tbsp rinsed capers instead of the lemon zest.

Herb mayonnaise

Finely chop a handful of fresh herbs, such as basil, coriander (cilantro) and tarragon, and stir into freshly made plain mayonnaise.

BASICS: FRUIT RELISHES, SWEET SAUCES AND FLAVOURED CREAMS

Tart fruit sauces and relishes are the perfect foil to fish, poultry and pork, as they nicely offset rich flavours and oily textures. The avocado salsa, laced with the juice of a lime, works well as an accompaniment to corn snacks, but is also delicious served on the side with pork, poultry or steak. After sampling these fruity flavours, move on to sheer indulgence with an irresistible selection of dessert sauces and creams. Sweetness is supplied by spices, syrups, soft fruits, chocolate and fortified wines.

Apple sauce

Serve with pork. Peel, core and slice 450g/1lb cooking apples and place in a pan. Add a splash of water, 15ml/1 tbsp caster (superfine) sugar and a few whole cloves. Cook the apples over a gentle heat, stirring occasionally, until the fruit becomes pulpy.

Quick cranberry sauce

Serve with roast chicken or turkey. Put 225g/8oz/2 cups cranberries in a pan with about 75g/3oz/scant ½ cup light muscovado (brown) sugar, 45ml/3 tbsp port and 45ml/3 tbsp orange juice. Bring to the boil, then simmer, uncovered, for 10 minutes, or until the cranberries are tender. Stir occasionally to stop the fruit from sticking.

Gooseberry relish

Serve this tart relish with oily fish, such as mackerel, or fatty meat such as pork. Put 225g/8oz fresh or frozen gooseberries in a pan with 225g/8oz/ generous 1 cup caster (superfine) sugar and 1 star anise. Add a splash of water

and a little white wine if you like. Bring to the boil and simmer, uncovered, for 10 minutes, stirring occasionally, until the fruit has broken down and the texture is soft and pulpy.

Avocado and cumin salsa

Serve this spicy Mexican-style salsa as an unusual accompaniment to a meat meal, or solo, with a large bowl of tortilla chips. They're the perfect shape for scooping up the chunky salsa. Peel, stone (pit) and roughly chop 1 ripe avocado. Transfer to a bowl and gently stir in 1 finely chopped fresh red chilli, 15ml/1 tbsp toasted crushed cumin seeds, 1 chopped ripe tomato, the juice of 1 lime, 45ml/3 tbsp olive oil and 30ml/2 tbsp chopped fresh coriander (cilantro). Season and serve.

SWEET SAUCES

These luscious sauces are perfect spooned over ice cream and can turn a store-bought dessert or slice of sponge cake into an indulgent treat.

White chocolate sauce

Break 150g/5oz white chocolate into squares. Heat 150ml/¼ pint/⅔ cup double (heavy) cream in a heavy pan. When almost boiling, stir in the white chocolate, a few pieces at a time, until melted and smooth. Remove from the heat and stir in 30ml/2 tbsp brandy or Cointreau. Serve the sauce hot.

Toffee chocolate sauce

This is perhaps the simplest sweet sauce to make of all. Roughly chop 2 Mars bars (chocolate toffee bars) and

put the pieces in a pan with 300ml/ ½ pint/1¼ cups double (heavy) cream. Stir over a gentle heat until the chocolate bars have melted. Serve hot with ice cream, or combine with 50g/2oz/1 cup corn flakes to make chocolate crispy cakes.

Raspberry and vanilla sauce

Scrape the seeds from a vanilla pod (bean) into a food processor. Add 175g/ 6oz/1 cup raspberries and 30ml/2 tbsp icing (confectioners') sugar. Process to a purée, adding a little water to thin, if necessary.

Chocolate fudge sauce

Put 175ml/6fl oz/¾ cup double (heavy) cream in a small pan with 45ml/3 tbsp golden (light corn) syrup, 200g/7oz/ scant 1 cup light muscovado (brown) sugar and a pinch of salt. Heat gently, stirring, until the sugar has dissolved. Add 75g/3oz/½ cup chopped plain (semisweet) chocolate and stir until melted. Simmer the sauce gently for about 20 minutes, stirring occasionally, until thickened. Keep warm in a heatproof bowl until ready to use.

FLAVOURED CREAMS

Cream is the perfect accompaniment for any dessert – whether it's a healthy fruit salad, a sumptuous plum tart or a warming baked apple. Flavoured creams are even better and can transform a tasty dessert into a truly luscious one.

Rosemary and almond cream

This fragrant cream has a lovely texture and is good served with fruit compotes, pies and tarts. Pour 300ml/½ pint/1¼ cups double (heavy) cream into a pan and add 2 fresh rosemary sprigs. Heat the mixture until just about to boil, then remove the pan from the heat and leave the mixture to infuse for 20 minutes. Remove the rosemary from the pan and discard. Pour the cream into a bowl and chill until cold. Whip the cold cream into soft peaks and stir in 30ml/2 tbsp chopped toasted almonds.

Rum and cinnamon cream

You can serve this versatile cream with most desserts. It goes particularly well with coffee, chocolate and fruit. Pour 300ml/½ pint/1¼ cups double (heavy) cream into a pan and add a cinnamon stick. Heat the mixture until it is just about to boil, then remove the pan from the heat and leave to infuse for about 20 minutes. Strain the cream through a fine sieve (strainer) and place in the refrigerator until cold. Whip the cold cream until it stands in soft peaks, then stir in 30ml/2 tbsp rum and 15ml/1 tbsp icing (confectioners') sugar, sifted if necessary, until thoroughly combined. Try a variation with 30ml/2 tbsp advocaat liqueur and 15ml/1 tbsp ginger conserve, too.

Marsala mascarpone

This sweet cream, based on a rich Italian cheese, is perfect for serving with grilled (broiled) fruit, tarts and hot desserts. Spoon 200g/7oz/scant 1 cup mascarpone into a large bowl and add 30ml/2 tbsp icing (confectioners') sugar and 45ml/3 tbsp Marsala. Beat the mixture until smooth. Another alcohol and sweet cream combo uses 45ml/3 tbsp Amaretto to 300ml/½ pint/1¼ cups whipped cream. Stir in 15ml/1 tbsp icing (confectioner's) sugar.

Cardamom cream

Warm, spicy cardamom pods make a wonderfully subtle, aromatic cream that is delicious served with fruit salads, compôtes, tarts and pies. It goes particularly well with tropical fruits such as mango. Pour 300ml/½ pint/1¼ cups double (heavy) cream into a pan and add 3 green cardamom pods. Heat the mixture gently until just about to boil, then remove the pan from the heat and leave to infuse for about 20 minutes. Pour the cream through a fine sieve (strainer) and place in the refrigerator until cold. Whip the cold cream until it stands in soft peaks, spoon it into a bowl and serve.

Praline cream

What could be more delicious than golden almond nut brittle, tasting of toffee but with a hint of bitterness from the nuts, blended with whipped cream? This is very good with poached apricots.

1 Put 115g/4oz/½ cup sugar and 75ml/5 tbsp water in a small, heavy pan. Stir over a gentle heat until the sugar has dissolved, then boil without stirring until the syrup is golden.

2 Remove from the heat, stir in 50g/2oz/⅓ cup whole blanched almonds and spread out on a lightly oiled baking sheet. Leave the nut syrup to cool until it turns glassy.

3 Scrape the hardened nut mixture off the surface of the baking tray and break into smaller pieces using your fingers, then put in a food processor. Process for about 1 minute, until finely chopped with the appearance of ground nuts.

4 In a large bowl, whip 300ml/½ pint/1¼ cups double (heavy) cream into soft peaks, then stir in the praline and serve immediately.

MAKING SIMPLE ACCOMPANIMENTS

When you've made a delicious main dish, you need to serve it with equally tasty accompaniments. The following section is full of simple, speedy ideas for fabulous side dishes – from creamy mashed potatoes, fragrant rice and spicy noodles to Italian-style polenta and simple, healthy vegetables.

MASHED POTATOES

Potatoes go well with just about any main dish. They can be cooked simply – boiled, steamed, fried or baked – but they are even better mashed with milk and butter.

Perfect mashed potatoes

Peel 675g/1½lb floury potatoes and cut them into large chunks. Place in a pan of salted boiling water. Return to the boil, then simmer for 15–20 minutes, or until completely tender. Drain the potatoes and return to the pan. Leave over a low heat for a couple of minutes, shaking the pan to drive off any excess moisture. Take the pan off the heat and, using a potato masher, mash the potatoes until smooth. Beat in 45–60ml/3–4 tbsp warm milk and a large knob (pat) of butter, then season with salt and pepper to taste.

Mustard mash

Make the mashed potatoes as directed above, then stir in 15–30ml/1–2 tbsp wholegrain mustard just before seasoning, and beat until smooth.

Parmesan and parsley mash

Make mashed potatoes as above, then stir in 30ml/2 tbsp freshly grated Parmesan and 15ml/1 tbsp chopped fresh flat leaf parsley.

Apple and thyme mash

Serve with pork. Make mashed potatoes as above. Heat 25g/1oz/2 tbsp butter in a pan and add 2 peeled, cored and sliced eating apples. Fry for 4–5 minutes, turning them often. Roughly mash, then fold into the potatoes, with 15ml/1 tbsp fresh thyme leaves.

Pesto mash

This is a simple way to dress up plain mashed potatoes. They have real bite and a lovely green-specked appearance. Make mashed potatoes as described above, then stir in 30ml/2 tbsp pesto sauce until thoroughly combined.

Masala mash

This tastes great with grilled (broiled) duck or pork. Put 15ml/1 tbsp mixed chopped fresh mint and coriander (cilantro) in a bowl. Add 5ml/1 tsp mango chutney, then stir in 5ml/1 tsp salt and 5ml/1 tsp crushed black peppercorns. Finely chop 1 fresh red and 1 fresh green chilli, removing the seeds if you like, and add to the mixture. Beat in 50g/2oz/¼ cup softened butter. Beat most of the herb mixture into the mashed potatoes and spoon the rest on top.

CRUSHED POTATOES

This chunky, modern version of mashed potatoes tastes fabulous. For all variations, simply crush the potatoes roughly, using the back of a fork.

Crushed potatoes with parsley and lemon

Cook 675g/1½lb new potatoes in salted boiling water for 15–20 minutes, until tender. Drain the potatoes and crush. Stir in 30ml/2 tbsp extra virgin olive oil, the grated rind and juice of 1 lemon and 30ml/2 tbsp chopped fresh flat leaf parsley. Season to taste.

Crushed potatoes with garlic and basil

Cook 675g/1½lb new potatoes in a pan of boiling salted water for 15–20 minutes until tender. Drain and crush. Stir in 30ml/2 tbsp extra virgin olive oil, 2 finely chopped garlic cloves and a handful of torn basil leaves. Season.

Crushed potatoes with pine nuts and Parmesan

Cook 675g/1½lb new potatoes in boiling salted water for 15–20 minutes until tender. Drain and crush. Stir in 30ml/2 tbsp extra virgin olive oil, 30ml/2 tbsp grated Parmesan cheese and 30ml/2 tbsp toasted pine nuts.

RICE

This versatile grain can be served simply – either boiled or steamed – or can be flavoured or stir-fried with different ingredients to make tasty, exciting accompaniments.

Easy egg-fried rice

Cook 115g/4oz/generous ½ cup long grain rice in a large pan of boiling water for 10–12 minutes, until tender. Drain well and refresh under cold running water. Spread out on a baking sheet and leave until completely cold. Heat 30ml/2 tbsp sunflower oil in a large frying pan and add 1 finely chopped garlic clove. Cook for 1 minute, then add the rice and stir-fry for 1 minute. Push the rice to the side of the pan and pour 1 beaten egg into the pan. Cook the egg until set, then break up with a fork and stir into the rice. Add a splash of soy sauce, and mix well.

Coconut rice

Put 225g/8oz/generous 1 cup basmati rice in a pan and pour in a 400ml/14oz can coconut milk. Cover with water, add some salt and bring to the boil. Simmer for 12 minutes, or until the rice is tender. Drain well and serve.

Coriander and spring onion rice

Cook 225g/8oz/generous 1 cup basmati rice in a large pan of salted boiling water for about 12 minutes, or until tender. Drain the rice well and return to the pan. Stir in 3 finely sliced spring onions (scallions) and a roughly chopped bunch of fresh coriander (cilantro) until well mixed, then serve.

NOODLES

There are many different types of noodles, all of which are quick to cook and make the perfect accompaniment to Chinese- and Asian-style stir-fries and curries. Serve them on their own, or toss them with a few simple flavourings. They can also be served cold as a simple salad.

Soy and sesame egg noodles

Cook a 250g/9oz packet of egg noodles according to the instructions on the packet. Drain well and tip the noodles into a large bowl. Drizzle over 30ml/ 2 tbsp dark soy sauce and 10ml/2 tsp sesame oil, then sprinkle over 15ml/ 1 tbsp toasted sesame seeds and toss well until thoroughly combined. These noodles will be delicious whether served hot, or cold as a salad.

Spicy peanut noodles

This simple and very tasty dish takes only minutes to make and is good on its own or with grilled (broiled) chicken. Cook a 250g/9oz packet of egg noodles according to the instructions on the packet, then drain. Heat 15ml/1 tbsp sunflower oil in a wok and add 30ml/ 2 tbsp crunchy peanut butter. Add a splash of cold water and a dash of soy sauce and stir the mixture over a gentle heat until thoroughly combined. Add the noodles to the pan and toss to coat in the peanut mixture. Sprinkle with fresh coriander (cilantro) to serve.

Chilli and spring onion noodles

Soak 115g/4oz flat rice noodles in cold water for 30 minutes, until softened. Tip into a colander and drain well. Heat 30ml/2 tbsp olive oil in a wok or large frying pan. Add 2 finely chopped garlic cloves and 1 seeded and finely chopped fresh red chilli and fry gently for 2 minutes. Slice a bunch of spring onions (scallions) and add to the pan. Cook for a minute or so, then stir in the rice noodles, combining them with the other ingredients until heated through. Season with salt and ground black pepper before serving.

POLENTA

This classic Italian dish made from cornmeal makes a swift and delicious accompaniment to many dishes and is a useful alternative to the usual potatoes, bread or pasta. It can be served in two ways – either soft, or set and cut into wedges and grilled (broiled) or fried. Soft polenta is rather like mashed potato, and like mashed potato, it can be layered with other ingredients and baked, or used as a topping. Grilled or fried polenta has a much firmer texture and a lovely crisp shell. Both types can be enjoyed plain, if you choose, or flavoured with other ingredients such as cheese, herbs and spices. Traditional polenta requires lengthy boiling and constant attention during cooking, but the quick-cook varieties, which are widely available in most large supermarkets, give excellent results and are much simpler and quicker to prepare.

Soft polenta with Cheddar cheese and thyme

Cook 225g/8oz/2 cups quick-cook polenta according to the instructions on the packet. As soon as the polenta is cooked, stir in 50g/2oz/½ cups grated Cheddar cheese and 30ml/2 tbsp chopped fresh thyme until thoroughly combined. Stir a large knob (pat) of butter into the cheesy polenta and season with salt and plenty of ground black pepper to taste before serving.

Grilled polenta with Gorgonzola

Cook 225g/8oz/2 cups quick-cook polenta according to the instructions on the packet. Check the seasoning, adding more if necessary, and spread the mixture out on an oiled baking sheet to a thickness of about 1cm/½in. Leave the polenta until cold and completely set, then chill for about 20 minutes. Turn the polenta out on to a board and cut it into large squares, then cut each square into 2 triangles. Pre-heat the grill (broiler) and arrange the polenta triangles on the grill pan. Cook for about 5 minutes, or until golden brown, then turn over and top each triangle with a sliver of Gorgonzola. Grill (broil) for a further 5 minutes, or until bubbling.

Baked polenta with two cheeses

Serve this simple bake with slices of prosciutto and a simple leaf and herb salad tossed with a lemon and honey dressing. Preheat the oven to 200°C/400°F/Gas 6. Grate 115g/4oz Cheddar cheese and crumble 115g/4oz soft Dolcelatte cheese. Mix the cheeses together in a bowl, using your fingers to combine them thoroughly. Cook 225g/8oz/2 cups quick-cook polenta according to the instructions on the packet. Spoon half the polenta into a baking dish and level the surface. Cover with half the cheese mixture, spoon the remaining polenta on top and sprinkle with the remaining cheese. Melt 50g/2oz/¼ cup butter in a pan and fry 2 chopped garlic cloves and a few chopped fresh sage leaves until golden. Drizzle over the polenta and grind black pepper over the top. Bake for 5 minutes until the cheese topping is bubbling.

Soft polenta

Cook 225g/8oz/2 cups quick-cook polenta according to the instructions on the packet. As soon as the polenta is cooked, stir in about 50g/2oz/¼ cup butter. Season with salt and black pepper to taste, then serve immediately.

Soft polenta with Parmesan and sage

Cook 225g/8oz/2 cups quick-cook polenta according to the instructions on the packet. As soon as the polenta is cooked, stir in 115g/4oz/1⅓ cups freshly grated Parmesan cheese and a handful of chopped fresh sage. Stir in a large knob (pat) of butter and season with salt and ground black pepper to taste before serving.

Fried chilli polenta triangles

Cook 225g/8oz/2 cups quick-cook polenta according to the instructions on the packet. Stir in 5ml/1 tsp dried chilli flakes, check the seasoning, adding more if necessary, and spread the mixture out on an oiled baking sheet to a thickness of about 1cm/½in. Leave the polenta until cold and completely set, then chill for about 20 minutes. Turn the polenta out on to a board and cut it into large squares, then cut each square into 2 triangles. Heat 30ml/2 tbsp olive oil in a large frying pan. Fry the triangles in the olive oil for 2–3 minutes on each side, until golden, then lift out and drain briefly on kitchen paper before serving.

QUICK AND SIMPLE VEGETABLES

Fresh vegetables are an essential part of our diet. They are delicious cooked on their own but they can also be combined with other ingredients.

Stir-fried cabbage with nuts and smoky bacon

Heat 30ml/2 tbsp sunflower oil in a wok or large frying pan and add 4 roughly chopped rashers (strips) smoked streaky (fatty) bacon. Stir-fry for about 3 minutes, until the bacon starts to turn golden, then add ½ shredded green cabbage to the pan. Stir-fry for 3–4 minutes, until the cabbage is just tender. Season with salt and ground black pepper, and stir in 25g/1oz/¼ cup roughly chopped toasted hazelnuts or almonds just before serving.

Creamy stir-fried Brussels sprouts

Shred 450g/1lb Brussels sprouts and add to the pan. Heat 15ml/1 tbsp sunflower oil in a wok or large frying pan. Add 1 chopped garlic clove and stir-fry for about 30 seconds. Stir-fry for 3–4 minutes, until just tender. Season with salt and black pepper and stir in 30ml/2 tbsp crème fraîche. Warm through for 1 minute.

Honey-fried parsnips and celeriac

Peel 225g/8oz parsnips and 115g/4oz celeriac. Cut both into matchsticks. Heat 30ml/2 tbsp olive oil in a wok or large frying pan and add the parsnips and celeriac. Fry over a gentle heat for 6–7 minutes, stirring occasionally, until golden and tender. Season with salt and ground black pepper and stir in 15ml/1 tbsp clear honey. Allow to bubble for 1 minute before serving.

Glazed carrots

Clear honey is the magic ingredient to use with this carrot side dish too. Cut three large carrots into matchsticks. Steam them over a pan of boiling water for 2–4 minutes until just tender. Meanwhile, heat 25g/1oz/2 tbsp butter in a heavy pan, add 1 crushed garlic clove and 15ml/1 tbsp chopped fresh rosemary leaves and cook for 1 minute or until the garlic is golden brown. Add 5ml/1 tsp Dijon mustard and 10ml/2 tsp clear honey. Stir over the heat until the honey has melted into the buttery sauce, then add the carrots. Cook, tossing the carrots to coat them with the mixture, for 2 minutes until the carrots are glazed. Season lightly with salt, if needed, and serve immediately.

SPECIALIST BREADS

Bread makes a simple accompaniment to many meals and is the perfect ready-made side dish when time is short. Look out for part-baked breads that you can finish off in the oven, so you can enjoy the taste of freshly baked bread in just a few minutes.

Ciabatta This chewy Italian bread is long and oval in shape and is commonly available in ready-to-bake form. Look out for ciabatta with added sun-dried tomatoes or olives.

Focaccia This flat, dimpled Italian bread is made with olive oil and has a softer texture than ciabatta. It is available plain but is also often flavoured with fresh rosemary and garlic.

Naan Traditionally cooked in a clay oven, this Indian bread is easy to find in supermarkets and makes a tasty accompaniment to curries. It is available plain, and also flavoured with spices.

Chapati This Indian flatbread is less heavy than naan and makes a good alternative. The small, round breads can be a little more difficult to find but are worth searching for.

Soda bread This traditional Irish bread is made using buttermilk and bicarbonate of soda (baking soda). It has a delicious flavour and is great for mopping up sauces or serving with soups.

Above: Rosemary focaccia has a crumbly texture and is perfect for sandwiches and for serving with a whole range of Italian-style dishes.

PLANNING A MENU: TIPS FOR THE COOK

Quick cooking does not necessarily mean throwing all your effort into a single dish. In fact, the bigger and better the meal, the more time you'll have to share food and swap news with family and friends. If you're planning a evening out, on the other hand, you'll need some light but nourishing fare to fuel the night ahead, A multi-faceted meal, full of different flavours, will remind you just how good food can be when you put in the effort. These well crafted menus will enable the quick cook to throw together memorable meals, each course complementing the other, without spending hours slaving in the kitchen, Above all, remember that the key to successful quick cooking is always to plan ahead.

• Make a list of all those you are cooking for to work out exactly how much food you will need. Check if anyone is vegetarian or has special dietary requirements such as an allergy to nuts or dairy products. If it's a special occasion, and there will be children present, remember to supply a range of drinks suitable for everyone.

• Decide what you are going to make, then be sure you have all the necessary equipment to hand. Choose courses that complement each other, and dishes you can cook with confidence. As you are short on time, it's best to stick to familiar techniques – few of us get a new recipe right the first go, and a group of hungry guests in the next room will only increase the pressure!

• Ensure you have enough space in the refrigerator for drinks, ingredients and dishes that need to be chilled. If necessary, have a clear-out beforehand to remove any unnecessary items.

• If you are serving up lots of courses, try to have as much as possible ready in advance. If some dishes can be made or part-prepared the day before, this is well worth doing.

• If possible, try to shop in advance for meals – it'll give you just that bit more energy when you come to cook.

• Recipes may need to be increased or reduced in quantity – sometimes at the last minute – depending on how many you are feeding. Dishes that can be most easily adapted in this way include soups, sauces for pasta and individual portions (such as a specific number of chicken portions).

• Accompanying sauces for hot dishes and dressings for salads do not have to be multiplied up as much as the main ingredients, if you need two or three times the number of portions specified. Similarly, do not multiply up herbs, spices and garlic as they may become overpowering.

• When eating *al fresco* with friends, remember to select dishes that are practical to serve and eat as well as easy to prepare. Dishes that can be piled neatly on plates are popular.

ENERGY-BOOSTING BREAKFAST

Knowing how important it is to eat a good breakfast and finding the time to make it are two different things. This menu proves it isn't just possible but is actually easy to start the day on a natural high that will see you right through the morning – without having to resort to quick sugar fixes.

PINEAPPLE, GINGER AND CARROT JUICE (PAGE 34)

Make this zingy drink the night before, if you like, although it takes so little time you could easily blitz it first thing. Use prepared pineapple to cut down on preparation time.

CANTALOUPE MELON SALAD (PAGE 39)

Simple but very sexy, this is a marvellous combination of chilled melon and caramelized strawberries. Get whoever is sharing your breakfast to cut up the melon to save time.

GRIDDLED TOMATOES ON SODA BREAD (PAGE 43)

Put the tomatoes on to cook while you prepare the melon salad. If you let them blacken slightly, they will acquire a wonderful, toffee-like flavour, which is enhanced by the balsamic vinegar.

WEEKEND BRUNCH

What better way to kick off a weekend outing or shopping trip than with this glorious brunch? This menu has everything: fruity zing, comforting carbs and even a nod to the traditional cooked breakfast. It's so easy to make, you'll be left with bags of energy for the rest of the day.

ZINGY PAPAYA FRUIT SALAD (PAGE 38)

You can make this in advance, but it is better served immediately after being freshly prepared. Slice and dress the papaya while the kidneys are cooking.

DEVILLED KIDNEYS ON BRIOCHE CROÛTES (PAGE 168)

Kidneys make a delicious breakfast food. They shouldn't be overcooked, so turn off the heat as soon as they are tender but still pink in the centre. They will hold while you serve the papaya fruit salad.

WARM PANCAKES WITH CARAMELIZED PEARS (PAGE 50)

If you're catering for vegetarians, this makes a great alternative to the devilled kidneys. If you're feeling indulgent, however, it also nicely rounds off the other two courses! Serve with milky coffee.

LIGHT BITE BEFORE A BUSY NIGHT

When you've got a hectic night ahead, perhaps because you are rushing out to the theatre, or planning to go to the gym in an hour or two, you want a meal that's sustaining without being so substantial as to slow you down. This three-course supper is ideal.

VITALITY JUICE (PAGE 35)

Pear, watercress and yogurt combine in this energy drink. For four people, double the recipe and serve in small glasses. If you're feeling jaded after a busy day, prepare as soon as you get home.

WARM SWORDFISH AND ROCKET SALAD (PAGE 188)

The swordfish benefits from being marinated for 5 minutes or so, during which time you can wrap some ciabatta in foil and put the loaf in a low oven to heat. The aromatic fish salad needs no other accompaniment, and it's light enough to help you sail through your evening's activities.

LEMON POSSET (PAGE 240)

This is one of the lightest desserts there is. It needs to be chilled, so make it ahead of time. Serve it on its own or with sponge fingers or similar dessert biscuits (cookies).

SUPER-QUICK SUPPER FOR FRIENDS

When you have a repertoire of really fast recipes, inviting friends home for an impromptu meal won't hold any terrors. It'll probably take longer to buy the ingredients than to cook the food.

BUTTER BEAN AND SUN-DRIED TOMATO SOUP (PAGE 63)

This hearty soup takes only minutes to make, and will happily sit on a low heat while you prepare the rest of the meal. Dispense with the bread if serving it as a first course, but add a few croûtons.

STIR-FRIED CHICKEN WITH THAI BASIL (PAGE 86)

A stir-fry is a great choice when you are entertaining, as friends will be content to chat while you put it together. Prepare the meat and vegetables in advance, and toss in some straight-to-wok noodles.

RHUBARB AND GINGER TRIFLES (PAGE 234)

These need to be chilled for at least half an hour before serving, so make them as soon as you get in from work, or have a spare moment after settling the children. Don't eat too many ginger snaps during the preparation!

EVERYDAY FAMILY FEAST

When you want to get the family together in the evening, serve a sumptuous meal that will keep everyone firmly in their seats. These dishes are economical, easily prepared, but above all memorable – proof that cooking on weekday nights need not mean humdrum food.

FOCACIA WITH SARDINES AND ROASTED TOMATOES (PAGE 67)

Although this works well as a lunch, it's also a great and informal way to kick off a family meal. Everyone will love the way the topping soaks in and flavours the bread.

CRUMBED CHICKEN WITH GREEN MAYONNAISE (PAGE 147)

Crisp-crumbed chicken is always popular, but it's the tangy caper mayonnaise that really rounds off this fine family main course. A lightly-spiced speciality, suitable for all palates.

BLUEBERRY MERINGUE CRUMBLE (PAGE 236)

Combining healthy fresh fruit with a treat of vanilla-flavoured cream and the surprise crunch of meringue, this wonderful dessert is a lovely way to cleanse the palate after a meal. Now all you need to do is get someone else to do the washing up.

AL FRESCO GATHERING

This flexible menu will get everyone into the garden this summer – cook, hosts and guests! Depending on how many of you there are, you can either prepare the whole menu, or just what suits at the time. This selection has a number of vegetarian options as well as the traditional meat feast.

MINI MOZZARELLA CIABATTA PIZZAS (PAGE 204)

A hit with adults and kids alike. These little pizzas make perfect finger food: ideal to nibble on while in conversation, or for little fingers to grab before running off to play. Go for a mixture of toppings but keep it simple: sliced black olives are a nice vegetarian substitute for the prosciutto.

HOME-MADE BURGERS WITH RELISH (PAGE 151)

These meaty treats are the perfect excuse to light the barbecue! Prepare them ahead of time, and have the buns ready too. Always cook thoroughly – test the temperature with a skewer before serving.

SWEET PEPPERS STUFFED WITH TWO CHEESES (PAGE 202)

Sweet peppers are wonderful roasted over coals, and the half-melting cheese is the perfect complement to the crisp skin and juicy texture. This is excellent vegetarian food, but don't cook them alongside the meat. Buy a separate, disposable barbecue or cook the peppers on a griddle.

LEMONY COUSCOUS SALAD (PAGE 79)

A fresh-tasting salad accompaniment that is great for piling on plates – just watch it disappear! Although you can serve it as soon as it is made, try to make it a little way in advance, if you can, so that the flavours have time to blend.

FRESH FRUIT SALAD (PAGE 246)

After all that hot, sultry summer fare, a simple fruit salad is the perfect way to round things off. This recipe is simply a blueprint for all kinds of sumptuous variations. Use the basic quantities suggested but add whichever fruits are in peak condition at the time.

SUPERB SUNDAY LUNCH

At weekends, it's something of a novelty to have a main meal in the middle of the day. This line-up of dishes looks daunting, but none are difficult and all are quick.

ARTICHOKE AND CUMIN DIP (PAGE 176)

A leisurely start to a meal that can be made in seconds if you keep canned artichokes in the cupboard. Serve it with everyone's favourite: pitta bread and black olives.

PAN-FRIED STEAKS WITH WHISKY AND CREAM (PAGE 105)

Ask your guests how they like their steak, so you can cater to individual preferences. Remember that the meat will carry on cooking for a few minutes while you make the delicious whisky sauce.

CARAMELIZED SHALLOTS (PAGE 225)

These are irresistible and go well with the steak. Making them ahead of time and reheating them will do them no harm at all. Don't let the liquid evaporate entirely until you return them to the heat for the last time.

CARROT AND PARSNIP PURÉE (PAGE 224)

A colourful and tasty mixture, this can also be made in advance and reheated in the microwave, if you have one. Serve alongside ready-prepared fine beans from the supermarket. These will cook in next to no time, and will add crisp texture and a contrasting colour

HONEY BAKED FIGS WITH HAZELNUT ICE CREAM (PAGE 243)

You can prepare these figs in advance and heat them through in the oven while you are serving the main course. If you don't want to bother with the ice cream, serve them with crème fraîche.

VEGETARIAN FEAST

This superb menu is as colourful as it is good to eat. Use red (bell) peppers instead of yellow ones for the stuffed peppers, and they will look lovely with the pasta and the dark green Brussels sprouts.

GRAPEFRUIT IN HONEY AND WHISKY (PAGE 245)

Although this is often served as a dessert, it also makes a delicious first course. The colours are gorgeous, and it has a lovely clean taste that is perfect when the main course is quite rich.

PUMPKIN AND PARMESAN PASTA (PAGE 133)

The original recipe included bacon, but this can easily be omitted. If you want to, substitute thinly sliced sun-dried tomato, although the pasta dish doesn't really need it. Serve with extra Parmesan.

STUFFED SWEET PEPPERS (PAGE 123)

Use a colourful combination of peppers as suggested. They need to steam for 15 minutes, so fill them ahead of time and put them on before making the pasta dish. For added crunch, serve stir-fried brussel sprouts, lightly cooked mangetouts (snow peas) or steamed broccoli on the side.

SYRUPY BRIOCHE SLICES WITH ICE CREAM (PAGE 242)

These are sheer indulgence. Make the orange syrup in advance, adding a little orange liqueur if you are feeling particularly extravagant, and assemble the dessert at the last moment.

THE PERFECT PICNIC

Food for the perfect picnic needs to be portable, easy to eat, filling enough to satisfy those who've been playing six-a-side football, and sufficiently varied to appeal to all ages. This menu has the lot.

TAPAS OF ALMONDS, OLIVES AND CHEESE (PAGE 174)

All these tasty snacks can be made days before being served – in fact, they benefit from early attention. Take them to the picnic in well-sealed plastic tubs, and pack plenty of paper napkins.

SMOKED MACKEREL PATÉ (PAGE 65) WITH CARROT AND CELERY STICKS

One of the easiest pâtés to make, this can be made the night before the picnic. Take it in a cool bag and serve it with Melba toast (the bought kind is fine) or with crudités.

ROAST CHICKEN PITTA POCKETS (PAGE 145)

If you buy a roast chicken, these are very quick and easy to assemble. Take the chicken, salad and tahini sauce separately to the picnic. The pittas will be just as delicious untoasted.

MEXICAN TORTAS (PAGE 73)

Hollow out bread rolls, pack them with a spicy filling and they become a delicious snack. If vegetarians are in the party, make some tortas without the pork; just substitute extra cheese. Serve with sweet cherry or cocktail tomatoes and crisp celery sticks for good measure.

CHOCOLATE AND PRUNE REFRIGERATOR BARS (PAGE 235)

Make these up to two days ahead of time, and transport them in a cool bag. Put the cool bag in the boot (trunk) of the car, or the chocolate bars may never make it all the way to the picnic grounds. Just in case they disappear fast, have some DRIED FRUIT SALAD (PAGE 246) on hand as a reserve.

SIMPLE SUMMER LUNCH

When the weather turns fine, you may want to invite friends or family to share a lovely garden lunch. Although a little more formal than a barbecue feast, this selection of fresh and flavourful dishes still require very little in the way of preparation and fuss.

CHILLED TOMATO SOUP WITH ROCKET PESTO (PAGE 60)

Made ahead of time, this refreshing appetizer is a very easy option. As the main course is quite light, for extra bulk you could serve it with warm sun-dried tomato bread.

GRILLED SOLE WITH CHIVE BUTTER (PAGE 190)

Make the chive butter early in the morning, and you'll have very little to do after your guests arrive. Sole cooks quickly, so don't leave it unattended while it is under the grill (broiler).

BRAISED LETTUCE AND PEAS (PAGE 221)

A delightful accompaniment made all the more special if you use freshly podded peas. Serve alongside baby new potatoes that can be cooked in the bag using a microwave.

SUMMER BERRIES IN WARM SABAYON GLAZE (PAGE 244)

Eating berries that have been coated in warm sabayon is like tasting freshly picked fruit you have picked yourself on a sunny day. The warmth really seems to bring out their flavour.

BREAKFASTS AND BRUNCHES

*Early mornings are the busiest time. Something has to give, and all too often that something is
breakfast. Nutritionists tell us how important this first meal of the day is, but still we skip it,
or settle for coffee and a doughnut when the mayhem has moderated. Not a good idea. With just
a few minutes to spare, you can make a delicious smoothie or a simple fruit compote.
Pineapple, Ginger and Carrot Juice will give you plenty of zing, and get you off to a good
start. Once you find out how good breakfast makes you feel, you'll want to revisit old
favourites like Cinnamon Toast or Griddled Tomatoes on Soda Bread. When the weekend
arrives and life is just a little less hectic, celebrate by making a special brunch. This is a great
meal for sharing with friends. Whatever you choose to cook won't take long, thanks to our
quick and easy recipes, so you'll soon be joining the party and accepting praise for your
delectable Kedgeree or excellent Eggs Benedict.*

PINEAPPLE, GINGER AND CARROT JUICE

YOU'RE NEVER TOO BUSY FOR BREAKFAST WHEN YOU HAVE RECIPES LIKE THIS ONE IN YOUR REPERTOIRE. GINGER ADDS A ZING TO THE SWEET, SCENTED MIXTURE OF FRESH PINEAPPLE AND CARROT. SERVED VERY COLD, THIS REFRESHING DRINK MAKES THE PERFECT START TO THE DAY.

Preparation: 5 minutes; Cooking: 0 minutes

MAKES ONE GLASS

INGREDIENTS
½ small pineapple
25g/1oz fresh root ginger
1 carrot
ice cubes

COOK'S TIP
This is one of the speediest breakfast snacks there is, but you can prepare it even more quickly if you buy ready-sliced fresh pineapple. This is sold in tubs and you will often find it in the chiller at the local supermarket.

1 Using a sharp knife, cut away the skin from the pineapple, then cut it into quarters and remove the core from each piece. Roughly slice the pineapple flesh and then chop into portions small enough to fit in the juicer.

2 Thinly peel the ginger, using a sharp knife or vegetable peeler, then chop the flesh roughly. Scrape or peel the carrot and cut it into rounds or chunks.

3 Push the carrot, ginger and pineapple through a juicer and pour into a glass. Add ice cubes and serve immediately.

Energy 108kcal/462kJ; Protein 1.3g; Carbohydrate 26.1g, of which sugars 25.8g; Fat 0.6g, of which saturates 0.1g; Cholesterol 0mg; Calcium 55mg; Fibre 4.2g; Sodium 23mg

VITALITY JUICE

THE CLUE IS IN THE NAME. THIS SPEEDY JUICE REALLY DOES PUT A SPRING IN YOUR STEP. WATERCRESS HAS A SLIGHTLY PEPPERY FLAVOUR WHEN EATEN ON ITS OWN, BUT BLENDING IT WITH PEAR, WHEATGERM AND YOGURT TAMES THE TASTE WHILE BOOSTING YOUR MORNING ENERGY LEVELS.

Preparation: 4 minutes; Cooking: 0 minutes

SERVES ONE

INGREDIENTS
    25g/1oz watercress
    1 large ripe pear
    30ml/2 tbsp wheatgerm
    150ml/¼ pint/⅔ cup natural
      (plain) yogurt
    15ml/1 tbsp linseeds (flax seeds)
    10ml/2 tsp lemon juice
    mineral water (optional)
    ice cubes

1 Roughly chop the watercress (you do not need to remove the tough stalks). Peel, core and roughly chop the pear.

2 Put the watercress and pear in a blender or food processor with the wheatgerm and blend until smooth. Scrape the mixture down from the side of the bowl if necessary.

3 Add the yogurt, seeds and lemon juice and blend until combined. Thin with a little mineral water if too thick.

4 Put several ice cubes in the bottom of a tall glass. Fill the glass to just below the brim with the Vitality Juice, leaving enough room to decorate with a few sprigs of chopped watercress on top.

VARIATIONS
For a non-dairy version of this delicious, refreshing drink, use yogurt made from goat's milk, sheep's milk or soya. A large apple can be used instead of the pear.

Energy 287kcal/1207kJ; Protein 17.8g; Carbohydrate 39.8g, of which sugars 31.2g; Fat 7.6g, of which saturates 1.6g; Cholesterol 2mg; Calcium 394mg; Fibre 8.8g; Sodium 144mg

MUESLI SMOOTHIE

LOVE MUESLI BUT DON'T LIKE THE TEXTURE? THIS DIVINELY SMOOTH DRINK HAS ALL THE GOODNESS BUT NONE OF THE LUMPY BITS. PURÉED APRICOTS AND STEM GINGER JUST ADD TO THE FLAVOUR.

Preparation: 4 minutes; Cooking: 0 minutes

SERVES TWO

INGREDIENTS
  50g/2oz/¼ cup ready-to-eat
    dried apricots
  1 piece preserved stem ginger,
    plus 30ml/2 tbsp syrup from the
    ginger jar
  40g/1½oz/scant ½ cup natural
    muesli (granola)
  about 200ml/7fl oz/scant 1 cup
    semi-skimmed (low-fat) milk

COOK'S TIP
Apricot and ginger are perfect partners in this divine drink. It makes an incredibly healthy, tasty breakfast, but is so delicious and indulgent that you could even serve it as a dessert after a summer meal. If serving it as a dessert, partner it with poached apricots.

1 Using a sharp knife, chop the dried apricots into slices or chunks. Chop the preserved ginger.

2 Put the apricots and ginger in a blender or food processor and add the syrup from the ginger jar with the muesli and milk.

3 Process until smooth, adding more milk if necessary, to make a creamy drink. Serve in wide glasses.

Energy 204kcal/865kJ; Protein 6.6g; Carbohydrate 39.1g, of which sugars 28.8g; Fat 3.4g, of which saturates 1.4g; Cholesterol 6mg; Calcium 150mg; Fibre 3.1g; Sodium 97mg

BREAKFAST IN A GLASS

THIS ENERGIZING BLEND IS SIMPLY BURSTING WITH GOODNESS — JUST WHAT YOU NEED WHEN YOU WAKE UP WISHING YOU COULD STAY IN YOUR COMFY BED FOR JUST AN HOUR OR SO LONGER.

Preparation: 5 minutes; Cooking: 0 minutes

SERVES TWO

INGREDIENTS
250g/9oz firm tofu
200g/7oz/1¾ cups strawberries
45ml/3 tbsp pumpkin or
   sunflower seeds, plus extra
   for sprinkling
30–45ml/2–3 tbsp clear honey
juice of 2 large oranges
juice of 1 lemon

VARIATION
Almost any other fruit can be used instead of the strawberries. Those with textures that blend well, such as mangoes, bananas, peaches, plums and raspberries, work particularly well as single variety substitutes, or you could try a mixture according to your taste. The juicy sweetness of mangoes and slightly tart tang of raspberries are a winning combination.

1 Roughly chop the tofu, then hull and roughly chop the strawberries. Reserve a few strawberry chunks.

2 Put all the ingredients in a blender or food processor and blend until completely smooth, scraping the mixture down from the side of the bowl, if necessary.

3 Pour into tumblers and sprinkle with extra seeds and strawberry chunks.

Energy 259kcal/1087kJ; Protein 13.3g; Carbohydrate 30.4g, of which sugars 28.2g; Fat 10.2g, of which saturates 1.1g; Cholesterol 0mg; Calcium 671mg; Fibre 1.8g; Sodium 19mg

ZINGY PAPAYA FRUIT SALAD

THIS REFRESHING, FRUITY SALAD MAKES A LOVELY LIGHT BREAKFAST, PERFECT FOR THE SUMMER MONTHS. CHOOSE REALLY RIPE, FRAGRANT PAPAYAS AND JUICY LIMES FOR THE BEST FLAVOUR.

Preparation: 5 minutes; Cooking: 0 minutes

SERVES FOUR

INGREDIENTS

   2 large ripe papayas
   juice of 1 fresh lime
   2 pieces preserved stem ginger,
     finely sliced

VARIATION

This fruit salad is delicious made with other tropical fruit. Try using passion fruit pulp instead of the ginger, or substitute two ripe, peeled and stoned (pitted) mangoes for the papaya.

1 Cut the papayas in half lengthways. Scoop out the seeds, using a teaspoon. With a sharp knife, cut the flesh into neat, thin slices.

2 Arrange the papaya slices on a platter. Squeeze the lime juice over the papaya and sprinkle with the sliced stem ginger. Serve immediately.

Energy 112kcal/475kJ; Protein 1.6g; Carbohydrate 27.3g, of which sugars 27.3g; Fat 0.3g, of which saturates 0g; Cholesterol 0mg; Calcium 72mg; Fibre 6.8g; Sodium 16mg

CANTALOUPE MELON SALAD

LIGHTLY CARAMELIZED STRAWBERRIES LOOK PRETTY AND TASTE DIVINE IN THIS SIMPLEST OF SALADS.
SERVE IT WITH A GLASS OF CHAMPAGNE TO WELCOME GUESTS AT A SOPHISTICATED SUMMER BRUNCH.

Preparation: 3 minutes; Cooking: 4–5 minutes

SERVES FOUR

INGREDIENTS
   115g/4oz/1 cup strawberries
   15ml/1 tbsp icing (confectioners')
   sugar, plus extra for dusting
   ½ cantaloupe melon

COOK'S TIP
When you need just a small amount of sifted icing (confectioners') sugar, use a tea strainer. Spoon the sugar into the strainer, then lightly tap the side with the spoon so that the sifted sugar drifts down evenly. Though tempting when you're in a hurry, mashing the sugar in the strainer with the spoon will not quicken the time it takes to sift through!

1 Preheat the grill (broiler) to high. Hull the strawberries and cut them in half. Arrange the fruit in a single layer, cut side up, on a baking sheet or in an ovenproof dish and dust with the icing sugar.

2 Grill (broil) the strawberries for 4–5 minutes, or until the sugar starts to bubble and turn golden.

3 Meanwhile, scoop out the seeds from the half melon using a spoon. Using a sharp knife, remove the skin, then cut the flesh into wedges.

4 Arrange the melon wedges attractively on a serving plate and sprinkle the lightly caramelized strawberries on top. Dust the salad with icing sugar and serve immediately.

Energy 34kcal/144kJ; Protein 0.7g; Carbohydrate 8g, of which sugars 8g; Fat 0.1g, of which saturates 0g; Cholesterol 0mg; Calcium 21mg; Fibre 1.1g; Sodium 8mg

CASHEW NUT SHAKE

THIS NUTRITIOUS DRINK TASTES SO CREAMY IT'S HARD TO BELIEVE THERE'S NOT A DROP OF MILK IN IT. CASHEW NUTS PROVIDE THE TASTE AND TEXTURE. CHILL IT BEFORE SERVING WITH PLENTY OF ICE.

Preparation: 5 minutes; Cooking: 0 minutes

1 Finely grind the cashew nuts in a food processor. Add the sugar and cinnamon and grind the mixture again to make a smooth nut paste.

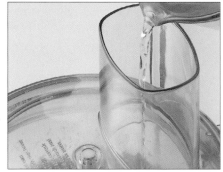

2 With the motor still running, gradually pour in 900ml/1½ pints/3¾ cups boiling water, until the drink becomes smooth and frothy. Scrape down the mixture occasionally, if necessary.

3 Pour the cashew nut milk into a jug (pitcher). Cover and chill. Stir well before serving in tall glasses, each with a couple of ice cubes on the bottom.

SERVES FOUR TO SIX

INGREDIENTS

400g/14oz/3½ cups blanched
   cashew nuts
225g/8oz/generous 1 cup caster
   (superfine) sugar
1.5ml/¼ tsp ground cinnamon

COOK'S TIP
For a smooth drink, make this the night before, allow it to stand in the refrigerator overnight, and strain before serving. If the mixture seems too thick, stir in a little water but remember that the ice will dilute it as it melts, giving it a lighter texture.

Energy 555kcal/2319kJ; Protein 13.9g; Carbohydrate 51.7g, of which sugars 42.9g; Fat 33.9g, of which saturates 6.7g; Cholesterol 0mg; Calcium 43mg; Fibre 2.1g; Sodium 196mg

CRANACHAN CRUNCH

THIS TASTY BREAKFAST DISH IS BASED ON A TRADITIONAL SCOTTISH RECIPE. THE TOASTED CEREAL
TASTES DELICIOUS WITH YOGURT AND A GENEROUS DRIZZLE OF HEATHER HONEY.

Preparation: 2 minutes; Cooking: 3–4 minutes

SERVES FOUR

INGREDIENTS
  75g/3oz crunchy oat cereal
  600ml/1 pint/2½ cups Greek
   (US strained plain) yogurt
  250g/9oz/1½ cups raspberries

1 Preheat the grill (broiler) to high.
Spread the oat cereal on a baking
sheet and place under the hot grill for
3–4 minutes until lightly toasted, stirring
regularly. Set aside to cool.

2 When the oat cereal has cooled
completely, fold it into the Greek yogurt,
then gently fold in 200g/7oz/generous
1 cup of the raspberries, being careful
not to crush the berries too much.

3 Spoon the yogurt mixture into four
serving glasses or dishes, top with the
remaining raspberries and serve
immediately.

Energy 222kcal/935kJ; Protein 10.1g; Carbohydrate 23g, of which sugars 13.3g; Fat 10.7g, of which saturates 6.7g; Cholesterol 21mg; Calcium 250mg; Fibre 3g; Sodium 236mg

CINNAMON TOAST

THIS IS AN OLD-FASHIONED SNACK THAT IS WARMING AND COMFORTING ON A COLD DAY. CINNAMON
TOAST IS PERFECT WITH A SPICY HOT CHOCOLATE DRINK OR WITH A FEW SLICES OF FRESH FRUIT.

Preparation: 2 minutes; Cooking: 2–3 minutes

SERVES TWO

INGREDIENTS
  75g/3oz/6 tbsp butter, softened
  10ml/2 tsp ground cinnamon
  30ml/2 tbsp caster (superfine) sugar,
    plus extra to serve
  4 slices bread
  prepared fresh fruit, such as
    peaches, plums, nectarines or
    mango (optional)

1 Place the softened butter in a bowl. Beat with a spoon until soft and creamy, then mix in the ground cinnamon and most of the sugar.

2 Toast the bread on both sides. Spread with the butter and sprinkle with a little remaining sugar. Serve at once, with pieces of fresh fruit, if you like.

COOK'S TIP
To round off this winter warmer, serve a quick cardamom hot chocolate with the cinnamon toast. Put 900ml/1½ pints/3¾ cups milk in a pan with two bruised cardamom pods and bring to the boil. Add 200g/7oz plain (semisweet) chocolate and whisk until melted. Using a slotted spoon, remove the cardamom pods just before serving.

Energy 461kcal/1921kJ; Protein 4.7g; Carbohydrate 41.6g, of which sugars 17.3g; Fat 31.8g, of which saturates 19.6g; Cholesterol 80mg; Calcium 72mg; Fibre 0.8g; Sodium 499mg

GRIDDLED TOMATOES ON SODA BREAD

NOTHING COULD BE SIMPLER THAN THIS BASIC DISH, TRANSFORMED INTO SOMETHING SPECIAL BY ADDING A DRIZZLE OF OLIVE OIL, BALSAMIC VINEGAR AND SHAVINGS OF PARMESAN CHEESE.

Preparation: 2 minutes; Cooking: 4–6 minutes

SERVES FOUR

INGREDIENTS
olive oil, for brushing and drizzling
6 tomatoes, thickly sliced
4 thick slices soda bread
balsamic vinegar, for drizzling
salt and ground black pepper
shavings of Parmesan cheese,
  to serve

COOK'S TIP
Using a griddle pan reduces the amount of oil required for cooking the tomatoes and gives them a barbecued flavour. The ridges on the pan brand the tomatoes, which look very attractive.

1 Brush a griddle pan with olive oil and heat. Add the tomato slices and cook for 4–6 minutes, turning once, until softened and slightly blackened. Alternatively, heat a grill (broiler) to high and line the rack with foil. Grill (broil) the tomato slices for 4–6 minutes, turning once, until softened.

2 While the tomatoes are cooking, lightly toast the soda bread. Place the tomatoes on top of the toast and drizzle each portion with a little olive oil and vinegar. Season to taste and serve immediately with thin shavings of Parmesan.

Energy 178kcal/751kJ; Protein 4.2g; Carbohydrate 26.3g, of which sugars 6.9g; Fat 7g, of which saturates 1g; Cholesterol 0mg; Calcium 66mg; Fibre 2.7g; Sodium 175mg

CHEESE TOASTIES

ALSO KNOWN AS BUBBLY CHEESE TOAST, BECAUSE OF THE WAY THE EGG AND CHEESE MIXTURE PUFFS UP DURING BAKING, THIS IS A NUTRITIOUS AND EASY SNACK THAT EVERYONE ENJOYS.

Preparation: 3–4 minutes; Cooking: 10–15 minutes

SERVES FOUR

INGREDIENTS
  2 eggs
  175–225g/6–8oz/1½–2 cups grated
   Cheddar cheese
  5–10ml/1–2 tsp wholegrain mustard
  4 slices bread, buttered
  2–4 halved tomatoes (optional)
  ground black pepper
  watercress or fresh parsley,
   to serve (optional)

COOK'S TIP
For the best flavour, use a mature (sharp) Cheddar cheese or a mixture of Cheddar and Leicester. To save time, buy packets of ready-grated cheese from the supermarket.

1 Preheat the oven to 230°C/450°F/ Gas 8 (the top oven of a range-type stove is ideal for this recipe). Whisk the eggs lightly and stir in the grated cheese, mustard and pepper.

2 Lay the buttered bread face down in a shallow baking dish.

3 Divide the cheese mixture among the slices of bread, spreading it out evenly.

4 Bake in the oven for 10–15 minutes, or until well risen and golden brown, adding the halved tomatoes for a few minutes, if using. Serve immediately, with the tomatoes, and garnish with sprigs of watercress or parsley.

Energy 357kcal/1484kJ; Protein 16.6g; Carbohydrate 13.4g, of which sugars 0.8g; Fat 25.8g, of which saturates 15.5g; Cholesterol 159mg; Calcium 369mg; Fibre 0.4g; Sodium 552mg

KIDNEY AND MUSHROOM TOASTS

MELTINGLY TENDER LAMB'S KIDNEYS ARE A TRADITIONAL BREAKFAST TREAT. COOKING THEM WITH MUSHROOMS IN MUSTARD BUTTER FLATTERS THEIR FLAVOUR, AND THEY TASTE GREAT ON TOAST.

Preparation: 5 minutes; Cooking: 4–6 minutes

SERVES TWO TO FOUR

INGREDIENTS

    4 large, flat field (portabello)
      mushrooms, stalks trimmed
    75g/3oz/6 tbsp butter, softened
    10ml/2 tsp wholegrain mustard
    15ml/1 tbsp chopped fresh parsley
    4 lamb's kidneys, skinned, halved
      and cored
    4 thick slices of brown bread, cut
      into rounds and toasted
    sprig of parsley, to garnish
    tomato wedges, to serve

COOK'S TIPS
• Kidneys are best served when they are still pink in the centre.
• Serve the mixture on halved, warm scones, if you prefer.

1 Wash the mushrooms, pat dry with kitchen paper and remove the stalks.

2 Mix the butter, wholegrain mustard and fresh parsley together.

3 Rinse the prepared lamb's kidneys well under cold running water, and pat dry with kitchen paper.

4 Melt about two-thirds of the butter mixture in a large frying pan and fry the mushrooms and kidneys for 2–3 minutes on each side.

5 When the kidneys are cooked to your liking spread with the remaining herb butter. Pile on the hot toast and serve with the tomato, garnished with parsley.

Energy 379kcal/1580kJ; Protein 20.1g; Carbohydrate 14.9g, of which sugars 1g; Fat 27.1g, of which saturates 15.9g; Cholesterol 353mg; Calcium 59mg; Fibre 1.7g; Sodium 560mg

CROQUE MONSIEUR

THIS CLASSIC FRENCH TOASTIE IS DELICIOUS SERVED AT ANY TIME OF DAY, BUT WITH A FOAMING CUP OF MILKY COFFEE IT MAKES A PARTICULARLY ENJOYABLE BRUNCH DISH.

Preparation: 5 minutes; Cooking: 5 minutes

SERVES FOUR

INGREDIENTS
  8 slices white bread
  softened butter
  4 large lean ham slices
  175g/6oz Gruyère or
    mild Cheddar cheese
  ground black pepper

1 Preheat the grill (broiler) to the highest setting. Arrange the bread on the grill rack and toast four slices on both sides and the other four slices on one side only.

2 Slice the cheese thinly. Butter the slices of bread that have been toasted on both sides and top with the ham, then the cheese. Season with plenty of ground black pepper. Transfer the topped bread slices to the grill pan.

3 Lay the remaining, half-toasted bread slices on top of the cheese, with the untoasted side uppermost. Grill (broil) the tops of the sandwiches until golden brown, then cut them in half using a sharp knife and serve.

Energy 336kcal/1409kJ; Protein 20.3g; Carbohydrate 26.9g, of which sugars 1.7g; Fat 16.2g, of which saturates 9.8g; Cholesterol 57mg; Calcium 385mg; Fibre 0.8g; Sodium 897mg.

EGGS BENEDICT

USING A GOOD-QUALITY BOUGHT HOLLANDAISE FOR THIS RECIPE SAVES TIME AND MAKES ALL THE DIFFERENCE TO THE RESULT. EGGS BENEDICT ARE DELICIOUS SERVED ON TOASTED ENGLISH MUFFINS.

Preparation: 2–3 minutes; Cooking: 4–6 minutes

SERVES FOUR

INGREDIENTS
  4 large (US extra large) eggs
  4 lean ham slices
  60ml/4 tbsp warm hollandaise sauce
  2 English muffins, split
  salt and ground black pepper

COOK'S TIP
Many people complain that it's near impossible to poach a perfectly round egg – too often the edges of the cooked whites look a bit ragged. You can try swirling the simmering water with a spoon just before adding the eggs – the little currents of water help to cement the shape of the whites. Failing this, simply use a sharp knife point to trim around the edges just before serving.

1 Pour cold water into a medium pan to a depth of about 5cm/2in and bring to a gentle simmer. Crack an egg into a saucer. Swirl the water in the pan with a spoon, then slide the egg carefully into the centre of the swirl.

2 Add the second egg to the pan. Simmer both eggs for 2–3 minutes, until the whites are set, but the yolks are still soft.

3 Meanwhile, toast the muffin halves. Place on four serving plates and arrange the ham slices on top. Remove the eggs from the pan using a slotted spoon and place on top of the ham on two of the plates. Poach two more eggs and top the remaining muffins.

4 Spoon the hollandaise sauce over the eggs, season and serve immediately.

Energy 276kcal/1154kJ; Protein 14.9g; Carbohydrate 15.9g, of which sugars 1.6g; Fat 17.7g, of which saturates 3.7g; Cholesterol 258mg; Calcium 81mg; Fibre 0.7g; Sodium 520mg

PANETTONE FRENCH TOAST

THICKLY SLICED STALE WHITE BREAD IS USUALLY USED FOR FRENCH TOAST, BUT THE SLIGHTLY DRY
TEXTURE OF PANETTONE MAKES A GREAT ALTERNATIVE. SERVE WITH FRESH SUMMER BERRIES.

Preparation: 2 minutes; Cooking: 4–6 minutes

SERVES FOUR

INGREDIENTS
    2 large (US extra large) eggs
    50g/2oz/¼ cup butter or 30ml/2 tbsp
        sunflower oil
    4 large slices panettone, halved
    30ml/2 tbsp caster (superfine) sugar
    fresh berries, to serve

COOK'S TIP
A generous portion of chilled mixed
berry fruits such as raspberries,
blackberries, morello cherries and
blueberries perfectly complements
the richness of this snack.

1 Break the eggs into a bowl and whisk
lightly, then tip them into a shallow
dish. Heat the butter or oil in a large
non-stick frying pan.

2 Dip the panettone slices in the egg
and fry for 2–3 minutes on each side,
until golden brown. Drain, dust with
sugar and serve with the berries.

Energy 369kcal/1550kJ; Protein 9.2g; Carbohydrate 47.4g, of which sugars 19.9g; Fat 17.3g, of which saturates 8.7g; Cholesterol 123mg; Calcium 103mg; Fibre 1.7g; Sodium 349mg

BUTTERMILK PANCAKES

IT IS TRADITIONAL TO HAVE THESE PLUMP PANCAKES ON THEIR OWN, WITH HONEY, BUT THEY ALSO TASTE GOOD AMERICAN-STYLE, WITH CRISP FRIED BACON AND A GENEROUS DRIZZLE OF MAPLE SYRUP.
Preparation: 2 minutes; Cooking: 12–18 minutes

MAKES ABOUT TWELVE

INGREDIENTS

225g/8oz/2 cups plain
   (all-purpose) flour
7.5ml/1½ tsp bicarbonate of
   soda (baking soda)
25–50g/1–2oz/2–4 tbsp sugar
1 egg
about 300ml/½ pint/1¼ cups
   buttermilk
butter and oil, mixed, or white
   vegetable fat (shortening), for frying
honey, to serve

COOK'S TIP
You will need to cook the pancakes in batches, so keep warm on a low oven temperature, tightly wrapped in foil.

1 In a food processor or a large mixing bowl, mix together the plain flour, the bicarbonate of soda and enough sugar to taste. Add the egg, blend or stir to mix, then gradually pour in just enough of the buttermilk to make a thick, smooth batter.

2 Heat a heavy pan and add the butter and oil, or white fat. Place spoonfuls of the batter on to the hot pan and cook for 2–3 minutes until bubbles rise to the surface. Flip the pancakes over and cook for a further 2–3 minutes. Remove from the pan and serve warm with honey.

Energy 90kcal/380kJ; Protein 3.2g; Carbohydrate 18.7g, of which sugars 4.4g; Fat 0.8g, of which saturates 0.2g; Cholesterol 17mg; Calcium 61mg; Fibre 0.6g; Sodium 18mg

WARM PANCAKES WITH CARAMELIZED PEARS

IF YOU CAN FIND THEM, USE WILLIAMS PEARS FOR THIS RECIPE BECAUSE THEY ARE SO JUICY. FOR A REALLY INDULGENT BREAKFAST, TOP WITH A SPOONFUL OF CRÈME FRAICHE OR FROMAGE FRAIS.

Preparation: 5 minutes; Cooking: 6 minutes

SERVES FOUR

INGREDIENTS
8 ready-made pancakes
50g/2oz/¼ cup butter
4 ripe pears, peeled, cored and thickly sliced
30ml/2 tbsp light muscovado (brown) sugar
crème fraîche or fromage frais, to serve

1 Preheat the oven to 150°C/300°F/ Gas 2. Tightly wrap the pancakes in foil and place in the oven to warm through.

VARIATION
This tastes just as good with sliced nectarines instead of pears.

2 Meanwhile, heat the butter in a large frying pan and add the pears. Fry for 2–3 minutes, until the undersides are golden. Turn the pears over and sprinkle with sugar. Cook for a further 2–3 minutes, or until the sugar dissolves and the pan juices become sticky.

3 Remove the pancakes from the oven and take them out of the foil. Divide the pears among them, placing them in one quarter. Fold each pancake in half over the filling, then into quarters and place two folded pancakes on each plate. Drizzle the pan juices over and serve with crème fraîche or fromage frais.

Energy 544kcal/2274kJ; Protein 7.7g; Carbohydrate 64.9g, of which sugars 42.4g; Fat 29.9g, of which saturates 6.5g; Cholesterol 27mg; Calcium 155mg; Fibre 4.3g; Sodium 144mg

OATMEAL PANCAKES WITH BACON

*WRAP AN OATMEAL PANCAKE AROUND A CRISP SLICE OF BEST BACON AND SAMPLE A NEW TASTE
SENSATION WITH YOUR TRADITIONAL COOKED BREAKFAST. IT MAKES A GREAT EGG DIPPER, TOO.*

Preparation: 2–3 minutes; Cooking: 12 minutes

MAKES FOUR PANCAKES

INGREDIENTS
    50g/2oz/½ cup fine wholemeal
       (whole-wheat) flour
    30ml/2 tbsp fine pinhead oatmeal
    pinch of salt
    1 egg
    about 150ml/¼ pint/⅔ cup
       buttermilk or milk
    butter or oil, for greasing
    4 rashers (strips) bacon

COOK'S TIP
The oatmeal in the batter gives it texture,
so these pancakes are firmer than
conventional crêpes. You can easily
double or treble the mixture and even
make it ahead of time. It will thicken
on standing, though, so thin it with
buttermilk or milk before use.

1 Mix the flour, oatmeal and salt in a
bowl, beat in the egg and add enough
buttermilk or milk to make a creamy
batter of the same consistency as that
used for ordinary pancakes.

2 Thoroughly heat a griddle or cast-iron
frying pan over a medium-hot heat.
When very hot, grease the surface
lightly with butter or oil.

3 Pour in the batter, about a ladleful at
a time. Tilt the frying pan to spread
evenly and cook the pancake for about
2 minutes until set and the underside
is browned. Turn over and cook for
1 minute until browned.

4 Keep the pancake warm while you
cook the others and fry the bacon. Roll
the pancakes around the bacon to serve.

Energy 148kcal/621kJ; Protein 9.7g; Carbohydrate 13.1g, of which sugars 2g; Fat 6.7g, of which saturates 2.2g; Cholesterol 64mg; Calcium 62mg; Fibre 1.5g; Sodium 469mg

SWEET BREAKFAST OMELETTE

FOR A HEARTY START TO A DAY WHEN YOU KNOW YOU'RE GOING TO BE TOO RUSHED TO HAVE MUCH MORE THAN AN APPLE FOR LUNCH, TRY THIS SWEET OMELETTE WITH A SPOONFUL OF JAM.

Preparation: 3 minutes; Cooking: 5 minutes

SERVES ONE

INGREDIENTS

   3 eggs
   10ml/2 tsp caster (superfine) sugar
   5ml/1 tsp plain (all-purpose) flour
   10g/¼oz/½ tbsp unsalted
    (sweet) butter
   bread and jam, to serve

COOK'S TIP

Although this recipe is stated to serve one, it is substantial enough for two not-very-hungry people. Omelettes are best eaten the moment they emerge from the pan, so if you are cooking for a crowd, get each to make their own and eat in relays.

1 Break the eggs into a large bowl, add the sugar and flour and beat until really frothy. Heat the butter in an omelette pan until it begins to bubble, then pour in the egg mixture and cook, without stirring, until it begins to set.

2 Run a wooden spatula around the edge of the omelette, then carefully turn it over and cook the second side for 1–2 minutes until golden. Serve hot or warm with thick slices of fresh bread and a bowlful of fruity jam.

Energy 351kcal/1465kJ; Protein 19.3g; Carbohydrate 14.4g, of which sugars 10.6g; Fat 24.9g, of which saturates 9.9g; Cholesterol 592mg; Calcium 100mg; Fibre 0.2g; Sodium 271mg

CHIVE SCRAMBLED EGGS IN BRIOCHES

THESE CREAMY SCRAMBLED EGGS ARE DELICIOUS AT ANY TIME OF DAY BUT, WHEN SERVED WITH FRANCE'S FAVOURITE BREAKFAST BREAD, THEY BECOME THE ULTIMATE BREAKFAST OR BRUNCH TREAT.

Preparation: 6 minutes; Cooking: 7 minutes

SERVES FOUR

INGREDIENTS

    4 individual brioches
    6 eggs, beaten
    45ml/3 tbsp chopped fresh chives,
      plus extra to serve
    25g/1oz/2 tbsp butter
    45ml/3 tbsp cottage cheese
    60–75ml/4–5 tbsp double
      (heavy) cream
    salt and ground black pepper

1 Preheat the oven to 180°C/350°F/ Gas 4. Cut the tops off the brioches and set to one side. Carefully scoop out the centre of each brioche, leaving a bread case. Put the brioche cases and lids on a baking sheet and bake for 5 minutes until hot and crisp.

2 Meanwhile, beat the eggs lightly and season to taste. Add about one-third of the chopped chives. Heat the butter in a medium pan until it begins to foam, then add the eggs and cook, stirring constantly with a wooden spoon until semi-solid.

3 Stir in the cottage cheese, cream and half the remaining chives. Cook for 1–2 minutes more, making sure that the eggs remain soft and creamy.

COOK'S TIP
Save the scooped-out brioche centres and freeze them in an airtight container. Partly defrost and blend or grate them to make crumbs for coating fish or pieces of chicken before frying.

4 To serve, spoon the eggs into the crisp brioche shells and sprinkle with the remaining chives.

VARIATION
If you do not happen to have brioches to hand, these wonderful herby eggs taste delicious on top of thick slices of toasted bread. Try them piled high on warm focaccia, or on toasted ciabatta, Granary (whole-wheat) bread or muffins.

Energy 414kcal/1731kJ; Protein 16.2g; Carbohydrate 32.5g, of which sugars 10.5g; Fat 25.5g, of which saturates 12g; Cholesterol 322mg; Calcium 154mg; Fibre 1.9g; Sodium 374mg

SCRAMBLED EGGS <u>WITH</u> ANCHOVIES

LIFTING THE SPIRITS ON THE DULLEST OF DAYS SCRAMBLED EGGS ARE TRUE COMFORT FOOD.
THIS VERSION COMBINES WITH ANCHOVIES, WHOSE SALTY TANG IS SUPERB WITH THE CREAMY EGG.
Preparation: 2–3 minutes; Cooking: 7 minutes

SERVES TWO

INGREDIENTS
    2 slices bread
    40g/1½oz/3 tbsp butter, plus
        extra for spreading
    anchovy paste, such as
        Gentleman's Relish, for spreading
    2 eggs and 2 egg yolks, beaten
    60–90ml/4–6 tbsp single (light)
        cream or milk
    ground black pepper
    anchovy fillets, cut into strips,
        and paprika, to garnish

COOK'S TIP
These creamy scrambled eggs are delicious in baked potatoes instead of on toast. Serve with a salad and a glass of crisp white wine for a tasty lunch.

1 Toast the bread, spread with butter and anchovy paste, then remove the crusts and cut into triangles. Keep warm.

2 Melt the rest of the butter in a medium non-stick pan, then stir in the beaten eggs, cream or milk, and a little ground pepper. Heat very gently, stirring constantly, until the mixture begins to thicken.

3 Remove the pan from the heat and continue to stir until the mixture becomes very creamy, but do not allow it to harden.

4 Divide the scrambled eggs among the triangles of toast and garnish each one with strips of anchovy fillet and a generous sprinkling of paprika. Serve immediately, while still hot.

Energy 405kcal/1680kJ; Protein 12.6g; Carbohydrate 14.1g, of which sugars 1.5g; Fat 33.7g, of which saturates 17.2g; Cholesterol 451mg; Calcium 112mg; Fibre 0.4g; Sodium 350mg

LOX WITH BAGELS AND CREAM CHEESE

THIS SOPHISTICATED DISH IS PERFECT FOR A WEEKEND BREAKFAST OR BRUNCH WITH FRIENDS. LOX IS THE JEWISH WORD FOR SMOKED SALMON, AND THIS DELI CLASSIC IS EASY TO MAKE AT HOME.

Preparation: 3 minutes; Cooking: 4–5 minutes

SERVES 2

INGREDIENTS
2 bagels
115–175g/4–6oz/½–¾ cup full-fat
   cream cheese
150g/5oz sliced best smoked salmon
ground black pepper
lemon wedges, to serve

1 Preheat the oven to 200°C/400°F/ Gas 6. Put the bagels on a large baking sheet and warm them in the oven for 4–5 minutes.

2 Remove the bagels from the oven, split them in two and spread each half generously with cream cheese. Pile the salmon on top of the bagel bases and grind over plenty of black pepper.

3 Squeeze over some lemon juice, then add the bagel tops, at an angle.

4 Place on serving plates with the lemon wedges. If you have time, wrap each lemon wedge in a small square of muslin (cheesecloth), tie with fine string and put it on the plate.

COOK'S TIP
It is essential to be generous with the smoked salmon and to use the best cream cheese you can find – absolutely not a low-fat version.

Energy 496kcal/2068kJ; Protein 25.9g; Carbohydrate 28.9g, of which sugars 3.3g; Fat 31.6g, of which saturates 17.7g; Cholesterol 81mg; Calcium 71mg; Fibre 1.2g; Sodium 1858mg

JUGGED KIPPERS

THE DEMAND FOR NATURALLY SMOKED KIPPERS IS EVER INCREASING. THEY ARE MOST POPULAR FOR BREAKFAST, WITH BUTTER, LEMON JUICE AND CRUSTY BREAD, AND ARE PREPARED IN MINUTES.

Preparation: 2–3 minutes; Cooking: 5–6 minutes

SERVES FOUR

INGREDIENTS
   4 kippers (smoked herrings),
      preferably naturally smoked,
      whole or filleted
   25g/1oz/2 tbsp butter
   ground black pepper
   lemon wedges, to serve

1 Select a heatproof glass jug (pitcher) tall enough for the kippers to be immersed when the water is added. If the heads are still on the kippers, remove them.

2 Put the fish into the jug, tails up, and then cover them with boiling water. Leave for about 5 minutes, until tender.

3 Drain well and serve on warmed plates with butter, a little black pepper and the lemon wedges.

Energy 248kcal/1025kJ; Protein 15.9g; Carbohydrate 0g, of which sugars 0g; Fat 20.4g, of which saturates 5.8g; Cholesterol 68mg; Calcium 49mg; Fibre 0g; Sodium 776mg

KEDGEREE

Energy 480kcal/2006kJ; Protein 23.5g; Carbohydrate 69.9g, of which sugars 0g; Fat 11.5g, of which saturates 4.9g; Cholesterol 224mg; Calcium 59mg; Fibre 0g; Sodium 536mg

IMPRESS HOUSE GUESTS BY RUSTLING UP THIS DELECTABLE DISH IN LESS TIME THAN IT TAKES THEM TO TAKE A SHOWER. KEDGEREE IS GREAT FOR BREAKFAST, BRUNCH OR SUPPER.
Preparation: 2–3 minutes; Cooking: 16 minutes

SERVES FOUR

INGREDIENTS
    350g/12oz/1½ cups basmati rice
    225g/8oz undyed smoked
        haddock fillet
    4 eggs
    25g/1oz/2 tbsp butter
    30ml/2 tbsp garam masala
    ground black pepper

1 Preheat the grill (broiler) to medium. Place the smoked haddock on a baking sheet and grill (broil) for 10 minutes, or until cooked through.

2 Meanwhile, place the eggs in a pan of cold water and bring to the boil. Cook for 6–7 minutes. At the same time as the eggs and haddock are cooking, cook the rice in a pan of boiling water for 10–12 minutes.

3 When the eggs are cooked, drain and place under cold running water until cool enough to handle. Shell the eggs and cut into halves or quarters.

4 Remove the baking sheet from under the grill and transfer the smoked haddock to a board. Remove the skin when cool enough to handle.

5 Using a fork, ease the flesh apart so that it separates into large flakes. Remove any remaining bones.

6 Drain the rice and tip it into a bowl. Melt the butter in a pan, stir in the garam masala and add the fish. When it has warmed through, add it to the rice with the smoked fish and eggs. Mix gently, taking care not to mash the eggs. Season and serve immediately.

LUNCHES ON THE GO

Sitting down to a leisurely meal is a luxury few of us allow ourselves these days. We read longingly about Mediterranean meals that start at 2 and end at 5, with the whole family sitting around a scrubbed wooden table in the garden, but the reality for most of us is that there are appointments to be kept and jobs to be finished. However, a fast-paced weekday routine need not mean running on empty until we can finally sit down to an evening meal. This chapter is packed with easy, tasty dishes, which can be rustled up with the minimum of fuss without losing any flavour. A simple meal of Gazpacho followed by Smoked Mackerel Pâté with Melba toast would make a delicious light meal — and perfect for those occasions where friends stop by for a quick bite to eat. If you prefer something hot to kick-start the afternoon, there is Smoked Salmon and Chive Omelette or Linguine with Rocket, plus there are a great range of fabulous salads that can be thrown together in minutes and easily packed for work.

CHILLED TOMATO SOUP WITH ROCKET PESTO

THIS SOUP TAKES HARDLY ANY TIME TO MAKE, BUT MUST BE CHILLED, SO BEAR THAT IN MIND WHEN PLANNING YOUR MENU. WHIZZ IT UP WHEN YOU WAKE, AND MAKE THE PESTO JUST BEFORE SERVING.

Preparation: 10 minutes; Cooking: 4–5 minutes; Chilling: 4–8 hours

SERVES FOUR

INGREDIENTS
225g/8oz cherry tomatoes, halved
225g/8oz baby plum
  tomatoes, halved
225g/8oz vine-ripened
  tomatoes, halved
2 shallots, roughly chopped
25ml/1½ tbsp sun-dried
  tomato purée (paste)
600ml/1 pint/2½ cups
  vegetable stock
salt and ground black pepper
ice cubes, to serve
For the rocket pesto
  15g/½oz rocket (arugula) leaves
  75ml/5 tbsp olive oil
  15g/½oz/2 tbsp pine nuts
  1 garlic clove
  25g/1oz/⅓ cup freshly grated
    Parmesan cheese

1 Purée all the tomatoes and the shallots in a food processor or blender. Add the sun-dried tomato paste and process until smooth. Press the purée through a sieve (strainer) into a pan.

2 Add the vegetable stock and heat gently for 4–5 minutes. Season well. Pour into a bowl, leave to cool, then chill for at least 4 hours.

3 For the rocket pesto, put the rocket, oil, pine nuts and garlic in a food processor or blender and process to form a paste. Transfer to a bowl and stir in the Parmesan cheese. (This can also be prepared using a mortar and pestle.)

4 Ladle the soup into bowls and add a few ice cubes to each. Spoon some of the rocket pesto into the centre of each portion and serve.

Energy 218kcal/902kJ; Protein 4.8g; Carbohydrate 7.5g, of which sugars 7.2g; Fat 19g, of which saturates 3.6g; Cholesterol 6mg; Calcium 100mg; Fibre 2.2g; Sodium 104mg

GAZPACHO

PROBABLY THE MOST FAMOUS CHILLED SOUP IN THE WORLD, THIS ORIGINATED IN SPAIN BUT NOW APPEARS ON MENUS EVERYWHERE. IT IS PERFECT FOR A SUMMER LUNCH IN THE GARDEN.

Preparation: 12 minutes; Cooking: 5–6 minutes; Chilling: 4–8 hours

SERVES SIX

INGREDIENTS
    900g/2lb ripe tomatoes, peeled
      and seeded
    1 cucumber, peeled and
      roughly chopped
    2 red (bell) peppers, seeded and
      roughly chopped
    2 garlic cloves, crushed
    1 large onion, roughly chopped
    30ml/2 tbsp white wine vinegar
    120ml/4fl oz/½ cup olive oil
    250g/9oz/4½ cups fresh white
      breadcrumbs
    450ml/¾ pint/scant 2 cups iced water
    salt and ground black pepper
    ice cubes, to serve
For the garnish
    30–45ml/2–3 tbsp olive oil
    4 thick slices bread, crusts removed,
      cut into small cubes
    2 tomatoes, peeled, seeded and
      finely diced
    1 small green (bell) pepper, seeded
      and finely diced
    1 small onion, very finely sliced
    a small bunch of fresh flat leaf
      parsley, chopped

1 In a large bowl, mix the tomatoes, cucumber, peppers, garlic and onion. Stir in the vinegar, oil, breadcrumbs and water until well mixed. Purée the mixture in a food processor or blender until almost smooth, and pour into a large bowl. Stir in salt and pepper to taste and chill for at least 4 hours.

2 To make the garnish, heat the oil in a frying pan and add the bread cubes.

3 Fry over a medium heat for 5–6 minutes, stirring occasionally to brown evenly. Lift out the cubes with a slotted spoon, drain on kitchen paper and put into a small bowl. Place the remaining garnishing ingredients in separate bowls or on a serving plate.

COOK'S TIP
If the vegetable and vinegar mixture seems very thick after puréeing, stir in a little water. Cover the bowl with clear film before chilling the soup.

4 Ladle the gazpacho into bowls and add ice cubes to each portion. Serve at once. Pass around the bowls of garnishing ingredients with the soup so that they can be added to taste.

Energy 412kcal/1730kJ; Protein 9.1g; Carbohydrate 55.6g, of which sugars 14.7g; Fat 18.6g, of which saturates 2.6g; Cholesterol 0mg; Calcium 109mg; Fibre 5g; Sodium 431mg

AVOCADO SOUP

THIS DELICIOUS SOUP HAS A FRESH, DELICATE FLAVOUR AND A WONDERFUL COLOUR. FOR ADDED ZEST, ADD A GENEROUS SQUEEZE OF LIME OR LEMON JUICE JUST BEFORE SERVING.

Preparation: 3 minutes; Cooking: 3–4 minutes

SERVES FOUR

INGREDIENTS
2 large ripe avocados
300ml/½ pint/1¼ cups sour cream
1 litre/1¾ pints/4 cups
  well-flavoured chicken stock
a small bunch of fresh coriander
  (cilantro), chopped
salt and ground black pepper

COOK'S TIP
Choose ripe avocados for this soup – they should feel soft when gently pressed. Keep very firm avocados at room temperature for 3–4 days until they soften. To speed ripening, place in a brown paper bag.

1 Cut the avocados in half, remove the peel and lift out the stones (pits). Chop the flesh coarsely and place it in a food processor with 45–60ml/3–4 tbsp of the sour cream. Process until smooth.

2 Heat the chicken stock in a pan. When it is hot, but still below simmering point, add the rest of the sour cream and stir gently to mix.

3 Gradually stir the avocado mixture into the hot stock. Heat gently but do not let the mixture approach boiling point. Add salt to taste.

4 Ladle the soup into heated bowls and sprinkle each portion with chopped coriander and black pepper. Serve immediately, as it will discolour on standing.

Energy 343kcal/1416kJ; Protein 4.4g; Carbohydrate 5.1g, of which sugars 3.6g; Fat 33.9g, of which saturates 13.4g; Cholesterol 45mg; Calcium 106mg; Fibre 4g; Sodium 41mg

BUTTER BEAN AND SUN-DRIED TOMATO SOUP

THIS SOUP IS QUICK AND EASY TO MAKE. THE KEY IS TO USE A GOOD QUALITY HOME-MADE OR BOUGHT FRESH STOCK WITH PLENTY OF PESTO AND SUN-DRIED TOMATO PURÉE.

Preparation: 2 minutes; Cooking: 12 minutes

SERVES FOUR

INGREDIENTS

2 x 400g/14oz cans butter (lima)
  beans, drained and rinsed
900ml/1½ pints/3¾ cups chicken
  or vegetable stock
60ml/4 tbsp sun-dried tomato
  purée (paste)
75ml/5 tbsp pesto

COOK'S TIP
For the busy cook, good-quality bought stocks are a blessing. Most large supermarkets now sell fresh stock in tubs. Another good product is concentrated liquid stock, sold in bottles. However, if you cannot find any of the above, a good-quality stock cube will do the job.

1 Put the butter beans in a pan. Stir in the stock and bring to the boil over a medium heat, stirring once or twice.

2 Stir in the tomato purée and pesto. Lower the heat and cook gently for 5 minutes.

3 Transfer six ladlefuls of the soup to a blender or food processor, scooping up plenty of the beans. Process until smooth, then return the purée to the pan.

4 Heat gently, stirring frequently, for 5 minutes, then season if necessary. Ladle into four warmed soup bowls and serve with warm crusty bread or breadsticks.

Energy 269kcal/1130kJ; Protein 15.6g; Carbohydrate 28.3g, of which sugars 4.5g; Fat 11.2g, of which saturates 2.5g; Cholesterol 6mg; Calcium 111mg; Fibre 9.7g; Sodium 944mg

CHOPPED EGGS AND ONIONS

QUICK AND EASY TO MAKE, THIS IS A SPEEDY LUNCH. YOU COULD EVEN PACK IT UP AND TAKE IT TO WORK, ALTHOUGH THE AROMA OF EGGS AND ONION MIGHT NOT PROVE IRRESISTIBLE TO EVERYONE.

Preparation: 3–4 minutes; Cooking: 12 minutes

SERVES FOUR TO SIX

INGREDIENTS
  8–10 eggs
  6–8 spring onions (scallions) and/or
   1 yellow or white onion, very finely
   chopped, plus extra to garnish
  60–90ml/4–6 tbsp mayonnaise
  mild French wholegrain mustard,
   to taste (optional)
  15ml/1 tbsp chopped fresh parsley
  salt and ground black pepper
  rye toasts or crackers, to serve

COOK'S TIP
Holding a freshly boiled egg under cold running water helps to prevent the yolk from acquiring a greenish tinge where it meets the white.

1 Put the eggs in a large pan and pour in cold water to cover. Heat the water. When it boils, reduce the heat and simmer the eggs for 10 minutes. Stir the eggs twice so they cook evenly.

2 Drain the eggs, hold them under cold running water, then remove the shells, dry the eggs and chop roughly.

3 Place the chopped eggs in a large bowl. Add the onions, season with salt and pepper and mix well. Add enough mayonnaise to bind the mixture together. Stir in the mustard, if using, and the chopped parsley, or sprinkle the parsley on top to garnish. If you have time, chill the mixture before serving with rye toasts or crackers.

Energy 170kcal/706kJ; Protein 8.7g; Carbohydrate 0.5g, of which sugars 0.5g; Fat 15.1g, of which saturates 3.2g; Cholesterol 261mg; Calcium 48mg; Fibre 0.3g; Sodium 140mg

SMOKED MACKEREL PATÉ

THIS TASTY PATÉ BENEFITS FROM BEING CHILLED FOR A COUPLE OF HOURS, BUT IF YOU HAVEN'T GOT TIME FOR THAT, SERVE IT RIGHT AWAY. IT WON'T BE AS FIRM, BUT WILL TASTE JUST AS DELICIOUS.

Preparation: 2–3 minutes; Cooking: 20 minutes; Chilling: 1–2 hours (optional)

SERVES SIX

INGREDIENTS

4 smoked mackerel fillets, skinned
225g/8oz/1 cup cream cheese
1–2 garlic cloves, finely chopped
juice of 1 lemon
30ml/2 tbsp chopped fresh chervil,
  parsley or chives
15ml/1 tbsp Worcestershire sauce
salt and cayenne pepper
fresh chives, to garnish
warmed Melba toast, to serve

VARIATION
Use peppered mackerel fillets for a more piquant flavour. This pâté is also delicious when prepared using smoked haddock or kipper (smoked herring) fillets.

1 Break up the smoked mackerel fillets and put them in a food processor. Add the cream cheese, chopped garlic and lemon juice.

2 Process the mixture for a few seconds, just long enough to mix the ingredients, then add the chopped chervil, parsley or chives.

3 Process the mixture until it is fairly smooth but still slightly chunky, then add Worcestershire sauce, salt and cayenne pepper to taste. Process again to mix.

4 Spoon the pâté into a dish, cover with clear film (plastic wrap) and chill. Garnish with chives and serve with Melba toast.

Energy 344kcal/1421kJ; Protein 10.7g; Carbohydrate 0.5g, of which sugars 0.4g; Fat 33.3g, of which saturates 14.3g; Cholesterol 88mg; Calcium 57mg; Fibre 0.1g; Sodium 518mg

WHITEFISH SALAD <u>WITH</u> TOASTED BAGELS

A TRADITIONAL DELI FAVOURITE, SMOKED WHITEFISH MAKES A SUPERB SALAD. IF YOU CAN'T FIND IT, USE SMOKED HALIBUT, BUT DON'T PASS UP THE BAGELS, WHICH ARE THE PERFECT ACCOMPANIMENT.

Preparation: 8–10 minutes; Cooking: 0 minutes

SERVES FOUR TO SIX

INGREDIENTS

1 smoked whitefish or halibut,
  skinned and boned
2 celery sticks, chopped
½ red, white or yellow onion
  or 3–5 spring onions
  (scallions), chopped
45ml/3 tbsp mayonnaise
45ml/3 tbsp sour cream
juice of ½–1 lemon
1 round lettuce
ground black pepper
5–10ml/1–2 tsp chopped fresh
  parsley, to garnish
toasted bagels, to serve

1 Break the smoked fish into bitesize pieces. In a bowl, combine the chopped celery, onion or spring onion, mayonnaise and sour cream, and add lemon juice to taste.

2 Fold the fish into the mixture and season with pepper. Arrange the lettuce leaves on serving plates, then spoon the smoked fish salad on top. Sprinkle with parsley and serve with bagels.

Energy 108kcal/450kJ; Protein 7.8g; Carbohydrate 1.6g, of which sugars 1.3g; Fat 7.9g, of which saturates 1.9g; Cholesterol 22mg; Calcium 29mg; Fibre 0.4g; Sodium 64mg

FOCACCIA WITH SARDINES AND ROAST TOMATOES

FRESH SARDINES NOT ONLY HAVE A LOVELY FLAVOUR AND TEXTURE, BUT ARE ALSO CHEAP TO BUY SO MAKE AN ECONOMICAL YET UTTERLY DELICIOUS LUNCH IN NEXT TO NO TIME.

Preparation: 3–4 minutes; Cooking: 15 minutes

SERVES FOUR

INGREDIENTS
20 cherry tomatoes
45ml/3 tbsp herb-infused olive oil
12 fresh sardine fillets
1 focaccia loaf
salt and ground black pepper

VARIATIONS
This rather sumptuous topping tastes great on focaccia, but a split French stick would work just as well. If you happen to have some cold boiled potatoes in the refrigerator, slice them and fry them quickly in oil, while the sardines are cooking. Abandon the bread and pile the sardines and tomatoes on top of the potatoes instead.

1 Preheat the oven to 190°C/375°F/ Gas 5. Put the cherry tomatoes in a small roasting pan and drizzle 30ml/ 2 tbsp of the herb-infused olive oil over the top.

2 Season the tomatoes with salt and pepper and roast for 10–15 minutes, shaking the pan gently once or twice so that the tomatoes cook evenly on all sides. When they are tender and slightly charred, remove from the oven and set aside.

3 While the tomatoes are cooking, preheat the grill (broiler) to high. Brush the sardine fillets with the remaining oil and lay them on a baking sheet. Grill (broil) for 4–5 minutes on each side, until cooked through.

4 Split the focaccia in half horizontally and cut each piece in half to give four equal pieces. Toast the cut side under the grill. Top with the sardines and tomatoes and an extra drizzle of oil. Season with black pepper and serve.

Energy 301kcal/1262kJ; Protein 15.8g; Carbohydrate 27.6g, of which sugars 3.1g; Fat 15g, of which saturates 2.9g; Cholesterol 0mg; Calcium 106mg; Fibre 1.7g; Sodium 334mg

WALNUT AND GOAT'S CHEESE ON BRUSCHETTA

THE COMBINATION OF TOASTED WALNUTS AND MELTING GOAT'S CHEESE IS LOVELY IN THIS SIMPLE LUNCHTIME SNACK, WHICH CAN BE SERVED WITH A DRESSED SALAD IF THE OCCASION CALLS FOR IT.

Preparation: 5 minutes; Cooking: 3–5 minutes

SERVES FOUR

INGREDIENTS

50g/2oz/½ cup walnut pieces
4 thick slices walnut bread
120ml/4fl oz/½ cup French dressing
200g/7oz chèvre or other semi-soft
  goat's cheese

COOK'S TIP
Walnut bread is sold in most large supermarkets and makes an interesting alternative to ordinary crusty bread, although a freshly baked loaf of the latter is fine if speciality breads are not available. If using crusty bread, try to find a slender loaf to slice, so that the portions are not too wide. If you can only buy a large loaf, cut the slices in half to make neat, chunky pieces.

1 Preheat the grill (broiler). Spread out the walnut pieces on a baking sheet. Lightly toast them, shivering the baking sheet once or twice so that they cook evenly, then remove and set aside.

2 Put the walnut bread on a foil-lined grill rack and toast on one side. Turn the slices over and drizzle each with 15ml/1 tbsp of the dressing.

3 Cut the goat's cheese into twelve slices and place three on each piece of bread. Grill (broil) for about 3 minutes, until the cheese is melting and beginning to brown.

4 Transfer the bruschetta to serving plates, sprinkle with the toasted walnuts and drizzle with the remaining French dressing. Serve the bruschetta immediately with salad leaves.

Energy 558kcal/2321kJ; Protein 16.7g; Carbohydrate 25.6g, of which sugars 2.2g; Fat 37.2g, of which saturates 12.7g; Cholesterol 47mg; Calcium 137mg; Fibre 1.2g; Sodium 841mg

ANCHOVY AND QUAIL'S EGG BRUSCHETTA

QUAIL'S EGGS TASTE MARVELLOUS WITH THE ANCHOVIES AND MILD RED ONION SLICES, ESPECIALLY WHEN THE MIXTURE IS PILED ON TOASTED CIABATTA WHICH HAS BEEN RUBBED WITH FRESH GARLIC.
Preparation: 15 minutes; Cooking: 3–5 minutes

SERVES FOUR TO SIX

INGREDIENTS
50g/2oz anchovy fillets in salt
milk, for soaking
12 quail's eggs
2–3 garlic cloves
1 ciabatta or similar loaf
coarse salt
1 red onion, halved and thinly sliced
10–15ml/2–3 tsp cumin seeds,
   roasted and ground
a small bunch of flat leaf parsley,
   roughly chopped
30–45ml/2–3 tbsp olive oil

1 Soak the anchovies in milk for 15 minutes to reduce the salty flavour.

2 Meanwhile, put the quail's eggs in a pan of cold water. Bring to the boil and cook for 2 minutes, then drain and plunge into cold water.

3 Remove the skin from the garlic cloves, halve, and crush using a pestle and mortar.

4 Preheat the grill (broiler) on the hottest setting. Slice the loaf of bread horizontally in half and toast the cut sides until golden.

5 Rub the toasted bread all over with the crushed garlic and sprinkle with a little salt. Don't overdo this, as the anchovies will be quite salty.

6 Cut each piece of bread into four or six equal pieces. Drain the quail's eggs, shell them and cut them in half. Drain the anchovy fillets. Pile the onion slices, quail's egg halves and anchovy fillets on the pieces of bread. Sprinkle liberally with the ground roasted cumin and chopped parsley and serve immediately.

Energy 181kcal/761kJ; Protein 8.8g; Carbohydrate 18.2g, of which sugars 1.7g; Fat 8.6g, of which saturates 1.6g; Cholesterol 100mg; Calcium 87mg; Fibre 1g; Sodium 543mg

MUSHROOMS <u>ON</u> SPICY TOAST

DRY-PANNING IS A QUICK WAY OF COOKING MUSHROOMS THAT MAKES THE MOST OF THEIR FLAVOUR.
THE JUICES RUN WHEN THE MUSHROOMS ARE HEATED, SO THEY BECOME REALLY MOIST AND TENDER.
Preparation: 2–3 minutes; Cooking: 4–5 minutes

SERVES FOUR

INGREDIENTS
  8–12 large flat field (portabello)
    mushrooms
  50g/1oz/2 tbsp butter
  5ml/1 tsp curry paste
  salt
  4 slices thickly-sliced white bread,
    toasted, to serve

1 Preheat the oven to 200°C/400°F/
Gas 6. Peel the mushrooms, if
necessary, and remove the stalks. Heat
a dry frying pan until very hot.

2 Place the mushrooms in the hot frying
pan, with the gills on top. Using half
the butter, add a piece the size of a
hazelnut to each one, then sprinkle all
the mushrooms lightly with salt.

3 Cook over a medium heat until the
butter begins to bubble and the
mushrooms are juicy and tender.

4 Meanwhile, mix the remaining butter
with the curry powder. Spread on the
bread. Bake in the oven for 10 minutes,
pile the mushrooms on top and serve.

VARIATIONS
• Using a flavoured butter makes these
mushrooms even more special. Try one of
the following:
• **Herb butter** Mix softened butter with
chopped fresh herbs such as parsley and
thyme, or marjoram and chopped chives.
• **Olive butter** Mix softened butter with diced
green olives and spring onions (scallions).
• **Tomato butter** Mix softened butter with
sun-dried tomato purée (paste).
• **Garlic butter** Mix softened butter with
finely chopped garlic.
• **Pepper and Paprika butter** Mix softened
butter with 2.5ml/½ tsp paprika and
2.5ml/½ tsp black pepper.

Energy 230kcal/966kJ; Protein 6.1g; Carbohydrate 25.1g, of which sugars 1.6g; Fat 12.5g, of which saturates 6.7g; Cholesterol 27mg; Calcium 63mg; Fibre 1.9g; Sodium 341mg

GOLDEN GRUYÈRE AND BASIL TORTILLAS

TORTILLA FLIP-OVERS ARE A GREAT INVENTION. ONCE YOU'VE TRIED THIS RECIPE, YOU'LL WANT TO EXPERIMENT WITH DIFFERENT FILLINGS AND LEFTOVERS WILL NEVER GO TO WASTE AGAIN.

Preparation: 1–2 minutes; Cooking: 4 minutes

SERVES TWO

INGREDIENTS
   15ml/1 tbsp olive oil
   2 soft flour tortillas
   115g/4oz Gruyère cheese,
      thinly sliced
   a handful of fresh basil leaves
   salt and ground black pepper

VARIATION
These crisp tortillas make excellent snacks to share with friends on a night in. If you have a few slices of ham or salami in the refrigerator, add these to the tortillas – or simply prepare a mixture of the two to satisfy a range of palates.

1 Heat the oil in a frying pan over a medium heat. Add one of the tortillas, and heat through for 1 minute.

2 Arrange the Gruyère cheese slices and basil leaves on top of the tortilla and season with salt and pepper.

3 Place the remaining tortilla on top to make a sandwich and flip the whole thing over with a metal spatula. Cook for a few minutes, until the underneath is golden.

4 Slide the tortilla sandwich on to a chopping board or plate and cut into wedges. Serve immediately.

Energy 354kcal/1474kJ; Protein 16.4g; Carbohydrate 15g, of which sugars 0.4g; Fat 24.6g, of which saturates 13.3g; Cholesterol 56mg; Calcium 453mg; Fibre 0.6g; Sodium 486mg

STEAK AND BLUE CHEESE ON CIABATTA

MANY PEOPLE PREFER THEIR STEAKS COOKED QUITE RARE IN THE CENTRE, BUT THEY ARE STILL DELICIOUS IF COOKED A LITTLE LONGER. ADD A COUPLE OF MINUTES TO THE COOKING TIME IF NECESSARY.

Preparation: 2–3 minutes; Cooking: 12–14 minutes

SERVES TWO

INGREDIENTS
1 part-baked ciabatta bread
2 ribeye steaks, about
 200g/7oz each
15ml/1 tbsp olive oil
115g/4oz Gorgonzola cheese, sliced
salt and ground black pepper

1 Bake the ciabatta according to the instructions on the packet. Remove from the oven and leave to rest while you cook the steak.

2 Heat a griddle pan until hot. Brush the steaks with the olive oil and lay them on the griddle pan. Cook for 2–3 minutes on each side, depending on the thickness of the steaks.

3 Remove the steaks and set them aside to rest. Meanwhile, cut the loaf in half and split each half horizontally.

4 Cut the steaks in half lengthways so each is only half as thick as before. Moisten the bread with the pan juices then make into sandwiches using the steak and cheese. Season well and serve.

COOK'S TIP
Part-baked bread cooks in about 8 minutes in a hot oven, but if even that is too long, just warm a regular baked ciabatta or French stick.

Energy 767kcal/3221kJ; Protein 66g; Carbohydrate 52g, of which sugars 3.1g; Fat 34.2g, of which saturates 15.8g; Cholesterol 161mg; Calcium 410mg; Fibre 2.3g; Sodium 1360mg

MEXICAN TORTAS

THE GOOD THING ABOUT HOLLOWING OUT A BREAD ROLL IS THAT YOU CAN PACK IN MORE FILLING. THIS MEXICAN SNACK USES ROAST PORK AND REFRIED BEANS BUT EXPERIMENTING IS EXPECTED.

Preparation: 5–6 minutes; Cooking: 0 minutes

SERVES FOUR

INGREDIENTS

  2 fresh jalapeño chillies
  juice of ½ lime
  2 French bread rolls or 2 pieces
    French bread
  75g/3oz/²/₃ cup canned refried beans
  150g/5oz roast pork
  2 small tomatoes, sliced
  115g/4oz Cheddar or Monterey Jack
    cheese, sliced
  a small bunch of fresh coriander
    (cilantro)
  30ml/2 tbsp crème fraîche

1 Cut the chillies in half, scrape out the seeds, then cut the flesh into thin strips. Put it in a bowl, pour in the lime juice and leave to stand.

VARIATION
Sliced chicken carved from the rotisserie is another popular Mexican torta filler.

2 If using rolls, slice them in half and remove some of the crumb so that they are slightly hollowed. If using French bread, slice each piece in half lengthways.

3 Set the top of each piece of bread or roll aside and spread the bottom halves with a nice thick layer of the refried beans. Make sure the paste is evenly spread, as it will help to hold the next layer in place.

4 Cut the pork into thin shreds and put these on top of the refried beans. Top with the tomato slices. Drain the jalapeño strips and put them on top of the tomato slices. Add the cheese and sprinkle with coriander leaves.

5 Turn the top halves of the bread or rolls over so that the cut sides are uppermost, and spread these with crème fraîche. Sandwich back together again and serve.

Energy 307kcal/1285kJ; Protein 22.8g; Carbohydrate 18.2g, of which sugars 2.9g; Fat 15.8g, of which saturates 9.4g; Cholesterol 78mg; Calcium 271mg; Fibre 2g; Sodium 485mg

SMOKED SALMON AND CHIVE OMELETTE

THE ADDITION OF A GENEROUS PORTION OF CHOPPED SMOKED SALMON GIVES A REALLY LUXURIOUS FINISH TO THIS SIMPLE, CLASSIC DISH, WHICH IS AN IDEAL QUICK LUNCH FOR TWO PEOPLE.

Preparation: 2–3 minutes; Cooking: 5–6 minutes

SERVES TWO

INGREDIENTS
  4 eggs
  15ml/1 tbsp chopped fresh chives or
    spring onions (scallions)
  a knob (pat) of butter
  50g/2oz smoked salmon,
    roughly chopped
  salt and ground black pepper

1 Break the eggs into a bowl. Beat with a fork until just combined, then stir in the chopped fresh chives or spring onions. Season with salt and a generous sprinkling of freshly ground black pepper, and set aside.

2 Heat the butter in a medium frying pan until foamy. Pour in the eggs and cook over a medium heat for 3–4 minutes, drawing the cooked egg from around the edge into the centre of the pan from time to time.

3 At this stage, you can either leave the top of the omelette slightly soft or finish it off under the grill (broiler), depending on how you like your omelette. Top with the smoked salmon, fold the omelette over and cut in half to serve.

Energy 221kcal/920kJ; Protein 19g; Carbohydrate 0.2g, of which sugars 0.2g; Fat 16.4g, of which saturates 5.9g; Cholesterol 400mg; Calcium 65mg; Fibre 0.1g; Sodium 641mg

PEA <u>AND</u> MINT OMELETTE

SERVE THIS DELICIOUSLY LIGHT OMELETTE WITH CRUSTY BREAD AND A GREEN SALAD FOR A FRESH AND TASTY LUNCH. WHEN THEY ARE IN SEASON, USE FRESHLY SHELLED PEAS INSTEAD OF FROZEN ONES.
Preparation: 2 minutes; Cooking: 8–10 minutes

SERVES TWO

INGREDIENTS
   50g/2oz/½ cup frozen peas
   4 eggs
   30ml/2 tbsp chopped fresh mint
   a knob (pat) of butter
   salt and ground black pepper

VARIATION
When young broad (fava) beans are in season, use them instead of peas. Shell the beans and cook them in boiling salted water for 3–4 minutes until just tender. Meanwhile, grill (broil) 3–4 slices of bacon. Add the beans to the egg mixture instead of the peas and crumble the bacon over the omelette when it is almost cooked.

1 Break the eggs into a large bowl and beat with a fork. Season well with salt and pepper and set aside.

2 Cook the peas in a large pan of salted boiling water for 3–4 minutes until tender. Drain well in a colander and add to the eggs in the bowl. Stir in the chopped fresh mint and swirl with a spoon until thoroughly combined.

3 Heat the butter in a medium frying pan until foamy. Pour in the egg mixture and cook over a medium heat for 3–4 minutes, drawing in the cooked egg from the edges from time to time, until the mixture is nearly set.

4 Finish off cooking the omelette under a hot grill (broiler) until set and golden. Carefully fold the omelette over, cut it in half and serve immediately.

Energy 208kcal/865kJ; Protein 14.6g; Carbohydrate 3.3g, of which sugars 0.6g; Fat 15.7g, of which saturates 5.8g; Cholesterol 391mg; Calcium 79mg; Fibre 1.2g; Sodium 172mg

WARM PASTA SALAD WITH ASPARAGUS

TAGLIATELLE DRESSED WITH A CREAMY ASPARAGUS SAUCE IS THE BASIS FOR THIS SUSTAINING SALAD. IF YOU'VE SPENT THE MORNING GARDENING OR PLAYING SPORT, THIS IS A GREAT QUICK LUNCH.

Preparation: 6 minutes; Cooking: 12 minutes

SERVES FOUR

INGREDIENTS

450g/1lb asparagus
450g/1lb dried tagliatelle
225g/8oz cooked ham, in 5mm/¼ in-
  thick slices, cut into fingers
2 eggs, hard-boiled and sliced
50g/2oz Parmesan cheese
salt and ground black pepper

For the dressing

50g/2oz cooked potato
75ml/5 tbsp olive oil
15ml/1 tbsp lemon juice
10ml/2 tsp Dijon mustard
120ml/4fl oz/½ cup vegetable stock

VARIATIONS

Use sliced chicken instead of the ham, or thin slices of softer Italian cheese, such as Fontina or Asiago.

1 Snap the asparagus spears and discard the tough woody ends. Cut the spears in half and cook the thicker halves in boiling salted water for 12 minutes, adding the tips after 6 minutes.

2 Meanwhile, boil the pasta in a large pan of salted water for 10–12 minutes until tender.

3 Drain the asparagus. Reserve the tips. Purée the remainder with the dressing ingredients until smooth.

4 Drain the pasta, toss with the asparagus sauce and cool slightly. Divide among four pasta plates. Top with the ham, hard-boiled eggs and asparagus tips. Shave Parmesan cheese over the top.

Energy 699kcal/2941kJ; Protein 35.4g; Carbohydrate 88.2g, of which sugars 6.6g; Fat 25.2g, of which saturates 6.3g; Cholesterol 140mg; Calcium 228mg; Fibre 5.3g; Sodium 852mg

BACON SALAD WITH CAMEMBERT DRESSING

FRIED APPLES AND BACON ARE PERFECT PARTNERS. HERE THEY ARE HEAPED OVER CRISP LETTUCE TO MAKE AN IRRESISTIBLE SALAD. A WARM TANGY CHEESE DRESSING ADDS THE FINISHING TOUCH.

Preparation: 5 minutes; Cooking: 4–5 minutes

SERVES FOUR

INGREDIENTS
30ml/2 tbsp olive oil
50g/2oz diced streaky (fatty) bacon slices, preferably dry-cured, diced
1 eating apple, cored and chopped
2 small heads cos or romaine lettuce
a squeeze of lemon juice
salt and ground black pepper
For the dressing
150ml/¼ pint/⅔ cup sour cream
15ml/1 tbsp cider
50g/2oz Camembert or similar cheese, chopped
a dash of cider vinegar

VARIATION
For a slightly tangier topping, replace the Camembert with a mild and creamy blue cheese, such as Cambozola.

1 Heat 15ml/1 tbsp of the olive oil in a large frying pan and add the diced streaky bacon. Cook over a medium heat until crisp and golden. Add the chopped apple and cook gently for 1–2 minutes until golden brown and softened.

2 Tear the cos or romain lettuce carefully into bitesize pieces.

3 To make the dressing, heat the sour cream, cider, cheese and vinegar together in a small pan over a low heat until smooth and creamy.

4 Toss the lettuce with the remaining oil and the lemon juice, season, then divide among four plates. Heap the warm apple and bacon on top, then drizzle over the dressing.

Energy 190kcal/785kJ; Protein 5.9g; Carbohydrate 3.5g, of which sugars 3.5g; Fat 16.7g, of which saturates 8.4g; Cholesterol 42mg; Calcium 76mg; Fibre 0.5g; Sodium 244mg

SALAD OF WILD GREENS AND OLIVES

THIS SIMPLE SALAD ONLY TAKES A FEW MINUTES TO PUT TOGETHER. USE AS WIDE A VARIETY OF GREENS AS YOU CAN FIND, MATCHING SWEET FLAVOURS WITH A FEW BITTER LEAVES FOR ACCENT.

Preparation: 6 minutes; Cooking: 0 minutes

SERVES FOUR

INGREDIENTS
- 115g/4oz wild rocket (arugula)
- 1 packet mixed salad leaves
- ¼ white cabbage, thinly sliced
- 1 cucumber, sliced
- 1 small red onion, chopped
- 2–3 garlic cloves, chopped
- 3–5 tomatoes, cut into wedges
- 1 green (bell) pepper, seeded and sliced
- 2–3 mint sprigs, sliced or torn
- 15–30ml/1–2 tbsp chopped fresh parsley and/or tarragon or dill
- pinch of dried oregano or thyme
- 45ml/3 tbsp extra virgin olive oil
- juice of ½ lemon
- 15ml/1 tbsp red wine vinegar
- 15–20 black olives
- salt and ground black pepper
- cottage cheese, to serve

1 In a large salad bowl, put the rocket, mixed salad leaves, sliced white cabbage, sliced cucumber, chopped onion and chopped garlic. Toss gently with your fingers to combine the leaves and vegetables.

COOK'S TIP
Try to find mixed salad leaves that include varieties such as lamb's lettuce, purslane and mizuna.

2 Arrange the tomatoes, pepper, mint, fresh and dried herbs, salt and pepper on top of the greens and vegetables. Drizzle over the oil, lemon juice and vinegar, stud with the olives and serve with a bowl of cottage cheese.

VARIATION
This is traditionally served with labneh or yogurt cheese, but tastes good with cottage cheese too.

Energy 150kcal/619kJ; Protein 3.3g; Carbohydrate 10.4g, of which sugars 9.8g; Fat 10.7g, of which saturates 1.6g; Cholesterol 0mg; Calcium 106mg; Fibre 4.2g; Sodium 338mg

LEMONY COUSCOUS SALAD

THIS POPULAR SALAD MIXES OLIVES, ALMONDS AND COURGETTES WITH FLUFFY COUSCOUS AND ADDS A HERB, LEMON JUICE AND OLIVE OIL DRESSING. IT HAS A DELICIOUSLY DELICATE FLAVOUR.

Preparation: 10 minutes; Cooking: 0 minutes

SERVES FOUR

INGREDIENTS

275g/10oz/1⅔ cups couscous
550ml/18fl oz/2½ cups boiling
 vegetable stock
2 small courgettes (zucchini)
16–20 black olives
25g/1oz/¼ cup flaked (sliced)
 almonds, toasted
60ml/4 tbsp olive oil
15ml/1 tbsp lemon juice
15ml/1 tbsp chopped fresh
 coriander (cilantro)
15ml/1 tbsp chopped fresh parsley
a good pinch of ground cumin
a good pinch of cayenne pepper

1 Place the couscous in a bowl and pour over the boiling stock. Stir with a fork and then set aside for 10 minutes until all the stock has been absorbed and the couscous has fluffed up.

2 Meanwhile, trim the courgettes and cut them into pieces about 2.5cm/1in long. Slice into fine julienne strips with a sharp knife. Halve the black olives, discarding the stones (pits).

3 Fluff up the couscous with a fork, then carefully mix in the courgettes, olives and almonds.

4 Whisk the olive oil, lemon juice, coriander, parsley, cumin and cayenne in a bowl. Stir into the salad and toss gently. Transfer to a large serving dish and serve.

Energy 319kcal/1322kJ; Protein 6.6g; Carbohydrate 36.9g, of which sugars 1.4g; Fat 16.9g, of which saturates 2.1g; Cholesterol 0mg; Calcium 68mg; Fibre 1.8g; Sodium 286mg

SPAGHETTI WITH LEMON

THIS IS THE DISH TO MAKE WHEN YOU RUSH HOME FOR A QUICK BITE TO EAT AND FIND THERE'S NOTHING IN THE HOUSE EXCEPT A LEMON, SOME GARLIC AND WHAT'S IN THE PANTRY.

Preparation: 2–3 minutes; Cooking: 15 minutes

SERVES FOUR

INGREDIENTS
    350g/12oz dried spaghetti
    90ml/6 tbsp extra virgin olive oil
    juice of 1 large lemon
    2 garlic cloves, cut into
      very thin slivers
    salt and ground black pepper

COOK'S TIP
Spaghetti is the best type of pasta for this recipe, because the olive oil and lemon juice cling to its long thin strands. If you are out of spaghetti, use another dried long pasta shape instead, such as spaghettini, linguine or tagliatelle.

1 Cook the pasta in a pan of lightly salted boiling water for 10–12 minutes, until tender, then drain well and return to the pan.

2 Pour the olive oil and lemon juice over the cooked pasta, sprinkle in the slivers of garlic and add seasoning to taste. Toss the pasta over a medium to high heat for 1–2 minutes. Serve immediately in four warmed bowls.

Energy 448kcal/1886kJ; Protein 10.5g; Carbohydrate 64.9g, of which sugars 3g; Fat 18.1g, of which saturates 2.5g; Cholesterol 0mg; Calcium 22mg; Fibre 2.6g; Sodium 3mg

LINGUINE WITH ROCKET

THIS FASHIONABLE LUNCH IS VERY QUICK AND EASY TO MAKE AT HOME. ROCKET HAS AN EXCELLENT PEPPERY FLAVOUR WHICH COMBINES BEAUTIFULLY WITH THE PARMESAN.

Preparation: 3–5 minutes; Cooking: 11–14 minutes

SERVES FOUR

INGREDIENTS

350g/12oz dried linguine
120ml/4fl oz/½ cup extra virgin
   olive oil
1 large bunch rocket (arugula), about
   150g/5oz, stalks removed, shredded
75g/3oz/1 cup freshly grated
   Parmesan cheese

4 Toss the mixture quickly to mix all the flavours together and ensure the pasta is well coated with the oil. Serve immediately, sprinkled with the remaining Parmesan.

COOK'S TIPS

• Fresh Parmesan keeps well in the refrigerator for up to a month, if wrapped in greaseproof paper.

• Linguine is an egg pasta and looks rather like flattened strands of spaghetti. Spaghetti, fettucine or pappardelle could be used instead. Dried pasta cooks in just over 10 minutes, but an even faster result can be obtained by using fresh pasta.

Simply add it to a large pan of boiling, lightly salted water, making sure that all the strands are fully submerged, and cook for 2–3 minutes. The pasta is ready when it rises to the top of the pan and is tender to the taste, with a slight firmness in the centre.

1 Cook the pasta in a large pan of lightly salted boiling water for 10–12 minutes, until tender, then drain thoroughly.

2 Heat about 60ml/4 tbsp of the olive oil in the pasta pan, then add the drained pasta and rocket. Toss over a medium heat for 1–2 minutes, or until the rocket is just wilted, then remove the pan from the heat.

3 Transfer the pasta and rocket to a large, warmed bowl. Add half the freshly grated Parmesan and the remaining olive oil. Add a little salt and black pepper to taste.

Energy 573kcal/2404kJ; Protein 19g; Carbohydrate 65.4g, of which sugars 3.5g; Fat 28g, of which saturates 6.9g; Cholesterol 19mg; Calcium 311mg; Fibre 3.3g; Sodium 260mg

MEATY MEALS
IN MINUTES

When you only have a little time to produce a first-class meal, you need to make sure your ingredients are of the finest quality. Slow simmering does wonders for tougher cuts, but for fast food you need tender chicken breast meat, thin slices of turkey or veal, well hung beef steak and strips of lamb or pork fillet (tenderloin). Befriending your butcher can be the best move you ever make. Describe what you plan to cook and ask for advice. Dishes like Pan-Fried Chicken with Pesto, Pork with Cream and Apple Sauce, and Steak with Warm Tomato Salsa are great for special occasions, while more everyday meals call for the no less tasty Stir-fried Turkey with Broccoli, Pasta Salad with Salami or Fried Lamb Meatballs. All the recipes are quick and easy to cook, and if you rope in a few kitchen helpers for the preparation, they'll be ready even more rapidly.

CHICKEN FRIED RICE

THIS STIR-FRY IS BASED ON COOKED RICE, SO IS IDEAL FOR USING UP YESTERDAY'S LEFTOVERS. ANY RICE WILL DO, BUT JASMINE HAS THE BEST FLAVOUR, ESPECIALLY IF COOKED IN COCONUT MILK.

Preparation: 4–5 minutes; Cooking: 10–12 minutes

SERVES FOUR

INGREDIENTS
  30ml/2 tbsp groundnut (peanut) oil
  1 small onion, finely chopped
  2 garlic cloves, chopped
  2.5cm/1in piece fresh root ginger,
    peeled and grated
  225g/8oz skinless, boneless chicken
    breast portions, cut into
    1cm/½in dice
  450g/1lb/4 cups cold cooked white
    long grain rice
  1 red (bell) pepper, seeded and sliced
  115g/4oz/1 cup drained canned
    whole kernel corn
  5ml/1 tsp chilli oil
  5ml/1 tsp hot curry powder
  2 eggs, beaten
  salt
  spring onion (scallion) shreds,
    to garnish

2 Push the onion mixture to the sides of the wok, add the chicken to the centre and stir-fry for 2 minutes. Add the rice and toss well. Stir-fry over a high heat for about 3 minutes more, until the chicken is cooked through.

3 Stir in the sliced red pepper, corn, chilli oil and curry powder, with salt to taste. Toss over the heat for 1 minute. Stir in the beaten eggs and cook for 1 minute more. Garnish with the spring onion shreds and serve.

1 Heat the oil in a wok. Add the onion and stir-fry over a medium heat for 1 minute, then add the garlic and ginger and stir-fry for 2 minutes more.

COOK'S TIP
If you don't have any cold cooked rice in the refrigerator, you can still make this stir-fry if you have a couple of pouches of instant or express long grain or basmati rice in the cupboard. This type of rice cooks in under 2 minutes. For a stir-fry, the rice should be cold, so spread it out on a baking sheet after cooking and fan it to cool it quickly.

Energy 356kcal/1500kJ; Protein 21g; Carbohydrate 46.4g, of which sugars 6.3g; Fat 10.9g, of which saturates 2.5g; Cholesterol 135mg; Calcium 46mg; Fibre 1.4g; Sodium 150mg

SPICED CHICKEN RISOTTO WITH MINT

A CLASSIC RISOTTO MUST BE STIRRED FOR AROUND 20 MINUTES, WHICH CAN BE A LABOUR OF LOVE,
BUT WHEN ROMANCE IS THE LAST THING ON YOUR MIND, THIS QUICK VERSION IS A GOOD ALTERNATIVE.

Preparation: 3–5 minutes; Cooking: 15–17 minutes

SERVES FOUR

INGREDIENTS

  250g/9oz skinless, boneless chicken
    breast portions, diced
  3 garlic cloves, chopped
  5ml/1 tsp ground turmeric
  30–45ml/2–3 tbsp olive oil
  2 medium carrots, diced
  seeds from 6–8 cardamom pods
  500g/1¼lb/2½ cups long grain rice
  250g/9oz tomatoes, chopped
  750ml/1¼ pints/3 cups
    chicken stock
For the lemon and mint relish
  3 tomatoes, diced
  1 bunch or large handful fresh
    mint, chopped
  5–8 spring onions (scallions),
    thinly sliced
  juice of 2 lemons
  salt

1 Mix the diced chicken with half the garlic and the turmeric. Heat a little of the oil in a pan, add the chicken and fry until the chicken has cooked through thoroughly. Remove from the pan and set aside.

2 Add the remaining oil, garlic and cardamom seeds with the carrots and rice. Stir-fry for 1–2 minutes.

3 Add the tomatoes and chicken stock to the pan and bring to the boil. Cover and simmer for about 10 minutes.

4 Meanwhile, make the relish by mixing all the ingredients in a bowl.

5 When the rice is almost cooked, fork in the chicken and heat through. Serve with the relish.

VARIATIONS
• Use the same quantity of pumpkin or butternut squash in place of the carrots.
• To make a vegetarian version, omit the chicken and add a drained 400g/14oz can of chickpeas to the rice just before the end of cooking.

Energy 600kcal/2511kJ; Protein 26g; Carbohydrate 105.9g, of which sugars 5.3g; Fat 7.4g, of which saturates 1.1g; Cholesterol 44mg; Calcium 73mg; Fibre 1.8g; Sodium 55mg

STIR-FRIED CHICKEN WITH THAI BASIL

ON THE TABLE IN UNDER 10 MINUTES – YOU CAN'T SAY BETTER THAN THAT. THIS THAI-INSPIRED STIR-FRY IS TASTY, COLOURFUL AND FULL OF FLAVOUR, PERFECT FOR ANY DAY OF THE WEEK.

Preparation: 2–3 minutes; Cooking: 5–7 minutes

SERVES FOUR

INGREDIENTS
4 skinless chicken breast fillets
2 red (bell) peppers
30ml/2 tbsp garlic-infused olive oil
1 small bunch fresh Thai basil
salt and ground black pepper

COOK'S TIP

Thai basil, sometimes called holy basil, has purple-tinged leaves and a more pronounced, slightly aniseedy flavour than the usual varieties. It is available in most Asian food stores but if you can't find any, use a handful of ordinary basil instead. Serve this fragrant stir-fry with plain steamed rice or boiled noodles and soy sauce on the side.

1 Using a sharp knife, slice the chicken breast portions into strips. Halve the peppers, remove the seeds, then cut each piece of pepper into strips.

2 Heat a wok or large frying pan. Add the oil. When it is hot, add the chicken and toss over the heat for 2 minutes.

3 Add the red peppers and continue to stir-fry the mixture over a high heat for about 3 minutes, until the chicken is golden and cooked through. Season with salt and ground black pepper.

4 Roughly tear up the basil leaves, add to the chicken and peppers and toss briefly to combine. Serve immediately.

Energy 211kcal/892kJ; Protein 37.8g; Carbohydrate 6.9g, of which sugars 5.4g; Fat 3.7g, of which saturates 0.8g; Cholesterol 105mg; Calcium 67mg; Fibre 1.4g; Sodium 97mg

CRÈME FRAICHE AND CORIANDER CHICKEN

THIS IS AN ANY-OCCASION MAIN COURSE DISH THAT CAN BE TURNED AROUND IN MINUTES. BE GENEROUS WITH THE CORIANDER LEAVES, AS THEY HAVE A WONDERFUL FRAGRANT FLAVOUR.

Preparation: 8 minutes; Cooking: 8 minutes

SERVES FOUR

INGREDIENTS
6 skinless, boneless chicken
thigh portions
60ml/4 tbsp crème fraîche
1 small bunch fresh coriander
(cilantro), roughly chopped
15ml/1 tbsp sunflower oil
salt and ground black pepper

COOK'S TIP

This recipe uses boneless chicken thighs, but boneless breast portions can be used instead. Simply cut into bitesize pieces and cook in the frying pan for 5–6 minutes, until just tender.

1 Using a sharp cook's knife or cleaver, cut each chicken thigh into three or four pieces.

2 Heat the oil in a large frying pan, add the chicken and cook for about 6 minutes, turning occasionally.

3 Add the crème fraîche to the pan and stir until melted, then allow the mixture to bubble for 1–2 minutes. Add the chopped coriander to the chicken and stir to combine. Season with salt and ground black pepper to taste, and serve immediately.

Energy 249kcal/1041kJ; Protein 32.1g; Carbohydrate 0.7g, of which sugars 0.6g; Fat 13.1g, of which saturates 5.6g; Cholesterol 174mg; Calcium 44mg; Fibre 0.6g; Sodium 143mg

PAN-FRIED CHICKEN WITH PESTO

WARM PESTO ACCOMPANYING PAN-FRIED CHICKEN MAKES A DELICIOUSLY QUICK MEAL. SERVE WITH BABY CARROTS AND CELERY, BRAISED IN STOCK IN A SEPARATE PAN WHILE THE CHICKEN IS COOKING.

Preparation: 2–3 minutes; Cooking: 18 minutes

SERVES FOUR

INGREDIENTS

  15ml/1 tbsp olive oil
  4 chicken breast fillets, skinned
  fresh basil leaves, to garnish
For the pesto
  90ml/6 tbsp olive oil
  50g/2oz/½ cup pine nuts
  50g/2oz/⅔ cup freshly grated
   Parmesan cheese
  50g/2oz/1 cup fresh basil leaves
  15g/½oz/¼ cup fresh parsley
  2 garlic cloves, crushed
  salt and ground black pepper

1 Heat the 15ml/1 tbsp oil in a frying pan. Add the chicken breasts and cook gently for about 15 minutes, turning several times until they are tender, lightly browned and thoroughly cooked.

2 Meanwhile, make the pesto. Place the olive oil, pine nuts, Parmesan cheese, basil leaves, parsley, garlic, and salt and pepper in a food processor and process until smooth and well mixed.

3 Remove the chicken from the pan, cover and keep hot. Reduce the heat slightly, then add the pesto to the pan and cook gently, stirring constantly, for a few minutes, or until the pesto has warmed through.

4 Put the cooked chicken on a plate, pour the warm pesto over the top, then garnish with basil leaves and serve immediately.

Energy 480kcal/1998kJ; Protein 43.2g; Carbohydrate 1g, of which sugars 0.9g; Fat 33.8g, of which saturates 6.4g; Cholesterol 118mg; Calcium 192mg; Fibre 1.1g; Sodium 232mg

GREEK-STYLE CHICKEN WITH FENNEL SEEDS

THE SAUCE FOR THE CHICKEN IS BASED ON AVGOLEMONO, AN EXQUISITE EGG AND LEMON MIXTURE WHICH IS ONE OF GREECE'S GIFTS TO GOOD COOKS EVERYWHERE. IT TASTES GREAT WITH THE FENNEL.

Preparation: 3–4 minutes; Cooking: 15 minutes

SERVES FOUR

INGREDIENTS

4 skinless, boneless chicken
  breast portions
plain (all-purpose) flour, for dusting
30–45ml/2–3 tbsp olive oil
1–2 onions, chopped
¼ fennel bulb, chopped (optional)
15ml/1 tbsp chopped fresh parsley,
  plus extra to garnish
7.5ml/1½ tsp fennel seeds
75ml/5 tbsp dry Marsala
120ml/4fl oz/½ cup chicken stock
300g/11oz/2¼ cups petits pois
  (baby peas)
juice of 1½ lemons
2 egg yolks
salt and ground black pepper

1 Season the chicken with salt and pepper, then dust generously with flour. Shake off the excess flour; set aside.

2 Heat 15ml/1 tbsp oil in a pan, add the onions, fennel (if using), parsley and fennel seeds. Cook for 3 minutes.

3 Add the remaining oil and the chicken to the pan and cook over a high heat for 5–6 minutes on each side, until lightly browned and cooked through. Remove from the pan and set aside.

4 Deglaze the pan by pouring in the Marsala and cooking over a high heat until reduced to about 30ml/2 tbsp, then pour in the stock. Add the peas and return the chicken and onion mixture to the pan. Cook over a very low heat while you prepare the egg mixture.

5 In a bowl, beat the lemon juice and egg yolks together, then slowly add about 120ml/4fl oz/½ cup of the hot liquid from the chicken and peas, stirring well to combine.

6 Return the mixture to the pan and cook over a low heat, stirring, until the mixture thickens slightly. (Do not allow the mixture to boil or the eggs will curdle and spoil the sauce.) Serve the chicken immediately, sprinkled with a little extra chopped fresh parsley.

Energy 301kcal/1260kJ; Protein 41.6g; Carbohydrate 10.4g, of which sugars 3.3g; Fat 8.4g, of which saturates 1.5g; Cholesterol 105mg; Calcium 34mg; Fibre 4.3g; Sodium 96mg

TURKEY WITH MARSALA CREAM SAUCE

MARSALA MAKES A VERY RICH AND TASTY SAUCE. THE ADDITION OF LEMON JUICE GIVES IT A SHARP EDGE, WHICH HELPS TO OFFSET THE RICHNESS CONTRIBUTED BY THE BUTTER AND CREAM.

Preparation: 6 minutes; Cooking: 12 minutes

SERVES SIX

INGREDIENTS
   6 turkey breast steaks
   45ml/3 tbsp plain (all-purpose) flour
   30ml/2 tbsp olive oil
   25g/1oz/2 tbsp butter
   60ml/4 tbsp lemon juice
   175ml/6fl oz/¾ cup dry Marsala
   175ml/6fl oz/¾ cup double
      (heavy) cream
   salt and ground black pepper
   lemon wedges and chopped fresh
      parsley, to garnish
   mangetouts (snow peas) and green
      beans, to serve

1 Put each turkey steak between two sheets of clear film (plastic wrap) and pound with a rolling pin to flatten and stretch the meat. Cut each in half, cutting away and discarding any sinew.

2 Put the flour in a shallow bowl. Season well and coat the meat.

COOK'S TIPS
• You can save a lot of time by cooking the turkey in an electric frying pan, which will hold considerably more pieces than a standard frying pan.
• Cook the mangetouts (snow peas) and beans while the sauce is heating. They will only need a few minutes.

3 Heat the oil and butter in a deep, heavy frying pan until sizzling. Add as many pieces of turkey as the pan will hold and sauté over a medium heat for 2–3 minutes on each side until crispy and tender. Lift the pieces of turkey out with tongs, transfer to a warmed serving dish and keep hot. Repeat with the remaining turkey.

4 Lower the heat. Mix the lemon juice and Marsala together, add to the pan and raise the heat. Bring to the boil, stirring in the sediment, then add the cream. Simmer, stirring constantly, until the sauce is reduced and glossy. Taste for seasoning. Spoon over the turkey, garnish with the lemon wedges and parsley and serve immediately with the mangetouts and green beans.

Energy 326kcal/1355kJ; Protein 25.3g; Carbohydrate 3.5g, of which sugars 1g; Fat 19.9g, of which saturates 12.2g; Cholesterol 106mg; Calcium 26mg; Fibre 0.1g; Sodium 85mg

STIR-FRIED TURKEY WITH BROCCOLI

FOR A DELICIOUS MEAL WITHOUT BREAKING THE BANK, TURKEY IS AN EXCELLENT CHOICE. IT IS RELATIVELY INEXPENSIVE, HAS LITTLE WASTE AND TASTES GREAT IN A STIR-FRY LIKE THIS ONE.

Preparation: 8 minutes; Cooking: 8 minutes

SERVES FOUR

INGREDIENTS
  115g/4oz broccoli florets
  4 spring onions (scallions)
  5ml/1 tsp cornflour (cornstarch)
  45ml/3 tbsp oyster sauce
  15ml/1 tbsp dark soy sauce
  120ml/4fl oz/½ cup chicken stock
  10ml/2 tsp lemon juice
  45ml/3 tbsp groundnut (peanut) oil
  450g/1lb turkey steaks, cut into
    strips about 5mm x 5cm/¼ x 2in
  1 small onion, chopped
  2 garlic cloves, crushed
  10ml/2 tsp grated fresh root ginger
  115g/4oz/1½ cups fresh shiitake
    mushrooms, sliced
  75g/3oz baby corn, halved
    lengthways
  15ml/1 tbsp sesame oil
  salt and ground black pepper
  egg noodles, to serve

1 Divide the broccoli florets into smaller sprigs and cut the stalks into thin diagonal slices.

2 Finely chop the white parts of the spring onions and slice the green parts into thin shreds.

3 Put the cornflour in a bowl. Stir in the oyster sauce to make a thin paste, then add the soy sauce, stock and lemon juice. Stir and set aside.

4 Heat a wok until it is hot, add 30ml/2 tbsp of the groundnut oil and swirl it around. Add the turkey and stir-fry for about 2 minutes, or until the strips are golden and crispy at the edges, and cooked through. Remove the turkey and keep the pieces warm.

5 Add the remaining groundnut oil to the wok and stir-fry the chopped onion, garlic and ginger over a medium heat for about 1 minute. Increase the heat to high, add the broccoli, mushrooms and corn and stir-fry for 2 minutes.

6 Return the turkey to the wok, then add the cornflour mixture with the chopped spring onion and seasoning. Cook, stirring, for about 1 minute, or until the sauce has thickened. Stir in the sesame oil. Serve immediately on a bed of egg noodles with the finely shredded spring onion sprinkled on top.

COOK'S TIP
For speed and convenience, use straight-to-wok noodles and toss them with the turkey stir-fry until heated through.

Energy 255kcal/1065kJ; Protein 30.3g; Carbohydrate 5.8g, of which sugars 5g; Fat 12.4g, of which saturates 2.4g; Cholesterol 64mg; Calcium 30mg; Fibre 1.7g; Sodium 725mg

SKEWERED DUCK WITH POACHED EGGS

YOU HAVE TO BE ORGANIZED TO MAKE THIS MEAL IN TWENTY MINUTES, BUT IT IS TRULY WORTH THE EFFORT. BOIL THE EGGS IF THAT'S EASIER.

Preparation: 8 minutes; Cooking: 11 minutes

SERVES FOUR

INGREDIENTS
3 skinless, boneless duck breasts, thinly sliced
30ml/2 tbsp soy sauce
30ml/2 tbsp balsamic vinegar
30ml/2 tbsp groundnut oil
25g/1oz/2 tbsp unsalted butter
1 shallot, finely chopped
115g/4oz/1½ cups chanterelle mushrooms
4 eggs
50g/2oz mixed salad leaves
salt and ground black pepper
extra virgin olive oil, to serve

1 Toss the duck in the soy sauce and balsamic vinegar. Cover and marinate for 8–10 minutes. Meanwhile, soak 12 bamboo skewers in water to help prevent them from burning during cooking.

2 Meanwhile, melt the butter in a frying pan and cook the finely chopped shallot until softened but not coloured. Add the chanterelle mushrooms and cook over a high heat for about 5 minutes, stirring occasionally. Leave the pan over a low heat while you cook the duck.

3 Preheat the grill (broiler). Thread the duck slices on to the skewers, pleating them neatly. Place on a grill pan and drizzle with half the oil.

4 Grill (broil) for 3–5 minutes, then turn the skewers and drizzle with the remaining oil. Grill for a further 3 minutes, or until the duck is cooked through and golden.

5 Poach the eggs while the duck is cooking. Half fill a frying pan with water, add salt and heat until simmering. Break the eggs one at a time into a cup before tipping carefully into the water. Poach the eggs gently for about 3 minutes, or until the whites are set. Use a slotted spoon to transfer the eggs to a warm plate and trim off any untidy white.

6 Arrange the salad leaves on serving plates, then add the chanterelles and skewered duck. Carefully add the poached eggs. Drizzle with olive oil and season with ground black pepper, then serve at once.

VARIATION
If you haven't got time to thread the duck strips on to skewers, simply stir-fry in a little oil for a few minutes until crisp and cooked through, then sprinkle over the salad leaves with the mushrooms.

Energy 269kcal/1125kJ; Protein 29.3g; Carbohydrate 1.8g, of which sugars 1.3g; Fat 18.2g, of which saturates 6.3g; Cholesterol 327mg; Calcium 53mg; Fibre 0.7g; Sodium 412mg

FRIED PORK WITH SCRAMBLED EGG

WHEN YOU NEED A TASTY MEAL BEFORE GOING OUT FOR THE EVENING, THIS QUICK AND EASY RICE DISH, WITH JUST A LITTLE MEAT, IS THE ANSWER.

Preparation: 5 minutes; Cooking: 12 minutes

SERVES FOUR

INGREDIENTS
  2 x 250g/9oz sachets quick-cook rice
  45ml/3 tbsp vegetable oil
  1 onion, chopped
  15ml/1 tbsp chopped garlic
  115g/4oz pork, cut into small cubes
  2 eggs, beaten
  30ml/2 tbsp Thai fish sauce
  15ml/1 tbsp dark soy sauce
  2.5ml/½ tsp caster (superfine) sugar
  4 spring onions (scallions),
    finely sliced, to garnish
  2 fresh red chillies, sliced, to garnish
  1 lime, cut into wedges, to garnish

1 Cook the rice according to the instructions on the packet. Spread out and leave to cool.

2 Heat the oil in a wok or large frying pan. Add the onion and garlic and cook for about 2 minutes, until softened.

3 Add the pork to the softened onion and garlic. Stir-fry until the pork changes colour and is cooked.

4 Add the eggs and cook until scrambled into small lumps.

5 Add the rice and continue to stir and toss, to coat it with the oil and prevent it from sticking.

6 Stir in the fish sauce, soy sauce and sugar and mix well. Continue to fry until the rice is thoroughly heated. Spoon into warmed individual bowls and serve, garnished with sliced spring onions, chillies and lime wedges.

Energy 602kcal/2512kJ; Protein 18.8g; Carbohydrate 101.3g, of which sugars 1.1g; Fat 12.8g, of which saturates 2.2g; Cholesterol 113mg; Calcium 45mg; Fibre 0.2g; Sodium 323mg

SWEET AND SOUR PORK THAI-STYLE

IT WAS THE CHINESE WHO ORIGINALLY CREATED SWEET AND SOUR COOKING, BUT THE THAIS ALSO DO IT VERY WELL. THIS VERSION HAS A FRESHER AND CLEANER FLAVOUR THAN THE CHINESE.

Preparation: 6 minutes; Cooking: 13 minutes

SERVES FOUR

INGREDIENTS
    350g/12oz lean pork
    30ml/2 tbsp vegetable oil
    4 garlic cloves, thinly sliced
    1 small red onion, sliced
    30ml/2 tbsp Thai fish sauce
    15ml/1 tbsp granulated sugar
    1 red (bell) pepper, seeded and diced
    ½ cucumber, seeded and very
      thinly sliced
    2 plum tomatoes, cut into wedges
    115g/4oz piece fresh pineapple,
      cut into small chunks
    2 spring onions (scallions), cut into
      short lengths
    ground black pepper
To garnish
    coriander (cilantro) leaves
    spring onions (scallions), shredded

1 Cut the pork into thin strips. This is easier to do if you freeze it for 30 minutes first.

2 Heat the oil in a wok or large frying pan. Add the garlic. Cook over a medium heat until golden, then add the pork and stir-fry for 4–5 minutes. Add the onion slices and toss to mix.

3 Add the fish sauce, sugar and ground black pepper to taste. Toss the mixture over the heat for 3–4 minutes more.

4 Stir in the red pepper, cucumber, tomatoes, pineapple and spring onions. Stir-fry for 3–4 minutes more, then spoon into a bowl. Garnish with the coriander and spring onions and serve.

Energy 211kcal/885kJ; Protein 20g; Carbohydrate 12.4g, of which sugars 11.8g; Fat 9.4g, of which saturates 2g; Cholesterol 55mg; Calcium 29mg; Fibre 1.8g; Sodium 68mg

PORK AND PINEAPPLE COCONUT CURRY

THE HEAT OF THIS CURRY BALANCES OUT ITS SWEETNESS TO MAKE A FRAGRANT DISH. IT TAKES LITTLE TIME TO COOK, SO IS IDEAL FOR A QUICK SUPPER BEFORE GOING OUT FOR THE EVENING.

Preparation: 3 minutes; Cooking: 17 minutes

SERVES FOUR

INGREDIENTS

400ml/14fl oz can or carton
  coconut milk
10ml/2 tsp Thai red
  curry paste
400g/14oz pork loin steaks,
  trimmed and thinly sliced
15ml/1 tbsp Thai fish sauce
5ml/1 tsp palm sugar or light
  muscovado (brown) sugar
15ml/1 tbsp tamarind juice, made
  by mixing tamarind paste with
  warm water
2 kaffir lime leaves, torn
½ medium pineapple
1 fresh red chilli, seeded and
  finely chopped

1 Pour the coconut milk into a bowl and let it settle, so that the cream rises to the surface. Scoop the cream into a measuring jug (cup). You should have about 250ml/8fl oz/1 cup. If necessary, add a little of the coconut milk.

2 Pour the coconut cream into a large pan and bring it to the boil.

3 Cook the coconut cream for about 8 minutes, until the cream separates, stirring frequently to prevent it from sticking to the base of the pan. Peel and chop the pineapple.

4 Ladle a little of the coconut cream into a bowl and stir in the red curry paste. Return the mixture to the pan and stir until well mixed. Cook, stirring occasionally, for about 3 minutes, until the paste is fragrant.

5 Add the sliced pork and stir in the fish sauce, sugar and tamarind juice. Cook, stirring constantly, for 2–3 minutes, until the sugar has dissolved and the pork is no longer pink.

6 Add the remaining coconut milk and the lime leaves. Bring to the boil, then stir in the pineapple. Reduce the heat and simmer gently for 3 minutes, or until the pork is fully cooked. Sprinkle over the chilli and serve.

Energy 187kcal/790kJ; Protein 22.2g; Carbohydrate 15.3g, of which sugars 15.3g; Fat 4.5g, of which saturates 1.6g; Cholesterol 63mg; Calcium 55mg; Fibre 1.2g; Sodium 449mg

PORK <u>WITH</u> CREAM <u>AND</u> APPLE SAUCE

TENDER NOISETTES OF PORK IN A CREAMY LEEK AND APPLE SAUCE MAKE A GREAT DINNER PARTY DISH.
USE THE SAME WHITE WINE AS THE ONE YOU PLAN TO SERVE WITH THE MEAL, OR TRY CIDER.
Preparation: 2 minutes; Cooking: 18 minutes

SERVES FOUR

INGREDIENTS
    30ml/2 tbsp plain (all-purpose) flour
    4 noisettes of pork, firmly tied
    25g/1oz/2 tbsp butter
    4 baby leeks, finely sliced
    5ml/1 tsp mustard seeds,
      coarsely crushed
    150ml/¼ pint/⅔ cup dry white wine
    2 eating apples
    150ml/¼ pint/⅔ cup double
      (heavy) cream
    30ml/2 tbsp chopped fresh parsley
    salt and ground black pepper

1 Place the flour in a bowl and add plenty of seasoning. Turn the noisettes in the flour mixture to coat them lightly.

2 Melt the butter in a heavy frying pan and cook the noisettes for 1 minute on each side.

3 Add the sliced leeks to the pan and cook for 3 minutes. Stir in the mustard seeds. Pour in the wine. Cook gently for 10 minutes, turning the pork occasionally. Peel, core and slice the apples.

VARIATION
Use thin slices of pork fillet (tenderloin) for even faster cooking.

4 Add the sliced apples and double cream and simmer for 3 minutes, or until the pork is fully cooked and the sauce is thick, rich and creamy. Taste for seasoning, then stir in the chopped parsley and serve at once.

Energy 415kcal/1724kJ; Protein 23.1g; Carbohydrate 8.8g, of which sugars 4.4g; Fat 29.5g, of which saturates 17.2g; Cholesterol 128mg; Calcium 45mg; Fibre 1.3g; Sodium 119mg

PASTA SALAD <u>WITH</u> SALAMI

THIS PASTA DISH IS EASY TO MAKE AND WOULD BE PERFECT FOR A PICNIC OR PACKED LUNCH.
TAKE THE DRESSING AND SALAD LEAVES SEPARATELY AND MIX EVERYTHING AT THE LAST MOMENT.

Preparation: 3–4 minutes; Cooking: 12 minutes

SERVES FOUR

INGREDIENTS
225g/8oz pasta twists
275g/10oz jar charcoal-roasted
 peppers in oil
115g/4oz/1 cup pitted black olives
4 drained sun-dried tomatoes
 in oil, quartered
115g/4oz Roquefort cheese,
 crumbled
10 slices peppered salami, cut
 into strips
115g/4oz packet mixed leaf salad
30ml/2 tbsp white wine vinegar
30ml/2 tbsp chopped fresh oregano
2 garlic cloves, crushed
salt and ground black pepper

1 Cook the pasta in a large pan of lightly salted boiling water for 12 minutes, or according to the instructions on the packet, until tender but not soft. Drain thoroughly and rinse with cold water, then drain again.

2 Drain the peppers and reserve 60ml/ 4 tbsp of the oil for the dressing. Cut the peppers into long, fine strips and mix them with the olives, sun-dried tomatoes and Roquefort in a large bowl. Stir in the pasta and peppered salami.

3 Divide the salad leaves among four individual bowls and spoon the pasta salad on top. Whisk the reserved oil with the vinegar, oregano, garlic and seasoning to taste. Spoon this dressing over the salad and serve at once.

VARIATION
Use chicken instead of the salami and cubes of Brie in place of the Roquefort.

Energy 429kcal/1797kJ; Protein 17.8g; Carbohydrate 46.7g, of which sugars 6.6g; Fat 20.3g, of which saturates 8.9g; Cholesterol 37mg; Calcium 188mg; Fibre 3.9g; Sodium 1341mg

HOME-MADE VENISON SAUSAGES

VENISON SAUSAGES HAVE AN EXCELLENT FLAVOUR, A MUCH LOWER FAT CONTENT THAN MOST SAUSAGES AND THEY'RE EASY TO MAKE IF YOU FORGET ABOUT SAUSAGE SKINS AND JUST SHAPE THE MIXTURE.

Preparation: 5 minutes; Cooking: 12 minutes

MAKES 1.4KG/3LB

INGREDIENTS
  900g/2lb finely minced
    (ground) venison
  450g/1lb finely minced
    (ground) belly of pork
  15ml/1 tbsp salt
  10ml/2 tsp ground black pepper
  1 garlic clove, crushed
  5ml/1 tsp dried thyme
  1 egg, beaten
  plain (all-purpose) flour, for dusting
  oil, for frying
  fried onions, grilled (broiled)
    tomatoes and field (portabello)
    mushrooms, to serve

1 Combine all the sausage ingredients, except the flour and oil, in a bowl. Take a small piece of the mixture and fry it in a little oil in a heavy frying pan, then taste to check the seasoning for the batch. Adjust if necessary.

2 Form the mixture into chipolata-size sausages using floured hands.

3 Heat the oil in a large, heavy frying pan and shallow-fry the sausages for 10 minutes or until they are golden brown and cooked right through.

4 If you use a large pan, you'll be able to fry some onion rings alongside the sausages. At the same time, grill (broil) mushrooms and halved tomatoes to serve on the side.

COOK'S TIP
If you find yourself with more sausages than you need for one meal, freeze the surplus in an airtight container for no more than a month. Be sure to thaw the sausages completely before cooking.

Energy 1747kcal/7356kJ; Protein 302.4g; Carbohydrate 0g, of which sugars 0g; Fat 65.3g, of which saturates 17.6g; Cholesterol 924mg; Calcium 105mg; Fibre 0g; Sodium 880mg

LAMB STEAKS ᵂᴵᵀᴴ REDCURRANT GLAZE

GOOD AND MEATY, BUT THIN ENOUGH TO COOK QUICKLY, LAMB LEG STEAKS ARE A GOOD CHOICE FOR THE COOK SHORT ON TIME. THE REDCURRANT AND ROSEMARY GLAZE LOOKS GORGEOUS.

Preparation: 2–3 minutes; Cooking: 10 minutes

SERVES FOUR

INGREDIENTS
- 4 large fresh rosemary sprigs
- 4 lamb leg steaks
- 75ml/5 tbsp redcurrant jelly
- 30ml/2 tbsp raspberry or
  red wine vinegar

1 Reserve the tips of the rosemary and finely chop the remaining leaves. Rub the chopped rosemary, salt and pepper all over the lamb.

2 Preheat the grill (broiler). Heat the redcurrant jelly gently in a small pan with 30ml/2 tbsp water and a little seasoning. Stir in the vinegar.

3 Place the lamb steaks on a foil-lined grill (broiler) rack and brush with a little of the redcurrant glaze. Cook under the grill for about 5 minutes on each side, until deep golden, brushing frequently with more redcurrant glaze.

4 Transfer the lamb to warmed plates. Tip any juices from the foil into the remaining glaze and heat through gently. Pour the glaze over the lamb and serve, garnished with the reserved rosemary sprigs.

COOK'S TIP
This is a good recipe for the barbecue. Wait until the fierce heat has subsided and the coals are dusted with white ash, then place the rosemary-rubbed steaks directly on the grill rack. Brush frequently with the glaze as they cook. If you grow your own rosemary, try sprinkling some over the coals. As the oil in the herb warms, the scent of rosemary will perfume the air.

Energy 362kcal/1518kJ; Protein 34.4g; Carbohydrate 13g, of which sugars 13g; Fat 19.6g, of which saturates 9.1g; Cholesterol 133mg; Calcium 16mg; Fibre 0g; Sodium 156mg

FRIED LAMB MEATBALLS

MEATBALLS COOK QUICKLY; THE FIDDLY BIT IS SHAPING THEM. MIXING EVERYTHING TOGETHER WITH YOUR HANDS IS VERY SATISFYING AND WILL HELP SPEED UP THE PROCESS TOO.
Preparation: 10–15 minutes; Cooking: 5 minutes

SERVES FOUR

INGREDIENTS
    2 medium slices of bread,
      crusts removed
    1 onion
    500g/1¼lb minced (ground) lamb
      or beef
    5ml/1 tsp each dried thyme
      and oregano
    45ml/3 tbsp chopped fresh flat leaf
      parsley, plus extra to garnish
    1 egg, lightly beaten
    salt and ground black pepper
    lemon wedges, to serve (optional)
For frying
    25g/1oz/¼ cup plain
      (all-purpose) flour
    30–45ml/2–3 tbsp vegetable oil

1 Soak the slices of bread in a shallow bowl of water for 5 minutes. While the bread is soaking, grate or very finely chop the onion.

2 Drain the bread. Using clean hands, squeeze it dry and put it in a large bowl. Add the meat, onion, dried herbs, parsley, egg, salt and pepper to the bread. Mix together, preferably using your hands, until well blended.

3 Shape the meat mixture into individual balls about the size of a walnut, and roll them in the flour to give them a light dusting, shaking off any excess coating.

4 Heat the oil in a large frying pan. When it is hot, add the meatballs and fry for about 5 minutes, turning them frequently, until they are cooked through and look crisp and brown.

5 Using a slotted spoon, lift out the meatballs and drain on a double sheet of kitchen paper, to get rid of the excess oil. Sprinkle with the remaining chopped parsley and serve with lemon wedges, if you like.

Energy 411kcal/1710kJ; Protein 28.4g; Carbohydrate 13g, of which sugars 1.5g; Fat 27.6g, of which saturates 9.7g; Cholesterol 123mg; Calcium 66mg; Fibre 1.1g; Sodium 192mg

LAMB'S KIDNEYS <u>WITH</u> MUSTARD SAUCE

THIS PIQUANT RECIPE IS SIMPLE AND FLEXIBLE, SO THE EXACT AMOUNTS OF ANY ONE INGREDIENT ARE UNIMPORTANT. IT MAKES A TASTY FIRST COURSE BUT WOULD BE EQUALLY SUITABLE AS A SUPPER DISH.

Preparation: 5 minutes; Cooking: 5 minutes

SERVES FOUR

INGREDIENTS

4–6 lamb's kidneys
butter, for frying
Dijon mustard or other mild mustard,
  to taste
250ml/8fl oz/1 cup white wine
5ml/1 tsp chopped fresh mixed
  herbs, such as rosemary, thyme,
  parsley and chives
1 small garlic clove, crushed
about 30ml/2 tbsp single
  (light) cream
salt and ground black pepper
fresh parsley, to garnish

COOK'S TIP
Look for kidneys that are firm, with a rich, even colour. Avoid those with dry spots or a dull surface.

1 Skin the kidneys and slice them horizontally. Remove the cores with scissors, and then wash them thoroughly in plenty of cold water. Drain and pat dry with kitchen paper.

2 Heat a little butter in a heavy frying pan and cook the kidneys for about 1½ minutes on each side. Be careful not to overcook. Remove the kidneys from the pan and keep warm.

3 Add a spoonful of mustard to the pan with the wine, herbs and garlic. Simmer gently to reduce the liquid by about half, then add enough cream to make a smooth sauce.

4 Return the kidneys to the pan and reheat gently in the sauce. Don't let them cook any further, or the kidneys will be tough. Serve garnished with parsley, and with rice or a green salad.

Energy 161kcal/675kJ; Protein 19.9g; Carbohydrate 0.6g, of which sugars 0.6g; Fat 4.4g, of which saturates 2g; Cholesterol 366mg; Calcium 22mg; Fibre 0g; Sodium 177mg

KOFTA LAMB PATTIES

FOR A QUICK AND EASY SUPPER, SIMPLY SLIDE THESE SPICY LITTLE PATTIES INTO CONES MADE BY ROLLING WARMED TORTILLAS. A DOLLOP OF THICK YOGURT OR CRÈME FRAICHE WOULDN'T GO AMISS.

Preparation: 8 minutes; Cooking: 10 minutes

SERVES FOUR

INGREDIENTS

450g/1lb minced (ground) lamb
1–2 large slices French bread,
  very finely crumbed
½ bunch fresh coriander (cilantro),
  finely chopped
5 garlic cloves, chopped
1 onion, finely chopped
juice of ½ lemon
5ml/1 tsp ground cumin
5ml/1 tsp paprika
15ml/1 tbsp curry powder
a pinch each of ground cardamom,
  turmeric and cinnamon
15ml/1 tbsp tomato purée (paste)
cayenne pepper or chopped fresh
  chillies (optional)
1 egg, beaten (optional)
salt and ground black pepper
flat bread and salads, to serve

1 Put the lamb, crumbed bread, coriander, garlic, onion, lemon juice, spices, tomato purée, cayenne pepper or chillies and seasoning in a large bowl. Mix well. If the mixture does not bind together, add the beaten egg and a little more bread.

2 With wet hands, shape the mixture into four large or eight small patties.

3 Heat a heavy non-stick frying pan, add the patties and cook for about 10 minutes, until browned. Turn once or twice, but make sure that they do not fall apart. Serve hot with flat bread and salads.

VARIATION
Mix a handful of raisins or sultanas (golden raisins) into the meat mixture before shaping it into patties.

Energy 298kcal/1249kJ; Protein 24.2g; Carbohydrate 16.5g, of which sugars 2.6g; Fat 15.5g, of which saturates 7.1g; Cholesterol 87mg; Calcium 57mg; Fibre 1.1g; Sodium 242mg

VEAL ESCALOPES WITH LEMON

POPULAR IN ITALIAN RESTAURANTS, THIS DISH IS VERY SIMPLE TO MAKE AT HOME. WHITE VERMOUTH AND LEMON JUICE MAKE THE PERFECT SAUCE FOR THE DELICATELY FLAVOURED MEAT.

Preparation: 3–4 minutes; Cooking: 15 minutes

SERVES FOUR

INGREDIENTS
    4 veal escalopes (scallops)
    30–45ml/2–3 tbsp plain
      (all-purpose) flour
    50g/2oz/¼ cup butter
    60ml/4 tbsp olive oil
    60ml/4 tbsp Italian dry white
      vermouth or dry white wine
    45ml/3 tbsp lemon juice
    salt and ground black pepper
    lemon wedges, grated lemon rind
      and fresh parsley, to garnish
    salad, to serve

VARIATIONS
• Use skinless boneless chicken breast portions instead of the veal. If they are thick, cut them in half before pounding.
• Substitute thin slices of pork fillet (tenderloin) for the veal and use orange juice instead of lemon.

1 Put each veal escalope between two sheets of clear film (plastic wrap) and pound with the side of a rolling pin or the smooth side of a meat mallet until the slices are very thin.

2 Cut the pounded escalopes in half or quarters. Season the flour with a little salt and pepper and use it to coat the escalopes on both sides. Shake off any excess seasoned flour.

3 Melt the butter with half the oil in a large, heavy frying pan until sizzling. Add as many escalopes as the pan will hold. Cook over a medium to high heat for about 2 minutes on each side until lightly coloured. Remove with a spatula and keep hot. Add the remaining oil to the pan and cook the remaining veal escalopes in the same way.

4 Remove the pan from the heat and add the vermouth or wine and the lemon juice. Stir vigorously to mix well with the pan juices, then return the pan to the heat.

5 Return all the veal escalopes to the pan. Spoon the sauce over to coat the veal. Heat through for about 2 minutes, shaking the pan occasionally. Serve immediately, garnished with lemon wedges, lemon rind and a sprinkling of parsley.

Energy 360kcal/1498kJ; Protein 29g; Carbohydrate 4.8g, of which sugars 0.6g; Fat 23.5g, of which saturates 8.9g; Cholesterol 92mg; Calcium 16mg; Fibre 0.2g; Sodium 151mg

STEAK WITH WARM TOMATO SALSA

A TANGY SALSA OF TOMATOES, SPRING ONIONS AND BALSAMIC VINEGAR MAKES A COLOURFUL TOPPING FOR CHUNKY, PAN-FRIED STEAKS COOKED JUST THE WAY YOU LIKE THEM.

Preparation: 2–3 minutes; Cooking: 8 minutes

SERVES TWO

INGREDIENTS
  2 steaks, about 2cm/¾in thick
  3 large plum tomatoes
  2 spring onions (scallions)
  30ml/2 tbsp balsamic vinegar

1 Trim any excess fat from the steaks, then season on both sides with salt and pepper. Heat a non-stick frying pan and cook the steaks for about 3 minutes on each side for medium rare. Cook for a little longer if you like your steak well cooked.

2 Meanwhile, put the tomatoes in a heatproof bowl, cover with boiling water and leave for 1–2 minutes.

3 When the tomato skins start to split, drain and peel them, then halve them and scoop out the seeds. Dice the tomato flesh.

4 When the steaks are cooked to your taste, remove from the pan with a fish slice, to drain off any excess oil, and transfer them to plates. Keep the steaks warm on a very low oven temperature while you prepare the salsa.

5 Thinly slice the spring onions and add them to the cooking juices in the frying pan with the diced tomato, balsamic vinegar, 30ml/2 tbsp water and a little seasoning. Stir briefly until warm, scraping up any meat residue. Spoon the salsa over the steaks to serve.

COOK'S TIP
Choose rump, sirloin or fillet steak (beef tenderloin). If you prefer to grill (broil) the steak, the timing will be the same as in the recipe, although you must take into account the thickness of the meat.

Energy 207kcal/872kJ; Protein 33.9g; Carbohydrate 3.4g, of which sugars 3.4g; Fat 6.5g, of which saturates 2.7g; Cholesterol 89mg; Calcium 17mg; Fibre 1.2g; Sodium 100mg

PAN-FRIED STEAKS with WHISKY and CREAM

A GOOD STEAK IS ALWAYS A POPULAR CHOICE FOR DINNER, AND TOP QUALITY MEAT PLUS TIMING ARE THE KEYS TO SUCCESS. CHOOSE SMALL, THICK STEAKS RATHER THAN LARGE, THIN ONES IF YOU CAN.

Preparation: 0 minutes; Cooking: 8 minutes

SERVES FOUR

INGREDIENTS

    4 x 225–350g/8–12oz sirloin steaks,
      at room temperature
    5ml/1 tsp oil
    15g/½oz/1 tbsp butter
    50ml/2fl oz/¼ cup Irish whiskey
    300ml/½ pint/1¼ cups double
      (heavy) cream
    salt and ground black pepper

1 Dry the steaks with kitchen paper and season with pepper. Heat a cast-iron frying pan, or other heavy pan, over high heat. When it is very hot, add the oil and butter. Add the steaks to the foaming butter, one at a time, to seal the meat quickly.

2 Lower the heat to moderate and continue to cook the steaks, allowing 3–4 minutes for rare, 4–5 minutes for medium or 5–6 minutes for well-done steaks.

3 To test if the timing is right, press down gently in the middle of the steak: soft meat will be rare; when there is some resistance but the meat underneath the outside crust feels soft, it is medium; if it is firm to the touch, the steak is well done.

COOK'S TIP
Turn the steaks only once during cooking to seal in the juices.

4 When the steaks are cooked to your liking, transfer them to warmed plates and keep warm. Pour off the fat from the pan and discard. Add the whiskey and stir around to scrape off all the sediment from the base of the pan.

5 Allow the liquid to reduce a little, then add the cream and simmer over a low heat for a few minutes, until the cream thickens. Season to taste, pour the sauce around or over the steaks, as you prefer, and serve immediately.

Energy 806kcal/3345kJ; Protein 65.9g; Carbohydrate 1.3g, of which sugars 1.3g; Fat 56.5g, of which saturates 32.6g; Cholesterol 251mg; Calcium 51mg; Fibre 0g; Sodium 232mg

GREEN BEEF CURRY <u>WITH</u> THAI AUBERGINES

THIS IS A VERY QUICK CURRY SO IT IS ESSENTIAL THAT YOU USE GOOD-QUALITY MEAT. SIRLOIN IS RECOMMENDED, BUT TENDER RUMP OR EVEN FILLET STEAK COULD BE USED INSTEAD.

Preparation: 2 minutes; Cooking: 16 minutes

SERVES FOUR TO SIX

INGREDIENTS
    450g/1lb beef sirloin
    15ml/1 tbsp vegetable oil
    45ml/3 tbsp Thai green curry paste
    600ml/1 pint/2½ cups coconut milk
    4 kaffir lime leaves, torn
    15–30ml/1–2 tbsp Thai fish sauce
    5ml/1 tsp palm sugar or light
      muscovado (brown) sugar
    150g/5oz small Thai aubergines
      (eggplant), halved
    a small handful of fresh Thai basil
    2 fresh green chillies, to garnish

1 Trim off any excess fat from the beef. Using a sharp knife, cut it into long, thin strips. This is easiest to do if it is well chilled. Set it aside.

2 Heat the oil in a large, heavy pan or wok. Add the curry paste and cook for 1–2 minutes, until it is fragrant.

3 Stir in half the coconut milk, a little at a time. Cook, stirring frequently, for about 5–6 minutes, until an oily sheen appears on the surface of the liquid.

4 Add the beef to the pan with the kaffir lime leaves, Thai fish sauce, sugar and aubergine halves. Cook for 2–3 minutes, then stir in the remaining coconut milk.

5 Bring back to a simmer and cook until the meat and aubergines are tender. Stir in the Thai basil just before serving.

6 To prepare the garnish, slit the fresh green chillies and scrape out the pith and seeds. Shred the chillies finely and sprinkle over the curry.

GREEN CURRY PASTE
To make the green curry paste, put 15 fresh green chillies, 2 chopped lemon grass stalks, 3 sliced shallots, 2 garlic cloves, 15ml/1 tbsp chopped galangal, 4 chopped kaffir lime leaves, 2.5ml/ ½ tsp grated kaffir lime rind, 5ml/1 tsp chopped coriander (cilantro) root, 6 black peppercorns, 5ml/1 tsp each roasted coriander and cumin seeds, 15ml/1 tbsp sugar, 5ml/1 tsp salt and 5ml/1 tsp shrimp paste into a food processor and process until smooth. Gradually add 30ml/2 tbsp vegetable oil, processing after each addition.

Energy 147kcal/619kJ; Protein 18.2g; Carbohydrate 6.4g, of which sugars 6.3g; Fat 5.6g, of which saturates 1.9g; Cholesterol 38mg; Calcium 36mg; Fibre 0.5g; Sodium 341mg

BEEF WITH BLUE CHEESE SAUCE

CELEBRATIONS CALL FOR SPECIAL DISHES, AND THIS ONE IS MORE SPECIAL THAN MOST. ROQUEFORT CHEESE, CREAM AND FILLET STEAK IS A RICH COMBINATION, SO KEEP THE REST OF THE MEAL SIMPLE.

Preparation: 2 minutes; Cooking: 8 minutes

SERVES FOUR

INGREDIENTS

   25g/1oz/2 tbsp butter
   30ml/2 tbsp olive oil
   4 fillet steaks, cut 5cm/2in thick,
     about 150g/5oz each
   salt and coarsely ground black pepper
   fresh flat leaf parsley, to garnish
For the blue cheese sauce
   30ml/2 tbsp brandy
   150ml/5fl oz/⅔ cup double
     (heavy) cream
   75g/3oz Roquefort cheese, crumbled

COOK'S TIP
Adding oil to the butter for frying means you can cook at a higher heat, essential for searing the meat.

1 Heat the butter and oil together in a heavy frying pan, over a high heat. Season the steaks well. Fry them for 1 minute on each side, to sear them.

2 Lower the heat slightly and cook for a further 2–3 minutes on each side, or according to your taste. Remove the steaks to a warm plate.

3 Reduce the heat and add the brandy, stirring to incorporate the pan juices. Add the cream and boil to reduce a little.

4 Add the crumbled cheese and mash it into the sauce using a spoon. Taste for seasoning. Serve in a small sauce jug (pitcher), or poured over the steaks. Garnish the beef with parsley.

Energy 573kcal/2374kJ; Protein 36.3g; Carbohydrate 0.7g, of which sugars 0.7g; Fat 45.4g, of which saturates 24.4g; Cholesterol 170mg; Calcium 117mg; Fibre 0g; Sodium 341mg

NO-FUSS
VEGETARIAN

Vegetarian dishes are often praised for making innovative use of simple ingredients, and in a collection of quick dishes they are the stars. Their typical components — glowing vegetables, tasty grains, herbs and spices — are generally easy to prepare and cook. What's more, they tend not to cost a great deal, so you can afford to buy the best and still have change left over for some of life's luxuries, like a bottle of good wine or a punnet of strawberries for dessert. This wide-ranging chapter has a recipe for every occasion, from a light-as-air soufflé omelette for a late night supper to a hearty bean chilli for hungry hikers. Some dishes demand a bit of forward planning and a trip to the market or delicatessen; others require nothing more than a raid on the refrigerator and store cupboard (pantry). Spaghetti with Garlic and Oil, for instance, is as accessible as it sounds, with just six essential ingredients, all of which you are likely to have at hand. It is perfect for those occasions when even putting the kettle on seems to require too much effort, and can be on the table in less than a quarter of an hour.

SOUFFLÉ OMELETTE WITH MUSHROOMS

A SOUFFLÉ OMELETTE MAKES AN IDEAL MEAL FOR ONE, ESPECIALLY WITH THIS DELICIOUS FILLING, BUT BE WARNED — WHEN OTHERS SMELL IT COOKING THEY ARE LIKELY TO DEMAND THEIR SHARE.

Preparation: 5 minutes; Cooking: 13–15 minutes

SERVES ONE

INGREDIENTS
    2 eggs, separated
    15g/½oz/1 tbsp butter
    flat leaf parsley or coriander
      (cilantro) leaves, to garnish
For the mushroom sauce
    15g/½oz/1 tbsp butter
    75g/3oz/generous 1 cup button
      (white) mushrooms, thinly sliced
    15ml/1 tbsp plain (all-purpose) flour
    85–120ml/3–4fl oz/⅓–½ cup milk
    5ml/1 tsp chopped fresh parsley
    salt and ground black pepper

COOK'S TIP
For extra flavour, add a few drops of soy sauce to the mushrooms.

1 To make the mushroom sauce, melt the butter in a pan or frying pan and add the sliced mushrooms. Fry gently for 4–5 minutes, stirring occasionally. The mushrooms will exude quite a lot of liquid, but this will rapidly be reabsorbed.

2 Stir in the flour, then gradually add the milk, stirring all the time. Cook until the sauce boils and thickens. Add the parsley, if using, and season with salt and pepper. Keep warm.

3 Make the omelette. Beat the egg yolks with 15ml/1 tbsp water and season with a little salt and pepper. Whisk the egg whites until stiff, then fold into the egg yolks. Preheat the grill (broiler).

4 Melt the butter in a large frying pan and pour in the egg mixture. Cook over a gentle heat for 2–4 minutes. Place the frying pan under the grill and cook for a further 3–4 minutes until the top is golden brown.

5 Slide the omelette on to a warmed serving plate, pour the mushroom sauce over the top and fold the omelette in half. Serve, garnished with parsley.

Energy 838kcal/3514kJ; Protein 45.5g; Carbohydrate 53.7g, of which sugars 42.1g; Fat 51.4g, of which saturates 28.3g; Cholesterol 497mg; Calcium 1150mg; Fibre 1.3g; Sodium 707mg

SPICY OMELETTE

THE ACCUSATION THAT EGG DISHES CAN BE A BIT BLAND COULD NEVER BE LEVELLED AT THIS SPICY, VEGETABLE-RICH DISH. IT COMES FROM INDIA, WHERE IT IS OFTEN SERVED FOR BREAKFAST.

Preparation: 6–7 minutes; Cooking: 10 minutes

SERVES FOUR TO SIX

INGREDIENTS

30ml/2 tbsp vegetable oil
1 onion, finely chopped
2.5ml/½ tsp ground cumin
1 garlic clove, crushed
1 or 2 fresh green chillies,
 finely chopped
a few coriander (cilantro) sprigs,
 chopped, plus extra, to garnish
1 firm tomato, chopped
1 small potato, cubed and boiled
25g/1oz/¼ cup cooked peas
25g/1oz/¼ cup cooked corn,
 or drained canned corn
2 eggs, beaten
25g/1oz/¼ cup grated cheese
salt and ground black pepper

1 Heat the vegetable oil in a wok, karahi or large pan, and fry the next nine ingredients for 2–3 minutes until they are well blended but the potato and tomato are still firm. Season with salt and ground black pepper.

2 Increase the heat and pour in the beaten eggs. Reduce the heat, cover and cook until the bottom of the omelette is golden brown. Sprinkle the omelette with the grated cheese. Place under a hot grill (broiler) and cook until the egg sets and the cheese has melted.

3 Garnish the omelette with sprigs of coriander and serve with salad for a light lunch or supper.

VARIATION
You can use any vegetable with the potatoes. Try adding thickly sliced mushrooms instead of the corn.

Energy 93kcal/388kJ; Protein 4g; Carbohydrate 3.7g, of which sugars 1.2g; Fat 7.1g, of which saturates 1.9g; Cholesterol 67mg; Calcium 46mg; Fibre 0.6g; Sodium 104mg

MEXICAN TOMATO RICE

VERSIONS OF THIS DISH — A RELATIVE OF SPANISH RICE — ARE POPULAR ALL OVER SOUTH AMERICA.
IT IS A DELICIOUS MEDLEY OF RICE, TOMATOES, PEAS AND AROMATIC FLAVOURINGS.
Preparation: 3 minutes; Cooking: 17 minutes

SERVES FOUR

INGREDIENTS
   400g/14oz can chopped tomatoes in
      tomato juice
   30ml/2 tbsp vegetable oil, preferably
      olive oil
   ½ onion, roughly chopped
   2 garlic cloves, roughly chopped
   500g/1¼lb/2½ cups long grain rice
   750ml/1¼ pints/3 cups
      vegetable stock
   2.5ml/½ tsp salt
   3 fresh chillies
   150g/5oz/1 cup frozen peas
   ground black pepper

COOK'S TIP
The rice makes a good filling for red or
orange (bell) peppers, which have been
halved, seeded and steamed for about
15 minutes, until tender.

1 Pour the tomatoes and juice into a
food processor or blender, and process
until smooth.

2 Heat the oil in a large, heavy pan,
add the onion and garlic and cook over
a medium heat for 2 minutes until
softened. Stir in the rice and stir-fry for
1–2 minutes.

3 Add the tomato mixture and stir over
a medium heat for 3–4 minutes until all
the liquid has been absorbed.

4 Stir in the stock, salt, whole chillies
and peas. Bring to the boil. Cover and
simmer for about 6 minutes, stirring
occasionally, until the rice is just tender.

5 Remove the pan from the heat, cover
it with a tight-fitting lid and leave it to
stand in a warm place for 5 minutes.

6 Remove the chillies, fluff up the rice
lightly with a fork, and serve in warmed
bowls, sprinkled with black pepper.
The chillies can be used as a garnish,
if you like.

Energy 552kcal/2305kJ; Protein 12.7g; Carbohydrate 108.3g, of which sugars 4.8g; Fat 7g, of which saturates 1g; Cholesterol 0mg; Calcium 43mg; Fibre 3g; Sodium 10mg

COUSCOUS <u>WITH</u> HALLOUMI

VERY OFTEN COUSCOUS IS CONSIDERED A SIDE DISH. HERE, IT PLAYS A LEADING ROLE AND IS TOPPED WITH GRIDDLED SLICED COURGETTES AND HALLOUMI, A MILD CHEESE FROM CYPRUS.

Preparation: 5 minutes; Cooking: 10–12 minutes

SERVES FOUR

INGREDIENTS

30ml/2 tbsp olive oil, plus extra
  for brushing
1 large red onion, chopped
2 garlic cloves, chopped
5ml/1 tsp mild chilli powder
5ml/1 tsp ground cumin
5ml/1 tsp ground coriander
5 cardamom pods, bruised
3 courgettes (zucchini), sliced
  lengthways into ribbons
225g/8oz halloumi cheese, sliced
1 bay leaf
1 cinnamon stick
275g/10oz/1⅔ cups couscous
50g/2oz/¼ cup whole shelled
  almonds, toasted
1 peach, stoned (pitted) and diced
25g/1oz/2 tbsp butter
salt and ground black pepper
chopped fresh flat leaf parsley,
  to garnish

1 Heat the oil in a large heavy pan, add the onion and garlic and sauté for 3–4 minutes until the onion has softened, stirring occasionally.

2 Stir in the chilli powder, cumin, coriander and cardamom pods, and leave the pan over a low heat to allow the flavours to mingle.

3 Meanwhile, brush the courgettes lightly with oil and cook them on a hot griddle or under a hot grill (broiler) for 2–3 minutes, until tender and slightly charred.

4 Turn the courgettes over, add the halloumi and continue cooking for a further 3 minutes, turning the halloumi over once.

5 While the vegetables are cooking, pour 300ml/½ pint/1¼ cups water into a large pan and add the bay leaf and cinnamon stick. Bring to the boil, remove from the heat and immediately add the couscous. Cover and allow to swell for 2 minutes.

6 Add the couscous to the spicy onion mixture, with the almonds, diced peach and butter. Toss over the heat for 2 minutes, then remove the whole spices, arrange the couscous on a plate and season well. Top with the halloumi and courgettes. Sprinkle the parsley over the top and serve.

COOK'S TIP
Look out for packets of flavoured instant couscous at the supermarket. They are very quick and easy to cook, come in a range of flavours and taste delicious. A spiced version would work well in this recipe.

Energy 515kcal/2138kJ; Protein 19.9g; Carbohydrate 42.7g, of which sugars 6.1g; Fat 30.3g, of which saturates 12.5g; Cholesterol 46mg; Calcium 290mg; Fibre 2.9g; Sodium 264mg

SPICED VEGETABLE COUSCOUS

THIS TASTY VEGETARIAN MAIN COURSE IS EASY TO MAKE AND CAN BE PREPARED WITH ANY NUMBER OF YOUNG SEASONAL VEGETABLES SUCH AS SPINACH, LEEKS, PEAS OR CORN.

Preparation: 5 minutes; Cooking: 15 minutes

SERVES SIX

INGREDIENTS

45ml/3 tbsp olive oil
1 large onion, finely chopped
2 garlic cloves, crushed
15ml/1 tbsp tomato purée (paste)
2.5ml/½ tsp ground turmeric
2.5ml/½ tsp cayenne pepper
5ml/1 tsp ground coriander
5ml/1 tsp ground cumin
225g/8oz/1½ cups cauliflower florets
225g/8oz baby carrots, trimmed
1 red (bell) pepper, seeded and diced
225g/8oz courgettes (zucchini), sliced
400g/14oz can chickpeas, drained
  and rinsed
4 beefsteak tomatoes, peeled
  and sliced
45ml/3 tbsp chopped fresh coriander
  (cilantro)
sea salt and ground black pepper
coriander sprigs, to garnish
For the couscous
2.5ml/½ tsp salt
450g/1lb/2⅔ cups couscous
50g/2oz/¼ cup butter

1 Heat 30ml/2 tbsp oil in a large pan, add the onion and garlic and cook until soft and translucent. Stir in the tomato purée, turmeric, cayenne, coriander and cumin. Cook, stirring, for 2 minutes.

2 Add the cauliflower, baby carrots and pepper, with enough water to come halfway up the vegetables. Bring to the boil and cook for 5 minutes.

3 Add the courgettes, chickpeas and tomatoes and cook for 5 minutes. Stir in the fresh coriander and season. Lower the heat to a bare simmer.

4 Cook the couscous. Bring about 475ml/16fl oz/2 cups water to the boil in a large pan. Add the remaining olive oil and the salt. Remove from the heat and add the couscous, stirring. Allow to swell for 2 minutes.

5 Add the butter, and heat through gently, stirring to separate the grains.

6 Turn the couscous out on to a warm serving dish and place the cooked vegetables on top, pouring over any liquid. Garnish with coriander sprigs and serve immediately.

Energy 419kcal/1749kJ; Protein 12.9g; Carbohydrate 61.8g, of which sugars 11.8g; Fat 14.8g, of which saturates 1.9g; Cholesterol 0mg; Calcium 87mg; Fibre 6.7g; Sodium 178mg

SPAGHETTI WITH GARLIC AND OIL

IT DOESN'T GET MUCH SIMPLER THAN THIS: SPAGHETTI TOSSED WITH THE VERY BEST OLIVE OIL, WITH CHILLI FOR A HINT OF HEAT AND PLENTY OF PARSLEY FOR A CONTRASTING COOL, FRESH FLAVOUR.

Preparation: 1 minute; Cooking: 4–12 minutes

SERVES FOUR

INGREDIENTS
  400g/14oz fresh or dried spaghetti
  90ml/6 tbsp extra virgin olive oil
  2–4 garlic cloves, crushed
  1 dried red chilli
  1 small handful fresh flat leaf
    parsley, roughly chopped
  salt

1 Cook the pasta in a large pan of lightly salted boiling water. Dried pasta will take 10–12 minutes; fresh pasta about 3 minutes. Fresh pasta is ready when it rises to the surface of the water.

2 Meanwhile, heat the oil very gently in a small frying pan. Add the crushed garlic and whole dried chilli and stir over a low heat until the garlic is just beginning to brown. Remove the chilli and discard.

3 Drain the pasta and tip it into a warmed large bowl. Pour on the oil and garlic mixture, add the parsley and toss vigorously until the pasta glistens. Serve immediately in warm bowls.

COOK'S TIPS
• Since the oil is such an important ingredient here, only use the very best cold-pressed extra virgin olive oil.
• Don't use salt in the oil and garlic mixture, because it will not dissolve sufficiently. This is why salt is recommended for cooking the pasta.
• In Rome, grated Parmesan is never served with this dish, nor is it seasoned with pepper.
• In summer, Romans use fresh chillies, which they grow in pots on their terraces and window ledges. As the chilli is mainly used for flavouring, you could use chilli oil instead.

Energy 498kcal/2097kJ; Protein 12.6g; Carbohydrate 75.3g, of which sugars 3.4g; Fat 18.3g, of which saturates 2.6g; Cholesterol 0mg; Calcium 27mg; Fibre 3.2g; Sodium 3mg

PASTA WITH SUN-DRIED TOMATOES

THIS IS A LIGHT, MODERN PASTA DISH OF THE KIND SERVED IN FASHIONABLE RESTAURANTS.
IT IS NOT ONLY QUICK AND EASY TO PREPARE, IT LOOKS STUNNING TOO.

Preparation: 3 minutes; Cooking: 13–15 minutes

SERVES FOUR TO SIX

INGREDIENTS
   45ml/3 tbsp pine nuts
   350g/12oz dried paglia e fieno (or
      two different colours of tagliatelle)
   45ml/3 tbsp extra virgin olive oil or
      sunflower oil
   30ml/2 tbsp sun-dried tomato
      purée (paste)
   2 pieces drained sun-dried tomatoes
      in olive oil, cut into very thin slivers
   40g/1½oz radicchio leaves,
      finely shredded
   4–6 spring onions (scallions), thinly
      sliced into rings
   salt and ground black pepper

1 Put the pine nuts in a non-stick frying pan and toss over a low to medium heat for 1–2 minutes or until they are lightly toasted and golden. Remove from the pan and set aside.

2 Cook the pasta in lightly salted water for 12–14 minutes or until tender, keeping the colours separate by using two pans.

3 While the pasta is cooking, heat 15ml/1 tbsp of the oil in a medium pan or frying pan. Add the sun-dried tomato paste and the sun-dried tomatoes, then stir in 2 ladlefuls of the water used for cooking the pasta. Simmer until the sauce is slightly reduced, stirring constantly.

4 Mix in the shredded radicchio, then taste and season if necessary. Keep on a low heat. Drain the paglia e fieno, keeping the colours separate, and return the pasta to the pans. Add about 15ml/1 tbsp oil to each pan and toss over a medium to high heat until the pasta is glistening with the oil.

5 Arrange a portion of green and white pasta in each of 4–6 warmed bowls, then spoon the sun-dried tomato and radicchio mixture in the centre. Sprinkle the spring onions and pine nuts over the top and serve immediately. Before eating, each diner should toss the sauce ingredients with the pasta.

COOK'S TIP
If you find the presentation too fussy, you can toss the tomato and raddichio mixture with the pasta in a large bowl before serving, then sprinkle the spring onions and toasted pine nuts on top.

Energy 309kcal/1302kJ; Protein 8.6g; Carbohydrate 44.9g, of which sugars 3.6g; Fat 11.8g, of which saturates 1.3g; Cholesterol 0mg; Calcium 23mg; Fibre 2.3g; Sodium 16mg

GARGANELLI PASTA WITH ASPARAGUS AND CREAM

WHEN FRESH ASPARAGUS IS ON SALE AT THE MARKET, THIS IS A WONDERFUL WAY TO SERVE IT. ANY TYPE OF PASTA CAN BE USED, BUT ONE THAT MIRRORS THE SHAPE OF THE ASPARAGUS WORKS BEST.

Preparation: 4–5 minutes; Cooking: 15 minutes

SERVES FOUR

INGREDIENTS

1 bunch fresh young asparagus,
  250–300g/9–11oz
350g/12oz/3 cups dried garganelli
25g/1oz/2 tbsp butter
200ml/7fl oz/scant 1 cup panna da
  cucina or double (heavy) cream
30ml/2 tbsp dry white wine
90–115g/3½–4oz/1–1⅓ cups freshly
  grated Parmesan cheese
30ml/2 tbsp chopped fresh mixed
  herbs, such as basil, flat leaf
  parsley, chervil, marjoram
  and oregano
salt and ground black pepper

4 Meanwhile, melt the butter in a heavy pan. Add the cream, with salt and pepper to taste, and bring to the boil. Simmer for a few minutes until the cream reduces and thickens.

5 Stir the asparagus, wine and about half the Parmesan into the sauce. Drain the pasta and return it to the clean pan. Add the sauce and herbs and toss. Serve with the remaining Parmesan.

1 Snap off and throw away the woody ends of the asparagus – after trimming, you should have about 200g/7oz asparagus spears. Cut the spears diagonally into pieces about the same length and shape as the garganelli.

2 Blanch the thicker asparagus pieces in a large pan of lightly salted boiling water for 2 minutes, the tips for 1 minute. Using a slotted spoon, transfer the blanched asparagus to a colander, rinse under cold water and set aside.

3 Bring the water in the pan back to the boil, add the pasta and cook for 12 minutes or until tender.

Energy 716kcal/2994kJ; Protein 22g; Carbohydrate 67g, of which sugars 5g; Fat 41.3g, of which saturates 24.8g; Cholesterol 104mg; Calcium 335mg; Fibre 3.6g; Sodium 298mg

FRITTATA WITH LEEKS AND RED PEPPER

SIMILAR TO A QUICHE, BUT WITHOUT THE CRUST, THIS FRITTATA INCORPORATES A MIXTURE OF LIGHTLY SPICED VEGETABLES IN AN EGG CUSTARD. SLICES ARE EASY TO PACK FOR A PICNIC OR WORKING LUNCH.

Preparation: 5 minutes; Cooking: 14 minutes

SERVES THREE TO FOUR

INGREDIENTS

30ml/2 tbsp olive oil
1 large red (bell) pepper, seeded
   and diced
2.5–5ml/½–1 tsp ground
   toasted cumin
3 leeks, about 450g/1lb, thinly sliced
150g/5oz small spinach leaves
45ml/3 tbsp pine nuts, toasted
5 large eggs
15ml/1 tbsp chopped fresh basil
15ml/1 tbsp chopped fresh flat
   leaf parsley
salt and ground black pepper
watercress, to garnish
50g/2oz Parmesan cheese, grated,
   to serve

1 Heat a frying pan and add the oil. Add the red pepper and cook over a medium heat, stirring occasionally, for 3–4 minutes, until soft and beginning to brown. Add 2.5ml/½ tsp of the cumin and cook for another 1–2 minutes.

2 Stir in the leeks, then part-cover the pan and cook gently for about 5 minutes, until the leeks have softened and collapsed. Season with salt and ground black pepper.

3 Add the spinach. Cover the pan and leave the spinach to wilt in the steam for 2 minutes, then stir to mix it into the vegetables. Add the pine nuts and stir to mix well.

4 Preheat the grill (broiler). Beat the eggs with salt, pepper, the remaining cumin, basil and parsley. Add to the pan and cook over a gentle heat until the bottom of the omelette sets and turns golden brown. Pull the edges of the omelette away from the sides of the pan as it cooks and tilt the pan so that the uncooked egg runs underneath.

5 Flash the frittata under the hot grill to set the egg on top, but do not let it become too brown. Cut the frittata into wedges and serve warm, garnished with watercress and sprinkled with Parmesan.

VARIATION

A delicious way to serve frittata is to pack it into a slightly hollowed-out loaf and then drizzle it with a little extra virgin olive oil. Wrap tightly in clear film (plastic wrap) and leave to stand for 1–2 hours before cutting into thick slices. A frittata-filled loaf is ideal picnic fare.

Energy 323kcal/1342kJ; Protein 17.6g; Carbohydrate 7.1g, of which sugars 6.2g; Fat 25.3g, of which saturates 6g; Cholesterol 250mg; Calcium 281mg; Fibre 4.2g; Sodium 280mg

MUSHROOM STROGANOFF

*THIS CREAMY MIXED MUSHROOM SAUCE TASTES GREAT AND IS IDEAL FOR A DINNER PARTY.
SERVE IT WITH TOASTED BUCKWHEAT, BROWN RICE OR A MIXTURE OF WILD RICES.*

Preparation: 3 minutes; Cooking: 15–17 minutes

SERVES FOUR

INGREDIENTS

- 25g/1oz/2 tbsp butter
- 900g/2lb/8 cups mixed mushrooms, cut into bite-size pieces
- 350g/12oz/1¾ cups white long grain rice
- 350ml/12fl oz/1½ cups white wine sauce
- 250ml/8fl oz/1 cup sour cream
- chopped chives, to garnish

1 Melt the butter in a large, heavy pan and add the mushrooms. Cook over a medium heat until the mushrooms give up their liquid. Continue cooking until they are tender and beginning to brown.

2 Meanwhile, bring a large pan of lightly salted water to the boil. Add the rice, partially cover the pan and cook over a medium heat for 13–15 minutes until the rice is just tender.

3 Add the wine sauce to the cooked mushrooms in the pan and bring to the boil, stirring. Stir in the sour cream and season to taste. Drain the rice well, spoon on to warm plates, top with the sauce and garnish with chives.

Energy 556kcal/2316kJ; Protein 13.3g; Carbohydrate 80.4g, of which sugars 7.2g; Fat 21.7g, of which saturates 11.4g; Cholesterol 51mg; Calcium 96mg; Fibre 2.5g; Sodium 897mg

TOFU AND GREEN BEAN RED CURRY

THIS IS ONE OF THOSE VERSATILE RECIPES THAT SHOULD BE IN EVERY COOK'S REPERTOIRE. THIS VERSION USES GREEN BEANS, BUT OTHER TYPES OF VEGETABLE WORK EQUALLY WELL.

Preparation: 2–3 minutes; Cooking: 7 minutes

SERVES FOUR TO SIX

INGREDIENTS
600ml/1 pint/2½ cups canned
  coconut milk
15ml/1 tbsp Thai red curry paste
10ml/2 tsp palm sugar or honey
225g/8oz/3¼ cups button
  (white) mushrooms
115g/4oz/scant 1 cup green
  beans, trimmed
175g/6oz firm tofu, rinsed, drained
  and cut into 2cm/¾in cubes
4 kaffir lime leaves, torn
2 fresh red chillies, seeded
  and sliced
fresh coriander (cilantro) leaves,
  to garnish

1 Pour about one-third of the coconut milk into a wok or pan. Cook until it starts to separate and an oily sheen appears on the surface.

2 Add the red curry paste and palm sugar or honey to the coconut milk. Mix thoroughly, then add the mushrooms. Stir and cook for 1 minute.

3 Stir in the remaining coconut milk. Bring back to the boil, then add the green beans and tofu cubes. Simmer gently for 4–5 minutes more.

4 Stir in the kaffir lime leaves and sliced red chillies. Spoon the curry into a serving dish, garnish with the coriander leaves and serve immediately.

Energy 59kcal/250kJ; Protein 3.8g; Carbohydrate 7.5g, of which sugars 7.1g; Fat 1.8g, of which saturates 0.4g; Cholesterol 0mg; Calcium 188mg; Fibre 0.8g; Sodium 291mg

STIR-FRIED CRISPY TOFU

VEGETARIAN GUESTS OFTEN DRAW THE SHORT STRAW AT DINNERS WHERE MEAT EATERS ARE IN THE MAJORITY. OFFER A DISH LIKE THIS ONE, AND THERE'LL BE ENVIOUS LOOKS FROM ACROSS THE TABLE.

Preparation: 3–4 minutes; Cooking: 12 minutes

SERVES ONE TO TWO

INGREDIENTS

  250g/9oz deep-fried tofu cubes
  30ml/2 tbsp groundnut (peanut) oil
  15ml/1 tbsp Thai green curry paste
  30ml/2 tbsp light soy sauce
  2 kaffir lime leaves, rolled into
    cylinders and thinly sliced
  30ml/2 tbsp granulated sugar
  150ml/¼ pint/⅔ cup vegetable stock
  250g/9oz asparagus, trimmed and
    sliced into 5cm/2in lengths
  30ml/2 tbsp roasted peanuts,
    finely chopped

VARIATION
Substitute slim carrot batons, baby leeks or small broccoli florets for the asparagus, if you like.

1 Preheat the grill (broiler) to medium. Place the tofu cubes in a grill pan and grill (broil) for 2–3 minutes, then turn them over and continue to cook until they are crisp and golden brown all over. Watch them carefully; they must not be allowed to burn.

2 Heat the oil in a wok or heavy frying pan. Add the green curry paste and cook over a medium heat, stirring constantly, for 1–2 minutes, until it gives off its aroma.

3 Stir the soy sauce, lime leaves, sugar and vegetable stock into the wok or pan and mix well. Bring to the boil over a high heat, then reduce the heat to low so that the curried stock is just simmering.

4 Add the asparagus and simmer gently for 5 minutes. Meanwhile, chop each piece of tofu into four, then add to the pan with the peanuts.

5 Toss to coat all the ingredients in the sauce, then spoon into a warmed dish and serve immediately.

Energy 551kcal/2287kJ; Protein 37.3g; Carbohydrate 7.8g, of which sugars 5.2g; Fat 41.4g, of which saturates 2.8g; Cholesterol 0mg; Calcium 1894mg; Fibre 3.1g; Sodium 1203mg

TOFU AND PEPPER KEBABS

A SIMPLE COATING OF GROUND, DRY-ROASTED PEANUTS PRESSED ON TO CUBED TOFU PROVIDES PLENTY OF ADDITIONAL FLAVOUR ALONG WITH THE PEPPERS. USE METAL OR BAMBOO SKEWERS.

Preparation: 6–8 minutes; Cooking: 10–12 minutes

SERVES FOUR

INGREDIENTS
  250g/9oz firm tofu
  50g/2oz/½ cup dry-roasted peanuts
  2 red and 2 green (bell) peppers
  60ml/4 tbsp sweet chilli
    dipping sauce

1 Pat the tofu dry on kitchen paper and then cut it into small cubes. Grind the peanuts in a blender or food processor and transfer to a plate.

COOK'S TIP
Don't forget to soak the bamboo skewers upright in a jar of water for about half an hour before using, so they don't scorch.

2 Preheat the grill (broiler) to medium. Using a sharp knife, halve and seed the red and green peppers, and cut them into large chunks. Turn the tofu cubes in the ground nuts to coat thoroughly on all sides.

3 Thread the chunks of pepper on to four large skewers with the tofu cubes and place on a foil-lined grill rack. Grill (broil) the kebabs, turning frequently, for 10–12 minutes, or until the peppers and peanuts are beginning to brown.

Energy 175kcal/730kJ; Protein 10g; Carbohydrate 12.9g, of which sugars 11.4g; Fat 9.6g, of which saturates 1.6g; Cholesterol 0mg; Calcium 339mg; Fibre 3.6g; Sodium 108mg

STUFFED SWEET PEPPERS

THIS IS AN UNUSUAL RECIPE IN THAT THE STUFFED PEPPERS ARE STEAMED RATHER THAN BAKED.
THE TECHNIQUE IS SPEEDY AND THE RESULT IS BEAUTIFULLY LIGHT AND TENDER.
Preparation: 5 minutes; Cooking: 15 minutes

SERVES FOUR

INGREDIENTS

3 garlic cloves, finely chopped
2 coriander (cilantro) roots,
 finely chopped
400g/14oz/3 cups
 mushrooms, quartered
5ml/1 tsp Thai red curry paste
1 egg, lightly beaten
15–30ml/1–2 tbsp light soy sauce
2.5ml/½ tsp granulated sugar
3 kaffir lime leaves, finely chopped
4 yellow (bell) peppers, halved
 lengthways and seeded

VARIATIONS
Use red or orange (bell) peppers if you
prefer, or a combination of the two.

1 In a mortar or spice grinder pound or
blend the garlic with the coriander
roots. Scrape into a bowl.

2 Put the mushrooms in a food
processor and pulse briefly until they
are finely chopped. Add to the garlic
mixture, then stir in the curry paste,
egg, sauces, sugar and lime leaves.

3 Place the pepper halves in a single
layer in a steamer basket. Spoon the
mixture loosely into the pepper halves.

4 Bring the water in the steamer to the
boil, then lower the heat to a simmer.
Steam the peppers for 15 minutes, or
until the flesh feels tender when tested
with a knife tip. Serve hot.

Energy 89kcal/374kJ; Protein 5.1g; Carbohydrate 10.6g, of which sugars 9.9g; Fat 3.2g, of which saturates 0.8g; Cholesterol 48mg; Calcium 27mg; Fibre 3.5g; Sodium 563mg

AUBERGINE, MINT AND COUSCOUS SALAD

PACKETS OF FLAVOURED COUSCOUS ARE AVAILABLE IN MOST SUPERMARKETS — YOU CAN USE WHICHEVER YOU LIKE, BUT GARLIC AND CORIANDER IS PARTICULARLY GOOD FOR THIS RECIPE.

Preparation: 3 minutes; Cooking: 6 minutes

SERVES TWO

INGREDIENTS
    1 large aubergine (eggplant)
    30ml/2 tbsp olive oil
    115g/4oz packet couscous flavoured
      with garlic and coriander (cilantro)
    30ml/2 tbsp chopped fresh mint
    salt and ground black pepper

VARIATION
For extra colour and flavour, add tomato to the salad. Grill (broil) about six baby plum tomatoes alongside the aubergine (eggplant).

1 Preheat the grill (broiler) to high. Cut the aubergine into large chunky pieces and toss them with the olive oil. Season with salt and pepper to taste and spread the aubergine pieces on a non-stick baking sheet. Grill (broil) for 5–6 minutes, turning occasionally, until golden brown.

2 Meanwhile, prepare the couscous according to the instructions on the packet.

3 Stir the grilled aubergine and chopped fresh mint into the garlic and coriander couscous, toss thoroughly and serve immediately.

Energy 251kcal/1044kJ; Protein 4.8g; Carbohydrate 32.5g, of which sugars 2g; Fat 12.1g, of which saturates 1.7g; Cholesterol 0mg; Calcium 53mg; Fibre 2g; Sodium 5mg

MIXED BEAN AND TOMATO CHILLI

*THE ONLY TALENT THIS REQUIRES IS THE ABILITY TO OPEN A CAN, CHOP A CHILLI AND STIR A SAUCE.
IT'S IDEAL FOR THOSE DAYS WHEN YOUR ENERGY LEVELS ARE ZERO AND YOU NEED FOOD FAST.*

Preparation: 2–3 minutes; Cooking: 12 minutes

SERVES FOUR

INGREDIENTS
   400g/14oz jar tomato and herb sauce
   2 x 400g/14oz cans mixed beans,
      drained and rinsed
   1 fresh red chilli
   a large handful of fresh coriander
      (cilantro)
   120ml/4fl oz/½ cup sour cream

1 Seed and thinly slice the chilli, then put it into a pan.

2 Pour the tomato sauce and mixed beans into a pan. Finely chop the fresh coriander. Set some aside for the garnish and add the remainder to the tomato and bean mixture. Stir the contents of the pan for a few seconds to mix all the ingredients together.

3 Bring the mixture to the boil, then quickly reduce the heat, cover and simmer gently for 10 minutes. Stir the mixture occasionally and add a dash of water if the sauce starts to dry out.

4 Ladle the chilli into warmed individual bowls and top with sour cream. Sprinkle with coriander and serve.

VARIATIONS
This chilli is great just as it is, served with chunks of bread, but you may want to dress it up a bit occasionally. Try serving it over a mixture of long grain and wild rice, piling it into split pitta breads or using it as a filling for baked potatoes. Serve with yogurt or crème fraîche instead of sour cream.

COOK'S TIP
Treat chillies with caution and wash your hands in soapy water after touching them. The capsaicin they contain is a powerful irritant and will cause eyes to sting if it comes into contact with them.

Energy 309kcal/1302kJ; Protein 16.7g; Carbohydrate 43.7g, of which sugars 14.1g; Fat 8.7g, of which saturates 4.2g; Cholesterol 18mg; Calcium 193mg; Fibre 12.4g; Sodium 1202mg

ENSALADILLA

ALSO KNOWN AS RUSSIAN SALAD, THIS MIXTURE OF COOKED AND RAW VEGETABLES IN A RICH GARLIC MAYONNAISE MAKES A USEFUL VEGETARIAN MAIN COURSE. IT TASTES GOOD WITH HARD-BOILED EGGS.

Preparation: 10 minutes; Cooking: 8 minutes

SERVES FOUR

INGREDIENTS

    8 new potatoes, scrubbed
      and quartered
    1 large carrot, diced
    115g/4oz fine green beans,
      cut into 2cm/¾in lengths
    75g/3oz/¾ cup peas
    ½ Spanish (Bermuda) onion, chopped
    4 cornichons or small
      gherkins, sliced
    1 small red (bell) pepper, seeded
      and diced
    50g/2oz/½ cup pitted black olives
    15ml/1 tbsp drained pickled capers
    15ml/1 tbsp freshly squeezed
      lemon juice
    30ml/2 tbsp chopped fresh fennel
      or parsley
    salt and ground black pepper
For the aioli
    2–3 garlic cloves, finely chopped
    2.5ml/½ tsp salt
    150ml/¼ pint/⅔ cup mayonnaise

1 Make the aioli. Put two or three garlic cloves, depending on their size, in a mortar. Add the salt and crush to a paste. Whisk or stir into the mayonnaise.

VARIATION
This salad is delicious using any combination of chopped, cooked vegetables. Use whatever is available.

2 Cook the potatoes and diced carrot in a pan of boiling lightly salted water for 5 minutes, until almost tender.

3 Add the beans and peas to the potatoes and carrot and cook for 2 minutes, or until all the vegetables are tender but the beans still retain some crunch. Drain and transfer to a bowl of iced water to cool quickly.

4 When cool, drain the vegetables, place them in a large bowl and add the onion, cornichons or gherkins, red pepper, olives and capers. Stir in the aioli and pepper and lemon juice to taste.

5 Toss the vegetables and aioli together until well combined, check the seasoning and chill well. Serve garnished with fennel or parsley.

Energy 395kcal/1636kJ; Protein 5.2g; Carbohydrate 25.6g, of which sugars 8.1g; Fat 30.9g, of which saturates 4.8g; Cholesterol 28mg; Calcium 68mg; Fibre 4.9g; Sodium 472mg

SIMPLE RICE SALAD

SOMETIMES CALLED CONFETTI SALAD, THIS FEATURES BRIGHTLY COLOURED CHOPPED VEGETABLES SERVED IN A WELL-FLAVOURED DRESSING. CHILL IT WELL IF YOU INTEND TO TAKE IT ON A PICNIC.
Preparation: 6 minutes; Cooking: 10–12 minutes

SERVES SIX

INGREDIENTS
275g/10oz/1½ cups long grain rice
1 bunch spring onions (scallions),
  finely sliced
1 green (bell) pepper, seeded and
  finely diced
1 yellow (bell) pepper, seeded and
  finely diced
225g/8oz tomatoes, peeled, seeded
  and chopped
30ml/2 tbsp chopped fresh flat leaf
  parsley or coriander (cilantro)
For the dressing
75ml/5 tbsp mixed olive oil and extra
  virgin olive oil
15ml/1 tbsp sherry vinegar
5ml/1 tsp strong Dijon mustard
salt and ground black pepper

1 Cook the rice in a large pan of lightly salted boiling water for 10–12 minutes, until tender but still *al dente*. Be careful not to overcook it.

2 Drain the rice well in a sieve (strainer), rinse thoroughly under cold running water and drain again. Leave the rice to cool while you prepare the ingredients for the dressing.

3 Meanwhile, make the dressing by whisking all the ingredients together. Transfer the rice to a bowl and add half the dressing to moisten it and cool it further.

4 Add the spring onions, peppers, tomatoes and parsley or coriander with the remaining dressing, and toss well to mix. Season with salt and pepper to taste.

Energy 276kcal/1150kJ; Protein 4.6g; Carbohydrate 41.9g, of which sugars 5.2g; Fat 9.9g, of which saturates 1.4g; Cholesterol 0mg; Calcium 29mg; Fibre 1.7g; Sodium 8mg

FAMILY
MEALS

This chapter sets out to show just how simple it can be to produce delicious dishes for all sorts

of family occasions with the minimum of fuss. There's something here for everyone, from

reluctant young eaters to teenagers, who trust you'll be able to produce good food fast even when

they've forgotten to tell you they are bringing home friends for supper. For occasions like those,

there are store-cupboard (pantry) specials like Four Cheese Ciabatta Pizza or Corned Beef

and Egg Hash, based on basic ingredients. When sitting down together proves an impossibility

because every member of the family is on a different schedule, good-tempered dishes such as

Roast Chicken Pitta Pockets can be relished in relays. There are even some extra-special treats

for celebrations, such as Crispy Five-Spice Chicken and Duck and Sesame Stir-fry.

All the recipes are quick and easy, and the nutritional analysis at the bottom of every page

makes it simple to keep a watching brief on what everyone is eating.

FIORENTINA PIZZA

AN EGG ADDS THE FINISHING TOUCH TO THIS CLASSIC ITALIAN SPINACH PIZZA; TRY NOT TO OVERCOOK IT THOUGH, AS IT'S BEST WHEN THE YOLK IS STILL SLIGHTLY SOFT IN THE MIDDLE.

Preparation: 2 minutes; Cooking: 18 minutes

2 Preheat the oven to 220°C/425°F/ Gas 7. Brush the pizza base with half the remaining olive oil. Spread the pizza sauce evenly over the base, using the back of a spoon, then top with the spinach mixture. Sprinkle over a little freshly grated nutmeg.

3 Thinly slice the mozzarella and arrange over the spinach. Drizzle over the remaining oil. Bake for 10 minutes, then remove from the oven.

4 Make a small well in the centre of the pizza topping and carefully break the egg into the hole. Sprinkle over the grated Gruyère cheese and return the pizza to the oven for a further 5–10 minutes until crisp and golden. Serve immediately.

VARIATION

A calzone is like a pizza but is folded in half to conceal the filling. Add the egg with the rest of the pizza topping, fold over the dough, seal the edges and bake for 20 minutes.

SERVES TWO TO THREE

INGREDIENTS

45ml/3 tbsp olive oil
1 small red onion, thinly sliced
175g/6oz fresh spinach,
  stalks removed
1 pizza base, about 25–30cm/
  10–12in in diameter
1 small jar pizza sauce
freshly grated nutmeg
150g/5oz mozzarella cheese
1 egg
25g/1oz/¼ cup Gruyère
  cheese, grated

1 Heat 15ml/1 tbsp of the oil and fry the onion until soft. Add the spinach and fry until wilted. Drain any excess liquid.

Energy 503kcal/2100kJ; Protein 20.8g; Carbohydrate 40.3g, of which sugars 5.9g; Fat 29.7g, of which saturates 10.9g; Cholesterol 101mg; Calcium 417mg; Fibre 2.8g; Sodium 668mg.

FOUR CHEESE CIABATTA PIZZA

FEW DISHES ARE AS SIMPLE — OR AS SATISFYING — AS THIS PIZZA MADE BY TOPPING A HALVED LOAF OF CIABATTA. THIS IS THE SORT OF THING CHILDREN COULD MAKE TO GIVE MUM AND DAD A BREAK.

Preparation: 4 minutes; Cooking: 10–12 minutes

SERVES TWO

INGREDIENTS

  1 loaf ciabatta bread
  1 garlic clove, halved
  30–45ml/2–3 tbsp olive oil
  about 90ml/6 tbsp passata (bottled
    strained tomatoes) or sugocasa
  1 small red onion, thinly sliced
  30ml/2 tbsp chopped pitted olives
  about 50g/2oz each of four cheeses,
    one mature/sharp (Parmesan or
    Cheddar), one blue-veined
    (Gorgonzola or Stilton), one mild
    (Fontina or Emmental) and a goat's
    cheese, sliced, grated or crumbled
  pine nuts or cumin seeds, to sprinkle
  salt and ground black pepper
  sprigs of basil, to garnish

1 Preheat the oven to 200°C/400°F/ Gas 6. Split the ciabatta bread in half. Rub the cut sides with the garlic, then brush over the oil. Spread with the passata or sugocasa, then add the onion slices and olives. Season to taste with salt and black pepper.

2 Divide the cheeses between the ciabatta halves and sprinkle over the pine nuts or cumin seeds. Bake for 10–12 minutes, until bubbling and golden brown. Cut the pizza into slices and serve immediately, garnished with the sprigs of fresh basil.

Energy 782kcal/3265kJ; Protein 34g; Carbohydrate 55.8g, of which sugars 6.2g; Fat 47.4g, of which saturates 22.8g; Cholesterol 86mg; Calcium 756mg; Fibre 3.4g; Sodium 1952mg

WARM PENNE WITH FRESH TOMATOES AND BASIL

WHEN YOU'RE HEADING OFF FOR A FAMILY BIKE RIDE OR A WALK ON THE BEACH, SOMETHING LIGHT AND FRESH, BUT WHICH KEEPS ENERGY LEVELS TOPPED UP OVER TIME, IS JUST WHAT YOU NEED.

Preparation: 2–3 minutes; Cooking: 12–14 minutes

SERVES FOUR

INGREDIENTS
500g/1¼lb dried penne
5 very ripe plum tomatoes
1 small bunch fresh basil
60ml/4 tbsp extra virgin olive oil
salt and ground black pepper

COOK'S TIP
If you cannot find ripe tomatoes, roast those you have to bring out their flavour. Put the tomatoes in a roasting pan, drizzle with oil and roast at 190°C/375°F/Gas 5 for 20 minutes, then mash roughly.

1 Cook the pasta in a large pan of lightly salted boiling water for 12–14 minutes, until tender. Meanwhile, roughly chop the tomatoes and tear up the basil leaves.

2 Drain the pasta thoroughly and return it to the clean pan. Toss with the tomatoes, basil and olive oil. Season with salt and freshly ground black pepper and serve immediately.

Energy 552kcal/2336kJ; Protein 16.3g; Carbohydrate 96.9g, of which sugars 8.3g; Fat 13.8g, of which saturates 2g; Cholesterol 0mg; Calcium 65mg; Fibre 5.5g; Sodium 19mg

PUMPKIN AND PARMESAN PASTA

THE SWEET FLAVOUR OF PUMPKIN IS NICELY BALANCED BY THE PARMESAN IN THIS CREAMY PASTA SAUCE, WHILE FRIED GARLIC BREADCRUMBS PROVIDE A WELCOME CRUNCH.

Preparation: 4 minutes; Cooking: 14 minutes

SERVES FOUR

INGREDIENTS

800g/1¾lb fresh pumpkin flesh,
  cut into small cubes
300g/11oz dried tagliatelle
65g/2½oz/5 tbsp butter
1 onion, sliced
115g/4oz rindless smoked back
  bacon, diced
15ml/1 tbsp olive oil
2 garlic cloves, crushed
75g/3oz/1½ cups fresh white
  breadcrumbs
150ml/¼ pint/⅔ cup single
  (light) cream
50g/2oz/⅔ cup freshly grated
  Parmesan cheese
freshly grated nutmeg
30ml/2 tbsp chopped fresh parsley
15ml/1 tbsp chopped fresh chives
salt and ground black pepper
sprigs of flat leaf parsley, to garnish

1 Bring two pans of lightly salted water to the boil. Place the pumpkin cubes in one pan and the pasta in the other. Cook for 10–12 minutes.

2 Meanwhile, heat one-third of the butter in a separate large pan. Fry the onion and bacon for 5 minutes.

3 Melt the remaining butter with the oil in a frying pan. Add the garlic and breadcrumbs. Fry gently until the crumbs are golden brown and crisp. Drain on kitchen paper and keep warm.

4 Drain the pumpkin and add it to the onion and bacon mixture, with the cream. Heat until the cream is just below boiling point.

5 Drain the pasta, add to the pan and heat through. Stir in the Parmesan, nutmeg, parsley, chives and seasoning. Serve sprinkled with the garlic breadcrumbs and garnished with parsley.

COOK'S TIP

Look out for tubs of diced bacon bits in the supermarket chiller. They're a real time-saver. If you find cubed pumpkin too, you're on to a winner.

Energy 691kcal/2897kJ; Protein 23.8g; Carbohydrate 76.6g, of which sugars 8.1g; Fat 34.2g, of which saturates 18.1g; Cholesterol 83mg; Calcium 293mg; Fibre 4.8g; Sodium 834mg

SPAGHETTI CARBONARA

THIS ITALIAN CLASSIC, FLAVOURED WITH PANCETTA AND A GARLIC AND EGG SAUCE THAT COOKS AROUND THE HOT SPAGHETTI, IS POPULAR WORLDWIDE. IT MAKES A GREAT LAST-MINUTE SUPPER.

Preparation: 3 minutes; Cooking: 15–17 minutes

3 Meanwhile, cook the spaghetti in a large pan of salted boiling water for 10–12 minutes, until just tender.

4 Put the eggs, crème fraîche and grated Parmesan in a bowl. Stir in plenty of black pepper, then beat together well.

5 Drain the pasta thoroughly, tip it into the pan with the pancetta or bacon and toss well to mix.

SERVES FOUR

INGREDIENTS
  30ml/2 tbsp olive oil
  1 small onion, finely chopped
  1 large garlic clove, crushed
  8 slices pancetta or rindless smoked
    streaky (fatty) bacon, cut into
    1cm/½in pieces
  350g/12oz fresh or dried spaghetti
  4 eggs
  90–120ml/6–8 tbsp crème fraîche
  60ml/4 tbsp freshly grated
    Parmesan cheese, plus extra
    to serve
  salt and ground black pepper

1 Heat the oil in a large pan, add the onion and garlic and fry gently for about 5 minutes until softened.

2 Add the pancetta or bacon to the pan. Cook for 10 minutes, stirring often.

6 Turn off the heat under the pan, then immediately add the egg mixture and toss thoroughly so that it cooks lightly and coats the pasta.

7 Season to taste, then divide the pasta among four warmed bowls and sprinkle with ground black pepper. Serve immediately, with extra grated Parmesan handed separately.

VARIATION
You can replace the crème fraîche with double (heavy) cream or sour cream, if you prefer.

Energy 708kcal/2966kJ; Protein 30.7g; Carbohydrate 66.6g, of which sugars 4.2g; Fat 37.5g, of which saturates 15.5g; Cholesterol 261mg; Calcium 250mg; Fibre 2.8g; Sodium 824mg

PENNE WITH CHICKEN, BROCCOLI AND CHEESE

CRISP-TENDER, LIGHTLY COOKED BROCCOLI GIVES THIS DISH COLOUR AND CRUNCH. IT IS ALSO AN EXCELLENT FOIL TO THE RICHNESS OF THE CREAMY GORGONZOLA CHEESE AND WINE SAUCE.

Preparation: 3–4 minutes; Cooking: 12–14 minutes

SERVES FOUR

INGREDIENTS

400g/14oz/3½ cups dried penne
115g/4oz/scant 1 cup broccoli
   florets, divided into tiny sprigs
50g/2oz/¼ cup butter
2 chicken breast fillets, skinned and
   cut into thin strips
2 garlic cloves, crushed
120ml/4fl oz/½ cup dry white wine
200ml/7fl oz/scant 1 cup panna da
   cucina or double (heavy) cream
90g/3½oz Gorgonzola cheese, rind
   removed, finely diced
salt and ground black pepper
freshly grated Parmesan cheese,
   to serve

1 Bring two pans of lightly salted water to the boil. Add the pasta to one pan and cook over a medium heat for 12–14 minutes or until tender.

2 Meanwhile, plunge the broccoli into the second pan of salted boiling water. Bring back to the boil and boil for 2 minutes, then drain in a colander and refresh under cold running water. Shake well to remove the surplus water and set aside to drain completely.

VARIATION
Use leeks instead of broccoli if you prefer. Fry them with the chicken strips.

3 While the pasta is cooking, melt the butter in a large frying pan and add the chicken and garlic, with salt and pepper to taste. Stir well. Fry over a medium heat, stirring frequently, for 3 minutes, or until the chicken becomes white.

4 Pour the wine and cream over the chicken mixture in the pan, stir to mix, then simmer, stirring occasionally, for about 5 minutes, or until the sauce has reduced and thickened and the chicken is cooked through.

5 Add the broccoli, increase the heat and toss to heat it through and mix it with the chicken. Taste for seasoning.

6 Drain the pasta and add it to the sauce. Add the Gorgonzola and toss well. Serve in warmed bowls and sprinkle each portion with grated Parmesan.

Energy 951kcal/3982kJ; Protein 47.8g; Carbohydrate 80.2g, of which sugars 8.6g; Fat 48.8g, of which saturates 28.5g; Cholesterol 165mg; Calcium 324mg; Fibre 10.2g; Sodium 433mg

SESAME NOODLES

THIS IS ONE OF THOSE QUICK, COMFORTING DISHES THAT BECOME FAMILY FAVOURITES. CHILDREN LOVE ITS SWEET-SOUR FLAVOURS AND THERE ARE SHARP SPICES.

Preparation: 10 minutes; Cooking: 4 minutes

SERVES FOUR

INGREDIENTS

450g/1lb fresh egg noodles
½ cucumber, sliced lengthways, seeded and diced
4–6 spring onions (scallions)
a bunch of radishes, about 115g/4oz
225g/8oz mooli (daikon), peeled
115g/4oz/2 cups beansprouts, rinsed, then left in iced water and drained
60ml/4 tbsp groundnut (peanut) oil or sunflower oil
2 garlic cloves, crushed
45ml/3 tbsp toasted sesame paste
15ml/1 tbsp sesame oil
15ml/1 tbsp light soy sauce
5–10ml/1–2 tsp sweet chilli sauce, to taste
15ml/1 tbsp rice vinegar
120ml/4fl oz/½ cup chicken stock
5ml/1 tsp sugar, or to taste
salt and ground black pepper
roasted cashew nuts, to garnish

1 Cook the fresh noodles in boiling water for 1 minute then drain well. Rinse the noodles in fresh water and drain again.

2 Place the cucumber in a colander or sieve (strainer), sprinkle with salt and leave to drain over a bowl for 10 minutes.

COOK'S TIP
Always check that guests do not have any nut allergies.

3 Meanwhile, cut the spring onions into fine shreds. Cut the radishes in half and slice finely. Coarsely grate the mooli. Rinse the cucumber, drain, pat dry and mix with all the vegetables in a salad bowl. Toss gently.

4 Heat half the oil in a wok or frying pan and stir-fry the noodles for about 1 minute. Using a slotted spoon, transfer the noodles to a large serving bowl and keep warm.

5 Add the remaining oil to the wok. When it is hot, fry the garlic to flavour the oil. Remove from the heat and stir in the sesame paste, with the sesame oil, soy and chilli sauces, vinegar and chicken stock.

6 Add a little sugar and season to taste. Warm through but do not overheat. Pour the sauce over the noodles and toss well. Garnish with the cashew nuts and serve with the vegetables.

Energy 633kcal/2658kJ; Protein 17.6g; Carbohydrate 84.5g, of which sugars 5.3g; Fat 27.2g, of which saturates 5g; Cholesterol 34mg; Calcium 139mg; Fibre 5.7g; Sodium 484mg

DUCK AND SESAME STIR-FRY

FOR A SPECIAL FAMILY MEAL THAT IS A GUARANTEED SUCCESS, THIS IS IDEAL. IT TASTES FANTASTIC AND COOKS FAST, SO YOU'LL BE EATING IN NO TIME.

Preparation: 3 minutes; Cooking: 5–7 minutes

SERVES FOUR

INGREDIENTS

250g/9oz boneless duck meat
15ml/1 tbsp sesame oil
15ml/1 tbsp vegetable oil
4 garlic cloves, finely sliced
2.5ml/½ tsp dried chilli flakes
15ml/1 tbsp Thai fish sauce
15ml/1 tbsp light soy sauce
120ml/4fl oz/½ cup water
1 head broccoli, cut into small florets
coriander (cilantro) and 15ml/1 tbsp
   toasted sesame seeds, to garnish

VARIATION

Pak choi (bok choy) or Chinese flowering cabbage can be used instead of broccoli.

1 Cut all the duck meat into bitesize pieces. Heat the oils in a wok or large, heavy frying pan and stir-fry the garlic over a medium heat until it is golden brown – do not let it burn. Add the duck to the pan and stir-fry for a further 2 minutes, until the meat begins to brown.

2 Stir in the chilli flakes, fish sauce, soy sauce and water. Add the broccoli and continue to stir-fry for about 2 minutes, until the duck is just cooked through.

3 Serve on warmed plates, garnished with coriander and sesame seeds.

Energy 165kcal/686kJ; Protein 17.4g; Carbohydrate 2.3g, of which sugars 2g; Fat 10.6g, of which saturates 1.8g; Cholesterol 69mg; Calcium 72mg; Fibre 2.9g; Sodium 345mg

FUSILLI <u>WITH</u> SAUSAGE

GETTING SAUSAGES, PASTA AND TOMATO SAUCE READY AT THE RIGHT MOMENT TAKES A BIT OF JUGGLING, BUT THE RESULT IS A DELICIOUS DISH THAT EVERY MEMBER OF THE FAMILY WILL LOVE.

Preparation: 4–5 minutes; Cooking: 12–15 minutes

SERVES FOUR

INGREDIENTS

400g/14oz spicy pork sausages
30ml/2 tbsp olive oil
1 small onion, finely chopped
2 garlic cloves, crushed
1 large yellow (bell) pepper, seeded
  and cut into strips
5ml/1 tsp paprika
5ml/1 tsp dried mixed herbs
5–10ml/1–2 tsp chilli sauce
400g/14oz can Italian plum tomatoes
250ml/8fl oz/1 cup vegetable stock
300g/11oz/2³/₄ cups dried fusilli
salt and ground black pepper
freshly grated Pecorino cheese,
  to serve

1 Grill (broil) the sausages for 10–12 minutes until they are browned on all sides.

2 Meanwhile, heat the oil in a large pan, add the onion and garlic and cook for 3 minutes. Add the yellow pepper, paprika, herbs and chilli sauce to taste. Cook for 3 minutes more, stirring occasionally.

3 Pour in the canned tomatoes, breaking them up with a wooden spoon, then add salt and pepper to taste and stir well. Cook over a medium heat for 10–12 minutes, adding the vegetable stock gradually. At the same time, cook the pasta in lightly salted water until tender – about 12–14 minutes.

4 While the tomato sauce and pasta are cooking, drain the cooked sausages on kitchen paper, and, when cool enough to touch, cut each one diagonally into 1cm/½in pieces.

5 Add the sausage pieces to the sauce and mix well. Drain the pasta and add it to the pan of sauce. Toss well, then divide among four warmed bowls, sprinkled with the grated Pecorino.

Energy 709kcal/2970kJ; Protein 20.9g; Carbohydrate 72.2g, of which sugars 10.5g; Fat 39.5g, of which saturates 13.3g; Cholesterol 47mg; Calcium 74mg; Fibre 4.6g; Sodium 774mg

FLAMENCO EGGS

THIS ADAPTABLE DISH IS A SWIRL OF RED, GREEN, YELLOW AND WHITE. YOU CAN USE DIFFERENT VEGETABLES, BUT SHOULD ALWAYS INCLUDE CHORIZO.

Preparation: 4–5 minutes; Cooking: 15 minutes

SERVES FOUR

INGREDIENTS
   30ml/2 tbsp olive oil
   115g/4oz diced smoked bacon
    or pancetta
   2 frying chorizos, cubed
   1 onion, chopped
   2 garlic cloves, finely chopped
   1 red and 1 green (bell) pepper,
    seeded and chopped
   500g/1¼lb tomatoes, chopped
   15–30ml/1–2 tbsp fino sherry
   45ml/3 tbsp chopped parsley
   8 large (US extra large) eggs
   salt, paprika and cayenne pepper
For the garlic crumbs
   4 thick slices stale bread
   oil, for frying
   2 garlic cloves, bruised

1 Preheat the oven to 180°C/350°F/Gas 4. Warm four individual baking dishes.

2 Heat the oil in a large pan and fry the diced bacon and chorizo until they yield their fat. Add the onion and garlic and cook gently until softened, stirring.

3 Add the peppers and tomatoes and cook to reduce, stirring occasionally. Add some paprika and stir in the sherry.

COOK'S TIP
The chorizo and vegetable mixture mustn't be too dry, so add a little more sherry if necessary.

4 Divide the vegetable mixture evenly among the baking dishes. Sprinkle with parsley. Swirl the eggs together with a fork (without overmixing) and season well with salt and cayenne. Pour over the vegetable mixture.

5 Bake the eggs and vegetables for 8 minutes, or until the eggs are just set.

6 Meanwhile make the garlic crumbs. Cut the crusts off the bread and reduce to crumbs in a food processor, or use a hand grater.

7 Heat plenty of oil in a large frying pan over a high heat, add the garlic cloves for a few moments to flavour it, then remove and discard them. Throw in the breadcrumbs and brown quickly, scooping them out on to kitchen paper with a slotted spoon. Season with a little salt and paprika, then sprinkle them around the edge of the eggs, when ready to serve.

Energy 597kcal/2485kJ; Protein 27.3g; Carbohydrate 28g, of which sugars 11.1g; Fat 42.4g, of which saturates 11.7g; Cholesterol 429mg; Calcium 163mg; Fibre 3.2g; Sodium 1116mg

CLASSIC FISH AND CHIPS

QUINTESSENTIALLY ENGLISH, THIS IS FISH AND CHIPS AS IT SHOULD BE COOKED, WITH TENDER FLAKES OF FISH IN A CRISP BATTER, AND DOUBLE-DIPPED CHIPS THAT ARE CHUNKIER THAN NORMAL FRIES.

Preparation: 5 minutes; Cooking: 14–15 minutes

SERVES FOUR

INGREDIENTS
   450g/1lb potatoes
   groundnut (peanut) oil,
      for deep-frying
   4 x 175g/6oz cod fillets, skinned
      and any tiny bones removed
For the batter
   75g/3oz/⅔ cup plain
      (all-purpose) flour
   1 egg yolk
   10ml/2 tsp oil
   175ml/6fl oz/¾ cup water
   salt

1 To make the chips, cut the potatoes into 5mm/¼in thick slices. Then cut the slices into 5mm/¼in fingers or chips. Rinse the chips thoroughly in cold water, drain them well and then dry them thoroughly in a clean dish towel.

2 Heat the oil in a deep fat fryer to 180°C/350°F. Add the chips in the basket to the fryer and cook for 3 minutes. Lift out and shake off excess fat.

3 To make the batter, sift the flour into a bowl. Add a pinch of salt. Make a well in the middle of the flour and place the egg yolk in this. Add the oil and a little of the water. Mix the yolk with the oil and water, then add the remaining water and incorporate the surrounding flour to make a smooth batter. Cover and set aside until ready to use.

4 Reheat the oil in the fryer and cook the chips again for about 5 minutes, until they are golden and crisp. Drain on kitchen paper and season with salt. Keep hot in a low oven while you cook the pieces of fish.

COOK'S TIP
Use fresh rather than frozen fish for the very best texture and flavour. If you have to use frozen fish, thaw it thoroughly and make sure it is dry before coating with batter. Partially-frozen fish is unlikely to cook in the middle, despite the high cooking temperatures reached during deep-frying.

5 Dip the pieces of fish fillet into the batter and turn them to make sure they are evenly coated. Allow any excess batter to drip off before carefully lowering the fish into the hot oil.

6 Cook the fish for 5 minutes, turning once, if necessary, so that the batter browns evenly. The batter should be crisp and golden. Drain on kitchen paper. Serve at once, with lemon wedges and the chips.

VARIATIONS
• Although cod is the traditional choice for fish and chips, other white fish can be used: haddock is a popular alternative. Rock salmon, sometimes sold as huss or dogfish, also has a good flavour. Pollock or hoki are also suitable. Thin fillets, such as plaice or sole, tend to be too thin and can be overpowered by the batter. An egg and breadcrumb coating is more suitable for thin fish.
• To coat fish with egg and breadcrumbs, dip the fillets in seasoned flour, then in beaten egg and finally in fine, dry white breadcrumbs. Repeat a second time if the fish is to be deep-fried.
• Chunky chips are traditional with thick battered fish. Cut the potatoes into thick fingers to make chunky chips and allow slightly longer for the second frying.

Energy 645kcal/2700kJ; Protein 32.6g; Carbohydrate 54.3g, of which sugars 0.7g; Fat 34.5g, of which saturates 4.2g; Cholesterol 0mg; Calcium 130mg; Fibre 3.4g; Sodium 294mg

FRIED PLAICE <u>WITH</u> TOMATO SAUCE

THIS SIMPLE DISH IS PERENNIALLY POPULAR WITH CHILDREN. IT WORKS EQUALLY WELL WITH LEMON SOLE OR DABS, WHICH DO NOT NEED SKINNING, OR FILLETS OF HADDOCK AND WHITING.

Preparation: 5 minutes; Cooking: 14 minutes

SERVES FOUR

INGREDIENTS

25g/1oz/¼ cup plain (all-purpose) flour
2 eggs, beaten
75g/3oz/¾ cup dried breadcrumbs,
  preferably home-made
4 small plaice or flounder, skinned
25g/1oz/2 tbsp butter
30ml/2 tbsp sunflower oil
salt and ground black pepper
fresh basil leaves, to garnish
1 lemon, quartered, to serve
For the tomato sauce
30ml/2 tbsp olive oil
1 red onion, finely chopped
1 garlic clove, finely chopped
400g/14oz can chopped tomatoes
15ml/1 tbsp tomato purée (paste)
15ml/1 tbsp torn fresh basil leaves

1 First make the tomato sauce. Heat the olive oil in a large pan, add the finely chopped onion and garlic and cook for about 2–3 minutes, until softened.

2 Stir in the chopped tomatoes and tomato purée and simmer for 10 minutes, or until the fish is ready to be served, stirring occasionally.

3 Meanwhile, spread out the flour in a shallow dish, pour the beaten eggs into another and spread out the breadcrumbs in a third.

4 Season the fish with salt and pepper. Hold a fish in your left hand and dip it first in flour, then in egg and finally in the breadcrumbs, patting the crumbs on with your dry right hand. Aim for an even coating that is not too thick. Shake off any excess crumbs and set aside while you prepare the frying pans.

5 Heat the butter and oil in two large frying pans until foaming. Fry the fish for about 5 minutes on each side, until golden brown and cooked through. Drain on kitchen paper. Season the tomato sauce, stir in the basil and serve with the fish, garnished with basil leaves. Offer lemon wedges separately.

Energy 417kcal/1738kJ; Protein 28.1g; Carbohydrate 17.7g, of which sugars 4.9g; Fat 26.4g, of which saturates 3.1g; Cholesterol 0mg; Calcium 113mg; Fibre 1.6g; Sodium 349mg

GRILLED HAKE <u>WITH</u> LEMON <u>AND</u> CHILLI

NOTHING COULD BE SIMPLER THAN PERFECTLY GRILLED FISH WITH A DUSTING OF CHILLI AND LEMON RIND. THIS IS AN IDEAL MEAL FOR THOSE OCCASIONS WHEN SOMETHING LIGHT IS CALLED FOR.

Preparation: 2 minutes; Cooking: 6–8 minutes

SERVES FOUR

INGREDIENTS
   4 hake fillets, each 150g/5oz
   30ml/2 tbsp olive oil
   finely grated rind and juice of
    1 lemon
   15ml/1 tbsp crushed chilli flakes
   salt and ground black pepper

VARIATION
Any firm white fish can be cooked in this simple, low-fat way. Try cod, halibut or hoki. If you haven't got any chilli flakes, brush the fish with chilli oil instead of olive oil.

1 Preheat the grill (broiler) to high. Brush the hake fillets all over with the olive oil and place them skin side up on a baking sheet.

2 Grill (broil) the fish for 4–5 minutes, until the skin is crispy, then carefully turn the fillets over in the pan, using a metal spatula.

3 Sprinkle the fillets with the lemon rind and chilli flakes and season with salt and ground black pepper.

4 Grill the fillets for a further 2–3 minutes, or until the hake is cooked through. (Test using the point of a sharp knife; the flesh should flake.) Squeeze over the lemon juice just before serving.

Energy 188kcal/786kJ; Protein 27g; Carbohydrate 0.1g, of which sugars 0.1g; Fat 8.8g, of which saturates 1.2g; Cholesterol 35mg; Calcium 22mg; Fibre 0g; Sodium 150mg

CHICKEN OMELETTE DIPPERS

HAVE YOU GOT A RELUCTANT EATER IN THE FAMILY? NOT ANY MORE. CHILDREN LOVE THESE PROTEIN-PACKED CHICKEN OMELETTE ROLLS. YOU MIGHT HAVE TO RATION THE KETCHUP, HOWEVER.

Preparation: 3 minutes; Cooking: 16 minutes

SERVES FOUR

INGREDIENTS

  1 skinless, boneless chicken thigh,
    about 115g/4oz, cubed
  40ml/8 tsp butter
  1 small onion, chopped
  ½ carrot, diced
  2 shiitake mushrooms, stems
    removed and chopped
  15ml/1 tbsp finely chopped
    fresh parsley
  225g/8oz/2 cups cooked long grain
    white rice
  30ml/2 tbsp tomato ketchup,
    plus extra to serve
  6 eggs, lightly beaten
  60ml/4 tbsp milk
  2.5ml/½ tsp salt, plus extra to season
  ground black pepper

3 Beat the eggs with the milk in a bowl. Stir in the measured salt, and add pepper. Melt 5ml/1 tsp of the remaining butter in an omelette pan. Pour in a quarter of the egg mixture and stir it briefly with a fork, then allow it to set for 1 minute. Top with a quarter of the rice mixture.

4 There are two ways of shaping the omelette. Either just flip it over the filling, then cut in half to make wedges, or roll the omelette around the filling and cut in half. Keep the filled omelette hot in a low oven while cooking three more. Serve two wedges or rolls per person, with a bowl of tomato ketchup on the side for dipping.

1 Season the chicken. Melt 10ml/2 tsp butter in a frying pan. Fry the onion for 1 minute, then add the chicken and fry until cooked. Add the mushrooms and carrot, stir-fry over a medium heat until soft, then add the parsley. Set aside. Wipe the pan with kitchen paper.

2 Melt 10ml/2 tsp butter in the frying pan, add the rice and stir well. Mix in the fried ingredients, ketchup and black pepper. Stir well, adding salt to taste. Keep the mixture warm.

VARIATION
A mixture of tomato ketchup and chutney makes a tasty alternative dipping sauce.

Energy 316kcal/1322kJ; Protein 18g; Carbohydrate 21.5g, of which sugars 3.7g; Fat 18.4g, of which saturates 8.1g; Cholesterol 338mg; Calcium 80mg; Fibre 0.5g; Sodium 322mg

ROAST CHICKEN PITTA POCKETS

FAMILIES OFTEN HAVE TO EAT IN RELAYS: A PARENT IS GOING TO BE HOME LATE; ONE CHILD HAS A MUSIC LESSON; ANOTHER IS OFF TO THE SKATE PARK. THIS SERVE-ANYTIME SNACK WILL SUIT THE LOT.

Preparation: 12–14 minutes; Cooking: 2 minutes

MAKES SIX

INGREDIENTS
  1 small cucumber, peeled and diced
  3 tomatoes, peeled, seeded
    and chopped
  2 spring onions (scallions), chopped
  30ml/2 tbsp olive oil
  a small bunch of flat leaf parsley,
    finely chopped
  a small bunch of mint,
    finely chopped
  ½ preserved lemon, finely chopped
  45–60ml/3–4 tbsp tahini
  juice of 1 lemon
  2 garlic cloves, crushed
  6 pitta breads
  ½ small roast chicken or
    2 large roast chicken breasts,
    cut into strips
  salt and ground black pepper

1 Place the cucumber in a strainer over a bowl, sprinkle with a little salt and leave for 5 minutes to drain. Rinse well and drain again, then place in a bowl with the tomatoes and spring onions. Stir in the olive oil, parsley, mint and preserved lemon. Season well.

2 In a small bowl, mix the tahini with the lemon juice, then thin the mixture down with a little water to the consistency of thick double (heavy) cream. Beat in the garlic and season.

COOK'S TIP
The chicken in these pitta breads can be hot or cold – either roast a small bird specially or use up the leftovers from a large roast chicken.

3 Preheat the grill (broiler) to hot. Lightly toast the pitta breads well away from the heat source until they puff up. (Alternatively, lightly toast the breads in a toaster.) Open the breads and stuff them liberally with the chicken and salad. Drizzle a generous amount of tahini sauce into each one and serve with any extra salad.

Energy 337kcal/1419kJ; Protein 21g; Carbohydrate 43.5g, of which sugars 4.4g; Fat 9.9g, of which saturates 1.5g; Cholesterol 35mg; Calcium 182mg; Fibre 3.5g; Sodium 369mg

CHICKEN STUFFED WITH HAM AND CHEESE

A CLASSIC THAT IS PERENNIALLY POPULAR, THIS CONSISTS OF BREASTS OF CHICKEN STUFFED WITH SMOKED HAM AND GRUYÈRE, THEN COATED IN EGG AND BREADCRUMBS AND FRIED UNTIL GOLDEN.

Preparation: 6–8 minutes; Cooking: 10–12 minutes

SERVES FOUR

INGREDIENTS

4 skinless, boneless chicken breasts,
  about 130g/4½oz each
4 very thin smoked ham slices,
  halved and rind removed
about 90g/3½oz Gruyère cheese,
  thinly sliced
plain flour, for coating
2 eggs, beaten
75g/3oz/¾ cup natural-coloured
  dried breadcrumbs
5ml/1 tsp dried thyme
75g/3oz/6 tbsp butter
60ml/4 tbsp olive oil
salt and ground black pepper
mixed leaf salad, to serve

3 Spoon the flour for coating into a shallow bowl. Pour the beaten eggs into another shallow bowl and mix the breadcrumbs with the thyme and seasoning in a third bowl.

4 Toss each stuffed breast in the flour, then coat in egg and breadcrumbs, shaking off any excess.

5 Place half the butter and half the oil in one pan, and the remaining half measures in the other, and heat separately

COOK'S TIP
If you are able to prepare these portions in advance, cover the crumbed breasts and chill them for about 1 hour in the refrigerator to set the coating. It's certainly a tip worth remembering for when you have more time on a recipe.

6 When the fat stops foaming, gently slide in the coated breasts, two in each pan. Shallow fry over a medium-low heat for about 5 minutes each side, turning over carefully with a spatula. Drain on kitchen paper for a few seconds to soak up the excess fat. Serve immediately with the mixed leaf salad.

1 Slit the chicken breasts about three-quarters of the way through, then open them up and lay them flat. Place a slice of ham on each cut side of the chicken, trimming to fit if necessary so that the ham does not hang over the edge.

2 Top with the Gruyère slices, making sure that they are well within the ham slices. Fold over the chicken and reshape, pressing well to seal and ensuring that no cheese is visible.

VARIATION
Instead of Gruyère, try one of the herb-flavoured hard cheeses, such as Double Gloucester with Chives.

Energy 599kcal/2496kJ; Protein 41.8g; Carbohydrate 14.8g, of which sugars 0.8g; Fat 41.5g, of which saturates 18.4g; Cholesterol 220mg; Calcium 222mg; Fibre 0.4g; Sodium 698mg

CRUMBED CHICKEN <u>WITH</u> GREEN MAYONNAISE

THE CONTRAST BETWEEN CRISP CRUMB AND TENDER CHICKEN IS WHAT MAKES THIS SO SUCCESSFUL.
CAPER MAYONNAISE IS TRADITIONAL BUT MAYO FLAVOURED WITH WASABI WOULD BE GOOD TOO.
Preparation: 4 minutes; Cooking: 12 minutes

SERVES FOUR

INGREDIENTS
4 skinless chicken breast fillets,
  each weighing about 200g/7oz
juice of 1 lemon
5ml/1 tsp paprika
plain (all-purpose) flour, for dusting
1–2 eggs
dried breadcrumbs, for coating
about 60ml/4 tbsp olive oil
salt and ground black pepper
lemon wedges (optional), to serve
For the mayonnaise
120ml/4fl oz/½ cup mayonnaise
30ml/2 tbsp pickled capers, drained
  and chopped
30ml/2 tbsp chopped fresh parsley

1 Skin the chicken breasts. Lay them outside down and, with a sharp knife, cut horizontally, almost through, from the rounded side. Open them up like a book. Press gently, to make a roundish shape the size of a side plate. Sprinkle with lemon juice and paprika.

2 Set out three shallow bowls. Sprinkle flour over one, seasoning it well. Beat the egg with a little salt and pour into the second. Sprinkle the third with dried breadcrumbs. Dip the breasts first into the flour on both sides, then into the egg, then into the breadcrumbs to coat them evenly.

3 Put the mayonnaise ingredients in a bowl and mix well to combine.

4 Heat the oil in a heavy frying pan over a high heat. Fry the breast portions two at a time, turning after 3 minutes, until golden on both sides. Add more oil for the second batch if needed. Serve immediately, with the mayonnaise and lemon wedges, if using.

Energy 582kcal/2428kJ; Protein 51.5g; Carbohydrate 10.3g, of which sugars 0.8g; Fat 37.6g, of which saturates 6g; Cholesterol 210mg; Calcium 43mg; Fibre 0.5g; Sodium 369mg

CRISPY FIVE-SPICE CHICKEN

STRIPS OF CHICKEN FILLET, WITH A SPICED RICE FLOUR COATING, BECOME DELICIOUSLY CRISP AND GOLDEN WHEN FRIED. THEY MAKE A GREAT MEAL WHEN SERVED ON STIR FRIED VEGETABLE NOODLES.

Preparation: 5 minutes; Cooking: 10–12 minutes

SERVES FOUR

INGREDIENTS
   200g/7oz thin egg noodles
   30ml/2 tbsp sunflower oil
   2 garlic cloves, very thinly sliced
   1 fresh red chilli, seeded and sliced
   ½ red (bell) pepper, very
      thinly sliced
   2 carrots, peeled and cut into
      thin strips
   300g/11oz Chinese broccoli or
      Chinese greens, roughly sliced
   45ml/3 tbsp hoisin sauce
   45ml/3 tbsp soy sauce
   5ml/1 tsp caster (superfine) sugar
   4 skinless chicken breast fillets,
      cut into strips
   2 egg whites, lightly beaten
   115g/4oz/1 cup rice flour
   15ml/1 tbsp five-spice powder
   salt and ground black pepper
   vegetable oil, for frying

1 Cook the noodles according to the packet instructions, drain and set aside.

2 Heat the sunflower oil in a wok, then add the garlic, chilli, red pepper, carrots and broccoli or greens and stir-fry over a high heat for 2–3 minutes.

3 Add the sauces and sugar to the wok and cook for a further 2–3 minutes. Add the drained noodles, toss to combine, then remove from the heat, cover and keep warm.

4 Dip the chicken strips into the egg white. Combine the rice flour and five-spice powder in a shallow dish and season. Add the chicken strips to the flour mixture and toss to coat.

5 Heat about 2.5cm/1½in oil in a clean wok. When hot, shallow-fry the chicken for 3–4 minutes until crisp and golden.

6 To serve, divide the noodle mixture between warmed plates or bowls and top each serving with the chicken.

VARIATION
Instead of the vegetables listed above for the stir-fry, try a mixture of mangetouts (snow peas), baby corn, orange (bell) peppers, spring onions (scallions) and celery.

Energy 574kcal/2419kJ; Protein 49.6g; Carbohydrate 68g, of which sugars 9.4g; Fat 12.3g, of which saturates 2.5g; Cholesterol 120mg; Calcium 83mg; Fibre 5.1g; Sodium 1210mg

CORNED BEEF AND EGG HASH

THIS IS TRADITIONAL FAMILY FARE AT ITS VERY BEST. WARM AND COMFORTING, AND MADE IN MINUTES, IT WILL BECOME A FIRM FAVOURITE VERY QUICKLY.

Preparation: 4–5 minutes; Cooking: 12–15 minutes

SERVES FOUR

INGREDIENTS
30ml/2 tbsp vegetable oil
25g/1oz/2 tbsp butter
1 onion, finely chopped
1 green (bell) pepper, seeded
and diced
2 large firm boiled potatoes, diced
350g/12oz can corned beef, cubed
1.5ml/¼ tsp grated nutmeg
1.5ml/¼ tsp paprika
4 eggs
salt and ground black pepper
parsley, deep-fried in oil, to garnish
sweet chilli sauce or tomato sauce,
  to serve

COOK'S TIP
Put the can of corned beef into the refrigerator to chill for about half an hour before using – it will firm up and be much easier to cut into cubes.

1 Heat the oil and butter together in a large frying pan. Add the onion and fry for 3–4 minutes until softened.

2 In a bowl, mix together the green pepper, potatoes, corned beef, nutmeg and paprika. Season well. Add to the pan and toss gently to distribute the cooked onion. Press down lightly and fry without stirring on a medium heat for about 3–4 minutes until a golden brown crust has formed on the underside.

3 Stir the mixture through to distribute the crust, then repeat the frying twice, until the mixture is well browned.

4 Make four wells in the hash and carefully crack an egg into each. Cover and cook gently for about 4–5 minutes until the egg whites are set.

5 Sprinkle with deep-fried parsley and cut into quarters. Serve hot with sweet chilli sauce or tomato sauce.

Energy 421kcal/1758kJ; Protein 30.9g; Carbohydrate 17g, of which sugars 5.4g; Fat 26.2g, of which saturates 10.6g; Cholesterol 277mg; Calcium 65mg; Fibre 1.7g; Sodium 871mg

MEXICAN TACOS

READY-MADE TACO SHELLS MAKE PERFECT EDIBLE CONTAINERS FOR SHREDDED SALAD, MEAT FILLINGS, GRATED CHEESE AND SOUR CREAM. THIS IS A SUPER SUPPER THAT SPARES THE COOK HARD LABOUR.

Preparation: 5 minutes; Cooking: 10–12 minutes

SERVES FOUR

INGREDIENTS
    15ml/1 tbsp olive oil
    250g/9oz lean minced (ground) beef
      or turkey
    2 garlic cloves, crushed
    5ml/1 tsp ground cumin
    5–10ml/1–2 tsp mild chilli powder
    8 ready-made taco shells
    ½ small iceberg lettuce, shredded
    1 small onion, thinly sliced
    2 tomatoes, chopped in chunks
    1 avocado, halved, stoned (pitted)
      and sliced
    60ml/4 tbsp sour cream
    125g/4oz/1 cup grated Cheddar or
      Monterey Jack cheese
    salt and ground black pepper

1 Heat the oil in a frying pan. Add the meat, with the garlic and spices, and brown over a medium heat, stirring frequently to break up any lumps. Season, cook for 10 minutes, then set aside to cool slightly.

2 Meanwhile, warm the taco shells according to the instructions on the packet. Do not let them get too crisp.

3 Spoon the lettuce, onion, tomatoes and avocado slices into the taco shells. Top with the sour cream followed by the minced beef or turkey mixture.

COOK'S TIP
Stir-fried strips of turkey, chicken or pork are excellent instead of the minced beef.

4 Sprinkle the grated Cheddar or Monterey Jack cheese into the tacos and serve immediately, just as the cheese is melting. Tacos are eaten with the fingers and there's usually a certain amount of fallout, so have plenty of paper napkins handy.

Energy 559kcal/2325kJ; Protein 24.6g; Carbohydrate 26g, of which sugars 3.2g; Fat 39.6g, of which saturates 16g; Cholesterol 77mg; Calcium 322mg; Fibre 3.8g; Sodium 610mg

HOME-MADE BURGERS <u>WITH</u> RELISH

MAKING YOUR OWN BURGERS MEANS YOU CONTROL WHAT GOES INTO THEM. THESE ARE FULL OF FLAVOUR AND ALWAYS PROVE POPULAR. THE TANGY RATATOUILLE RELISH IS VERY EASY TO MAKE.

Preparation: 6 minutes; Cooking: 14 minutes

SERVES FOUR

INGREDIENTS

2 shallots, chopped
450g/1lb lean minced (ground) beef
30ml/2 tbsp chopped parsley
30ml/2 tbsp tomato ketchup
1 garlic clove, crushed
1 fresh green chilli, finely chopped
  and seeded
15ml/1 tbsp olive oil
400g/14oz can ratatouille
4 burger buns
lettuce leaves
salt and ground black pepper, to taste

1 Put the shallots in a bowl with boiling water to cover. Leave for 1–2 minutes, then slip off the skins and chop the shallots finely.

2 Mix half the shallots with the beef in a bowl. Add the chopped parsley and tomato ketchup, with salt and pepper to taste. Mix well with clean hands. Divide the mixture into four. Knead each portion into a ball, then flatten it into a burger.

3 Make a spicy relish by cooking the remaining shallot with the garlic and green chilli in the olive oil for 2–3 minutes, until softened.

4 Add the canned ratatouille to the pan containing the vegetables. Bring to the boil, then simmer for 5 minutes.

VARIATION
Set these burgers on individual plates with spicy corn relish on the side. To make the relish, heat 30ml/2 tbsp oil in a pan and fry 1 onion, 2 crushed garlic cloves and 1 seeded red chilli until soft. Add 10ml/2 tsp garam masala and cook for 2 minutes, then mix in a 320g/ 11¼oz can whole kernel corn and the grated rind and juice of 1 lime.

5 Meanwhile, preheat the grill (broiler) and cook the burgers for about 5 minutes on each side, until browned and cooked through. Meanwhile, split the burger buns. Arrange lettuce leaves on the bun bases, add the burgers and top with warm relish and the bun tops.

Energy 484kcal/2021kJ; Protein 27.9g; Carbohydrate 30.2g, of which sugars 7.7g; Fat 28.8g, of which saturates 9.3g; Cholesterol 68mg; Calcium 120mg; Fibre 2.2g; Sodium 473mg

SPEEDY SUPPERS

When you're weary, what you want most is for someone else to cook for you. Failing that, you want quick, easy recipes that will enable you to put together a fabulous meal as quickly as possible. The recipes in this chapter do just that. They're fun to cook, will boost flagging energy levels and are a great deal more exciting than the takeaway you may have been considering. Pasta dishes like Pansotti with Walnut Sauce, and Penne with Cream and Smoked Salmon take only minutes to put together, but look great on the plate and taste marvellous. Stir-fried Duck with Pineapple is a wonderful blend of textures, with crisp duck matched against satin-smooth sesame noodles, and Devilled Kidneys on Brioche Croûtes is as sophisticated as it is swift to produce. For those who think no meal is complete without meat, Russian Hamburgers and Beef Stroganov will fit the bill, while vegetarians will appreciate the delicious Courgette Rissoles and Corn Fritters. There are also several superb salads, so you will be spoilt for choice.

FETTUCINE ALL'ALFREDO

THIS SIMPLE RECIPE WAS INVENTED BY A ROMAN RESTAURATEUR CALLED ALFREDO, WHO BECAME FAMOUS FOR SERVING IT WITH A GOLD FORK AND SPOON.

Preparation: 1–2 minutes; Cooking: 10–12 minutes

SERVES FOUR

INGREDIENTS
  50g/2oz/¼ cup butter
  200ml/7fl oz/scant 1 cup double
    (heavy) cream
  50g/2oz/⅔ cup freshly grated
    Parmesan cheese, plus
    extra to serve
  350g/12oz fresh fettucine

1 Melt the butter in a large pan. Add the cream and bring it to the boil. Simmer for 5 minutes, stirring constantly, then add the Parmesan cheese, with salt and freshly ground black pepper to taste, and turn off the heat under the pan.

2 Bring a large pan of salted water to the boil. Drop in the pasta all at once and quickly bring the water back to the boil, stirring occasionally. Cook the pasta for 2–3 minutes, or until it rises to the surface of the water and is tender. Drain well.

3 Turn on the heat under the pan of cream to low, add the cooked pasta all at once and toss until it is thoroughly coated in the sauce. Taste the sauce for seasoning. Serve immediately, with extra grated Parmesan cheese handed around separately.

Energy 697kcal/2912kJ; Protein 16.3g; Carbohydrate 65.8g, of which sugars 3.8g; Fat 42.8g, of which saturates 26g; Cholesterol 108mg; Calcium 199mg; Fibre 2.6g; Sodium 226mg

PANSOTTI <u>WITH</u> WALNUT SAUCE

RECIPES DON'T COME MUCH EASIER THAN THIS. WALNUTS, GARLIC OIL AND CREAM MAKE A
STUNNINGLY SUCCESSFUL SAUCE FOR STUFFED PASTA. FOR SPEED AND FLAVOUR, USE FRESH PASTA.

Preparation: 4 minutes; Cooking: 4–5 minutes

SERVES FOUR

INGREDIENTS

    90g/3½oz/scant 1 cup shelled
      walnuts or walnut pieces
    60ml/4 tbsp garlic-flavoured olive oil
    120ml/4fl oz/½ cup double
      (heavy) cream
    350g/12oz cheese and herb-filled
      pansotti or other stuffed pasta

1 Put the walnuts and garlic oil in a food processor and process to a paste, adding up to 120ml/4fl oz/½ cup warm water through the feeder tube to slacken the consistency. Spoon the mixture into a large bowl and add the cream. Beat well to mix, then season to taste with salt and black pepper.

2 Cook the pansotti or stuffed pasta in a large pan of salted boiling water for 4–5 minutes, or according to the instructions on the packet. Meanwhile, put the walnut sauce in a large warmed bowl and add a ladleful of the pasta cooking water to thin it.

3 Drain the pasta and tip it into the bowl of walnut sauce. Toss well, then serve immediately.

COOK'S TIP
Walnuts become rancid quite quickly, so you shouldn't store open packets in the pantry for long periods. For a sauce like this one, or anything else for which the walnuts are ground, buy the more economical walnut pieces.

VARIATION
Don't worry if you can't locate pansotti; tortellini will work just as well. The best place to buy the pasta for this recipe is a specialist deli where pasta is made on the premises.

Energy 702kcal/2931kJ; Protein 14.3g; Carbohydrate 66.1g, of which sugars 4g; Fat 44.1g, of which saturates 13g; Cholesterol 41mg; Calcium 58mg; Fibre 3.3g; Sodium 11mg

PASTA WITH FRESH PESTO

BOTTLED PESTO IS A USEFUL INGREDIENT, BUT YOU CAN MAKE YOUR OWN IN LESS TIME THAN IT TAKES TO BOIL THE PASTA THAT ACCOMPANIES IT. ANY SPARE PESTO WILL KEEP FOR A FEW DAYS.

Preparation: 4 minutes; Cooking: 12–14 minutes

SERVES FOUR

INGREDIENTS
  400g/14oz/3½ cups dried pasta
  50g/2oz/1⅓ cups fresh basil leaves,
    plus extra, to garnish
  2–4 garlic cloves
  60ml/4 tbsp pine nuts
  120ml/4fl oz/½ cup extra virgin
    olive oil
  115g/4oz/1⅓ cups freshly grated
    Parmesan cheese, plus extra
    to serve
  25g/1oz/⅓ cup freshly grated
    Pecorino cheese
  salt and ground black pepper

1 Bring a large pan of lightly salted water to the boil. Add the pasta and cook for 12–14 minutes or according to the instructions on the packet, until just tender but still firm to the bite.

2 Meanwhile, put the basil leaves, garlic and pine nuts in a blender or food processor. Add 60ml/4 tbsp of the olive oil. Process until the ingredients are finely chopped, scraping down the sides of the bowl twice.

3 With the motor running, slowly pour the remaining oil in a thin, steady stream through the feeder tube.

4 Scrape the mixture into a large bowl and beat in the cheeses with a wooden spoon. Taste and add salt and pepper if necessary.

5 Drain the pasta well, then add it to the bowl of pesto and toss to coat. Serve immediately, garnished with the fresh basil leaves. Hand shaved Parmesan around separately.

Energy 783kcal/3279kJ; Protein 27.9g; Carbohydrate 74.7g, of which sugars 3.9g; Fat 43.5g, of which saturates 10.9g; Cholesterol 35mg; Calcium 447mg; Fibre 3.2g; Sodium 385mg

PENNE WITH CREAM AND SMOKED SALMON

NO SUPPER DISH COULD BE SIMPLER. FRESHLY COOKED PASTA IS TOSSED WITH CREAM, SMOKED SALMON AND THYME TO MAKE A LOVELY, LIGHT DISH THAT LOOKS AS GOOD AS IT TASTES.

Preparation: 2 minutes; Cooking: 12–14 minutes

SERVES FOUR

INGREDIENTS

350g/12oz/3 cups dried penne
115g/4oz thinly sliced smoked
  salmon
2–3 fresh thyme sprigs
25g/1oz/2 tbsp butter
150ml/¼ pint/⅔ cup double
  (heavy) cream
salt and ground black pepper

VARIATION
Substitute low-fat cream cheese for half the cream in the sauce, for a less rich mixture that still tastes very good.

1 Bring a large pan of lightly salted water to the boil. Add the pasta and cook for 12–14 minutes, or according to the instructions on the packet, until tender but still firm to the bite.

2 Meanwhile, using kitchen scissors or a small, sharp knife, cut the smoked salmon into thin strips, each about 5mm/¼in wide, and place on a plate. Strip the leaves from the thyme sprigs.

3 Melt the butter in a large pan. Stir in the cream with a quarter of the salmon and thyme leaves, then season with pepper. Heat gently for 3–4 minutes, stirring constantly. Do not allow the sauce to boil. Taste for seasoning.

4 Drain the pasta and toss it in the cream and salmon sauce. Divide among four warmed bowls and top with the remaining salmon and thyme leaves.

Energy 573kcal/2403kJ; Protein 18.5g; Carbohydrate 65.5g, of which sugars 3.6g; Fat 28.2g, of which saturates 16.2g; Cholesterol 75mg; Calcium 47mg; Fibre 2.6g; Sodium 589mg

CORN FRITTERS

SOMETIMES IT IS THE SIMPLEST DISHES THAT TASTE THE BEST. THESE FRITTERS, PACKED WITH CORN, ARE EASY TO PREPARE AND GO WELL WITH EVERYTHING FROM GAMMON TO NUT RISSOLES.

Preparation: 5 minutes; Cooking: 8 minutes

MAKES TWELVE

INGREDIENTS

3 corn cobs, total weight about
  250g/9oz
1 garlic clove, crushed
a small bunch of fresh coriander
  (cilantro), chopped
1 small fresh red or green chilli,
  seeded and finely chopped
1 spring onion (scallion),
  finely chopped
15ml/1 tbsp soy sauce
75g/3oz/¾ cup rice flour or plain
  (all-purpose) flour
2 eggs, lightly beaten
60ml/4 tbsp water
oil, for shallow-frying
salt and ground black pepper
sweet chilli sauce, to serve

1 Using a sharp knife, slice the kernels from the cobs using downward strokes. Rinse to remove any clinging debris from the cob and place in a bowl.

2 Add the garlic, chopped coriander, red or green chilli, spring onion, soy sauce, flour, beaten eggs and water to the corn and mix well. Season with salt and pepper to taste and mix again. The mixture should be firm enough to hold its shape, but not stiff.

3 Heat the oil in a large frying pan. Add spoonfuls of the corn mixture, gently spreading each one out with the back of the spoon to make a roundish fritter. Cook for 1–2 minutes on each side.

4 Drain the first batch of fritters on kitchen paper and keep hot on a foil-covered dish while frying more in the same way. Serve the fritters hot with sweet chilli sauce – arrange on a large plate around the sauce, if you like.

Energy 76kcal/314kJ; Protein 2.1g; Carbohydrate 7.6g, of which sugars 0.5g; Fat 4.1g, of which saturates 0.7g; Cholesterol 32mg; Calcium 14mg; Fibre 0.6g; Sodium 102mg

COURGETTE RISSOLES

THIS IS AN INGENIOUS WAY OF TRANSFORMING BLAND-TASTING COURGETTES INTO A DISH THAT CAPTIVATES EVERYONE WHO TRIES IT. SERVE THE RISSOLES WITH A TOMATO AND ONION SALAD.

Preparation: 5–6 minutes; Cooking: 14 minutes

SERVES THREE TO FOUR

INGREDIENTS
   500g/1¼lb courgettes (zucchini)
   120ml/4fl oz/½ cup extra virgin
     olive oil
   1 large onion, finely chopped
   2 spring onions (scallions), green and
     white parts finely chopped
   1 garlic clove, crushed
   3 medium slices proper bread
     (not from a pre-sliced loaf)
   2 eggs, lightly beaten
   200g/7oz feta cheese, crumbled
   50g/2oz/½ cup freshly grated Greek
     Graviera or Italian Parmesan cheese
   45–60ml/3–4 tbsp finely chopped
     fresh dill or 5ml/1 tsp dried oregano
   50g/2oz/½ cup plain
     (all-purpose) flour
   salt and ground black pepper
   lemon wedges, to serve

1 Bring a pan of lightly salted water to the boil. Slice the courgettes into 4cm/1½in lengths and drop them into the boiling water. Cover and cook for about 10 minutes, or until very soft. Drain in a colander until they are cool enough to handle.

2 Heat 45ml/3 tbsp of the olive oil in a frying pan, add the onion and spring onions and sauté until translucent. Add the garlic, then, as soon as it becomes aromatic, take the pan off the heat.

3 Squeeze the courgettes with your hands, to extract as much water as possible, then place them in a large bowl. Add the fried onion and garlic mixture and mix well.

4 Toast the bread, cut off and discard the crusts, then break up the toast and crumb it in a food processor. Add the crumbs to the courgette mixture, with the eggs, feta, and grated Graviera or Parmesan.

5 Stir in the dill or oregano and add salt and pepper to taste. Mix well, using your hands to squeeze the mixture and make sure that all the ingredients are combined evenly. If the courgette mixture seems too wet, add a little flour.

6 Take about a heaped tablespoon of the courgette mixture, roll it into a round ball and press it lightly to make the typical rissole shape. Make more rissoles in the same way.

7 Coat the rissoles lightly in the flour and dust off any excess. Heat the remaining olive oil in a large non-stick frying pan and fry the rissoles, in batches if necessary, until they are crisp and brown, turning them over once or twice during cooking.

8 Drain the rissoles on a double layer of kitchen paper and serve on a warmed platter or on individual plates, with the lemon wedges for squeezing.

Energy 528kcal/2194kJ; Protein 22g; Carbohydrate 28.8g, of which sugars 7.9g; Fat 36.9g, of which saturates 13g; Cholesterol 143mg; Calcium 436mg; Fibre 3g; Sodium 1001mg

WARM SALAD OF HAM AND NEW POTATOES

WITH A LIGHTLY SPICED NUTTY DRESSING, THIS WARM SALAD IS AS DELICIOUS AS IT IS FASHIONABLE, AND AN EXCELLENT CHOICE FOR A CASUAL SUMMER SUPPER WITH FRIENDS.

Preparation: 3 minutes; Cooking: 15–17 minutes

SERVES FOUR

INGREDIENTS

225g/8oz new potatoes, halved
  if large
50g/2oz green beans
115g/4oz young spinach leaves
2 spring onions (scallions), sliced
4 eggs, hard-boiled and quartered
50g/2oz cooked ham, cut into strips
juice of ½ lemon
salt and ground black pepper

For the dressing
60ml/4 tbsp olive oil
5ml/1 tsp ground turmeric
5ml/1 tsp ground cumin
50g/2oz/⅓ cup shelled hazelnuts

1 Cook the potatoes in boiling salted water for 10–15 minutes, or until tender. Meanwhile, cook the beans in boiling salted water for 2 minutes.

2 Drain the potatoes and beans. Toss with the spinach and spring onions.

3 Arrange the hard-boiled egg quarters on the salad and sprinkle the strips of ham over the top. Drizzle with the lemon juice and season with plenty of salt and pepper.

4 Heat the dressing ingredients in a large frying pan and continue to cook, stirring frequently, until the nuts turn golden. Pour the hot, nutty dressing over the salad and serve immediately.

VARIATION
An even quicker salad can be made by using a 400g/14oz can of mixed beans and pulses instead of the potatoes. Drain and rinse the beans and pulses, then drain again.

Energy 318kcal/1319kJ; Protein 12.4g; Carbohydrate 11g, of which sugars 2.2g; Fat 25.4g, of which saturates 4g; Cholesterol 198mg; Calcium 106mg; Fibre 2.3g; Sodium 268mg

WARM DRESSED SALAD WITH POACHED EGGS

SOFT POACHED EGGS, CHILLI, HOT CROÛTONS AND COOL, CRISP SALAD LEAVES MAKE A LIVELY AND UNUSUAL COMBINATION. THIS SIMPLE SALAD IS PERFECT FOR A MID-WEEK SUPPER

Preparation: 2–3 minutes; Cooking: 10–12 minutes

SERVES TWO

INGREDIENTS
½ small loaf wholemeal
  (whole-wheat) bread
45ml/3 tbsp chilli oil
2 eggs
115g/4oz mixed salad leaves
45ml/3 tbsp extra virgin olive oil
2 garlic cloves, crushed
15ml/1 tbsp balsamic or
  sherry vinegar
50g/2oz Parmesan cheese, shaved
ground black pepper

1 Carefully cut the crust from the Granary loaf and discard. Cut the bread into neat slices and then into 2.5cm/1in cubes.

2 Heat the chilli oil in a large frying pan. Add the bread cubes and cook for about 5 minutes, tossing the cubes occasionally, until they are crisp and golden brown all over.

3 Meanwhile, bring a pan of water to the boil. Break each egg into a jug and carefully slide into the water, one at a time. Gently poach the eggs for about 4 minutes until lightly cooked.

4 Divide the salad leaves between two plates. Remove the croûtons from the pan and arrange them over the leaves.

5 Wipe the pan clean with kitchen paper. Then heat the olive oil in the pan, add the garlic and vinegar and cook over high heat for 1 minute. Pour the warm dressing over the salads.

6 Place a poached egg on each salad. Top with thin Parmesan shavings and a little ground black pepper.

Energy 697kcal/2907kJ; Protein 25.9g; Carbohydrate 41.3g, of which sugars 2.8g; Fat 49g, of which saturates 11.5g; Cholesterol 215mg; Calcium 408mg; Fibre 6.3g; Sodium 914mg

OMELETTE WRAPS

CUT OPEN THESE NEAT PARCELS TO REVEAL THE FLAVOURSOME PORK FILLING. THEY ARE PERFECT FOR AN IMPROMPTU SUPPER AND ARE SO EASY TO MAKE THAT YOU WON'T MIND OFFERING SECONDS.

Preparation: 2–4 minutes; Cooking: 16–18 minutes

SERVES FOUR

INGREDIENTS
   30ml/2 tbsp vegetable oil
   2 garlic cloves, finely chopped
   1 small onion, finely chopped
   225g/8oz/2 cups minced
     (ground) pork
   30ml/2 tbsp Thai fish sauce
   5ml/1 tsp sugar
   2 tomatoes, peeled and chopped
   15ml/1 tbsp chopped fresh
     coriander (cilantro)
   ground black pepper
   sprigs of coriander and fresh red
     chillies, sliced, to garnish
For the omelettes
   5–6 eggs
   15ml/1 tbsp Thai fish sauce
   30ml/2 tbsp vegetable oil

1 Heat the oil in a wok, add the garlic and onion, and fry for 2 minutes until soft. Add the pork and fry for about 8 minutes until lightly browned.

2 Stir in the fish sauce, sugar, tomatoes and black pepper; simmer until slightly thickened. Mix in the fresh coriander.

3 To make the omelettes, whisk together the eggs and fish sauce.

4 Heat 15ml/1 tbsp of the oil in an omelette pan or wok. Add half the beaten egg mixture and tilt the pan to spread the egg into a thin, even sheet.

5 Cook until the omelette is just set, then spoon half the filling into the centre. Fold into a neat square parcel by bringing the opposite sides of the omelette towards each other – first the top and bottom, then the right and left sides.

6 Slide the parcel on to a warm serving dish, folded side down. Repeat with the rest of the oil, eggs and filling to make a second omelette parcel. Garnish with sprigs of coriander and red chillies. Cut each omelette in half to serve.

COOK'S TIP
For a milder flavour, discard the seeds and membrane of the chillies, where most of their heat resides. Wash your hands after handling chillies.

Energy 319kcal/1327kJ; Protein 20.7g; Carbohydrate 3.8g, of which sugars 3.4g; Fat 25g, of which saturates 5.7g; Cholesterol 323mg; Calcium 55mg; Fibre 0.7g; Sodium 147mg

OMELETTE ARNOLD BENNETT

CONTRIVING TO BE CREAMY AND FLUFFY AT THE SAME TIME, THIS SMOKED HADDOCK SOUFFLÉ OMELETTE IS DELICIOUS. NO WONDER THE AUTHOR ARNOLD BENNETT LOVED IT SO MUCH.

Preparation: 2 minutes; Cooking: 12 minutes

SERVES TWO

INGREDIENTS
175g/6oz smoked haddock fillet
  (preferably undyed if available)
50g/2oz/4 tbsp butter, diced
175ml/6fl oz/¾ cup whipping or
  double (heavy) cream
4 eggs, separated
40g/1½oz/⅓ cup mature (sharp)
  Cheddar cheese, grated
ground black pepper
watercress, to garnish

1 Put the haddock in a shallow pan with water to cover and poach over a medium heat for 8–10 minutes or until the fish flakes easily when tested with the tip of a knife. Drain well.

2 Remove the skin and any bones from the haddock fillet and discard. Carefully flake the flesh using a fork.

3 Melt half the butter with 60ml/4 tbsp of the cream in a fairly small non-stick pan, then add the flaked fish and stir together gently. Cover the pan and remove from the heat. Preheat the grill (broiler).

4 Mix the egg yolks with 15ml/1 tbsp of the cream. Season with pepper, then stir into the fish. Mix the cheese and the remaining cream. Whisk the egg whites until stiff, then fold into the fish mixture. Heat the remaining butter in an omelette pan, add the fish mixture and cook until browned underneath. Pour the cheese mixture over and grill (broil) until bubbling. Garnish and serve.

Energy 821kcal/3396kJ; Protein 36.1g; Carbohydrate 2.6g, of which sugars 2.6g; Fat 74g, of which saturates 42.6g; Cholesterol 577mg; Calcium 280mg; Fibre 0g; Sodium 1123mg

HADDOCK IN CIDER SAUCE

FIRST CLASS FISH DOESN'T NEED ELABORATE TREATMENT. THE CIDER SAUCE SERVED WITH THE HADDOCK IS BASED ON THE POACHING LIQUID, ENRICHED BY JUST A WHISPER OF CREAM.

Preparation: 2 minutes; Cooking: 13 minutes

SERVES FOUR

INGREDIENTS
675g/1½lb haddock fillet
1 medium onion, thinly sliced
1 bay leaf
2 parsley sprigs
10ml/2 tsp lemon juice
450ml/¾ pint/2 cups dry (hard) cider
25g/1oz/¼ cup cornflour (cornstarch)
30ml/2 tbsp single (light) cream
salt and ground black pepper

VARIATION
Try cod or hake or another white fish with firm flesh instead of haddock.

1 Cut the haddock fillet into four equal portions and place in a pan big enough to hold them neatly in a single layer. Add the onion, bay leaf, parsley and lemon. Season with salt.

2 Pour in most of the cider, reserving 30ml/2 tbsp for the sauce. Cover and bring to the boil, reduce the heat and simmer for 10 minutes, or until the fish is just cooked.

3 Strain 300ml/½ pint/1¼ cups of the cooking liquid into a measuring jug (cup). Cover the pan containing the fish and remove from the heat. In a small pan, mix the cornflour with the reserved cider, then gradually whisk in the measured cooking liquid and bring to the boil. Whisk until smooth and thick.

4 Whisk in more of the cooking liquid, if necessary, to make a pouring sauce. Remove the pan from the heat, stir in the cream and season to taste with salt and ground black pepper.

5 To serve, remove any skin from the fish, arrange on individual hot serving plates and pour the sauce over. Serve with a selection of vegetables.

Energy 216kcal/918kJ; Protein 32.5g; Carbohydrate 9.4g, of which sugars 3.5g; Fat 2.5g, of which saturates 1.1g; Cholesterol 65mg; Calcium 43mg; Fibre 0.1g; Sodium 127mg

HERRING FILLETS IN OATMEAL WITH APPLES

FRESH HERRINGS MAKE AN INEXPENSIVE AND TASTY SUPPER FISH. COATING THEM IN OATMEAL BEFORE FRYING GIVES THEM A CRISP OUTER EDGE THAT CONTRASTS WELL WITH THE TENDER APPLE SLICES.

Preparation: 3–4 minutes; Cooking: 6 minutes

SERVES FOUR

INGREDIENTS
    8 herring fillets
    seasoned flour, for coating
    1 egg, beaten
    115g/4oz/1 cup fine pinhead oatmeal
      or oatflakes
    oil, for frying
    2 eating apples
    25g/1oz/2 tbsp butter

1 Wash the fish and pat dry with kitchen paper. Skin the fillets and check that all bones have been removed.

2 Toss the herring fillets in the seasoned flour, then dip them in the beaten egg and coat them evenly with the oatmeal or oatflakes.

3 Heat a little oil in a heavy frying pan and fry the fillets, a few at a time, until golden brown. Drain on kitchen paper and keep warm.

4 Core the apples, but do not peel. Slice them quite thinly. In another pan, melt the butter and fry the apple slices gently until just softened. Serve the apple with the coated fish fillets.

VARIATIONS
• Mackerel fillets can be cooked in the same way.
• A fruit sauce – apple, gooseberry or rhubarb – could be served instead of the sliced apples. Cook 225g/8oz of your preferred fruit with 90ml/6 tbsp cold water until just softened. Purée and serve with the fish.
• Try serving this with crisp grilled (broiled) bacon slices or follow the fruit theme by wrapping strips of bacon around pitted prunes that have been soaked in port, then grilling (broiling) the bacon rolls.
• Poached nectarine slices would also be a good accompaniment.

Energy 566kcal/2361kJ; Protein 35.6g; Carbohydrate 24.3g, of which sugars 3.4g; Fat 37g, of which saturates 9.9g; Cholesterol 146mg; Calcium 128mg; Fibre 2.6g; Sodium 270mg

STIR-FRIED DUCK <u>WITH</u> PINEAPPLE

THE FATTY SKIN ON DUCK MAKES IT IDEAL FOR STIR-FRYING: AS SOON AS THE DUCK IS ADDED TO THE HOT PAN THE FAT RUNS, CREATING DELICIOUS CRISP SKIN AND TENDER FLESH WHEN COOKED.

Preparation: 5 minutes; Cooking: 10 minutes

SERVES FOUR

INGREDIENTS
    250g/9oz fresh sesame noodles
    2 duck breasts, thinly sliced
    3 spring onions (scallions),
      cut into strips
    2 celery sticks, cut into
      matchstick strips
    1 fresh pineapple, peeled, cored and
      cut into strips
    300g/11oz carrots, peppers,
      beansprouts and cabbage, shredded
    90ml/6 tbsp plum sauce

1 Bring a pan of water to the boil and add the noodles. Cook for approximately 3 minutes then drain over the pan using a colander. Set aside.

2 Meanwhile, heat a wok. Add the duck and stir-fry for 2 minutes, until crisp. Drain off all but 30ml/2 tbsp of the fat. Add the spring onions and celery and stir-fry for 2 minutes. Remove the ingredients from the wok and set aside.

3 Add the pineapple strips and mixed vegetables and stir-fry for 2 minutes.

4 Add the cooked noodles to the wok with the plum sauce, then replace the duck mixture.

5 Stir-fry the duck mixture for about 2 minutes more, or until the noodles and vegetables are hot and the duck is cooked through. Serve at once.

COOK'S TIP
Fresh sesame noodles can be bought from large supermarkets – you'll find them in the chiller cabinets alongside fresh pasta. If they aren't available use fresh egg noodles instead and cook according to the instructions on the packet. For extra flavour, add a little sesame oil to the cooking water.

Energy 455Kcal/1927kJ; Protein 28.3g; Carbohydrate 69g, of which sugars 22.6g; Fat 11g, of which saturates 1.4g; Cholesterol 110mg; Calcium 81mg; Fibre 5.7g; Sodium 143mg.

SPICY FRIED NOODLES WITH CHICKEN

THIS IS A WONDERFULLY VERSATILE DISH AS YOU CAN ADJUST IT TO INCLUDE YOUR FAVOURITE INGREDIENTS — JUST AS LONG AS YOU KEEP A BALANCE OF FLAVOURS, TEXTURES AND COLOURS.

Preparation: 6 minutes; Cooking: 8–10 minutes

SERVES FOUR

INGREDIENTS
    225g/8oz egg thread noodles
    60ml/4 tbsp vegetable oil
    2 garlic cloves, finely chopped
    175g/6oz pork fillet (tenderloin),
        sliced into thin strips
    1 skinless, boneless chicken breast
        portion (about 175g/6oz), sliced
        into thin strips
    115g/4oz/1 cup peeled cooked
        prawns (shrimp)
    45ml/3 tbsp fresh lemon juice
    45ml/3 tbsp Thai fish sauce
    30ml/2 tbsp soft light brown sugar
    2 eggs, beaten
    ½ fresh red chilli, seeded and
        finely chopped
    50g/2oz/⅔ cup beansprouts
    60ml/4 tbsp roasted peanuts, chopped
    3 spring onions (scallions), cut into
        5cm/2in lengths and shredded
    45ml/3 tbsp chopped fresh
        coriander (cilantro)

1 Cook the noodles in a large pan of boiling water, then leave for 5 minutes.

2 Meanwhile, heat 45ml/3 tbsp of the oil in a wok or large frying pan, add the garlic and cook for 30 seconds. Add the pork and chicken and stir-fry until lightly browned, then add the prawns and stir-fry for 2 minutes.

3 Stir in the lemon juice, then add the fish sauce and sugar. Stir-fry until the sugar has dissolved.

5 Pour the beaten eggs over the noodles and stir-fry until almost set, then add the chilli and beansprouts.

4 Drain the noodles and add to the wok or pan with the remaining 15ml/1 tbsp oil. Toss all the ingredients together.

6 Divide the roasted peanuts, spring onions and coriander leaves into two equal portions, add one portion to the pan and stir-fry for about 2 minutes.

7 Transfer the noodles to a serving platter. Sprinkle on the remaining roasted peanuts, spring onions and chopped coriander and serve immediately.

COOK'S TIP
Store beansprouts in the refrigerator and use within a day of purchase, as they tend to lose their crispness and become slimy and unpleasant quite quickly. The most commonly used beansprouts are sprouted mung beans, but you could use other types of beansprouts instead.

Energy 605kcal/2537kJ; Protein 39.8g; Carbohydrate 52.1g, of which sugars 11.5g; Fat 27.9g, of which saturates 5.5g; Cholesterol 226mg; Calcium 83mg; Fibre 3.1g; Sodium 1052mg

DEVILLED KIDNEYS ON BRIOCHE CROÛTES

THE TRICK WITH LAMB'S KIDNEYS IS NOT TO OVERCOOK THEM, SO THIS RECIPE IS A GIFT FOR THE QUICK COOK. CREAM TAMES THE FIERY SAUCE, MAKING A MIXTURE THAT TASTES GREAT ON CROUTES.

Preparation: 5 minutes; Cooking: 12–14 minutes

SERVES FOUR

INGREDIENTS
    8 mini brioche slices
    25g/1oz/2 tbsp butter
    1 shallot, finely chopped
    2 garlic cloves, finely chopped
    115g/4oz/1½ cups mushrooms,
      halved
    1.5ml/¼ tsp cayenne pepper
    15ml/1 tbsp Worcestershire sauce
    8 lamb's kidneys, halved and trimmed
    150ml/¼ pint/⅔ cup double
      (heavy) cream
    30ml/2 tbsp chopped fresh parsley

1 Preheat the grill (broiler) and toast the brioche slices until golden brown on both sides. Keep warm.

2 Melt the butter in a frying pan. Add the shallot, garlic and mushrooms and cook for 5 minutes, or until the shallot has softened. Stir in the cayenne pepper and Worcestershire sauce and simmer for 1 minute.

3 Add the kidneys to the pan and cook for 3–5 minutes on each side. Finally, stir in the cream and simmer for about 2 minutes, or until the sauce has heated through and has thickened slightly.

4 Remove the brioche croûtes from the wire rack and place on warmed plates. Top with the kidneys. Sprinkle with chopped parsley and serve immediately.

COOK'S TIPS
If you can't find mini brioches, you can use a large brioche instead. Slice it thickly and stamp out croûtes using a 5cm/2in round cutter. If you prefer, the brioche croûtes can be fried rather than toasted. Melt 25g/1oz/2 tbsp butter in a frying pan and fry the croûtes until crisp and golden on both sides.

Energy 575kcal/2412kJ; Protein 37.7g; Carbohydrate 40.7g, of which sugars 13.2g; Fat 30.3g, of which saturates 16.3g; Cholesterol 623mg; Calcium 122mg; Fibre 2g; Sodium 599mg

CRUNCHY SALAD <u>WITH</u> BLACK PUDDING

HIGHLY FLAVOURED BLACK PUDDING IS A SPICY SAUSAGE ENRICHED WITH BLOOD. THIS PUTS SOME PEOPLE OFF, WHICH IS A PITY AS IT HAS A GREAT FLAVOUR. IT IS THE STAR OF THIS SIMPLE SALAD.

Preparation: 4 minutes; Cooking: 8–12 minutes

SERVES FOUR

INGREDIENTS
   250g/9oz black pudding
     (blood sausage), sliced
   1 focaccia loaf, plain or flavoured
     with sun-dried tomatoes, garlic
     and herbs, cut into chunks
   45ml/3 tbsp olive oil
   1 cos or romaine lettuce, torn into
     bitesize pieces
   250g/9oz cherry tomatoes, halved
For the dressing
   juice of 1 lemon
   90ml/6 tbsp olive oil
   10ml/2 tsp French mustard
   15ml/1 tbsp clear honey
   30ml/2 tbsp chopped fresh herbs,
     such as coriander (cilantro),
     chives and parsley
   salt and ground black pepper

1 Dry-fry the black pudding in a large, non-stick frying pan for 5–10 minutes, or until browned and crisp, turning occasionally. Remove the black pudding from the pan using a slotted spoon and drain on kitchen paper. Set the black pudding aside and keep warm.

VARIATION
If black pudding (blood sausage) isn't your thing, try this recipe with spicy chorizo or Kabanos sausages instead. Cut them into thick diagonal slices before cooking. Use a similar type of crusty bread, such as ciabatta, for the croûtons, if you prefer.

2 Cut the focaccia into chunks. Add the oil to the juices in the frying pan and cook the focaccia cubes in two batches, turning often, until golden on all sides. Lift out the focaccia chunks and drain on kitchen paper.

3 Mix together all the focaccia, black pudding, lettuce and cherry tomatoes in a large bowl. Mix together the dressing ingredients and season with salt and pepper. Pour the dressing over the salad. Mix well and serve at once.

Energy 641kcal/2674kJ; Protein 15.1g; Carbohydrate 55g, of which sugars 8.1g; Fat 41.6g, of which saturates 9.4g; Cholesterol 43mg; Calcium 196mg; Fibre 3.2g; Sodium 1001mg

RUSSIAN HAMBURGERS

THESE TASTY HAMBURGERS CAN BE MADE VERY QUICKLY AND YET STILL TASTE DIVINE.
SERVE THEM SOLO, WITH SAUCE, OR JUST SLIDE THEM INTO BUNS.
Preparation: 6 minutes; Cooking: 12–14 minutes

SERVES FOUR

INGREDIENTS
  2 thick slices white bread,
    crusts removed
  45ml/3 tbsp milk
  450g/1lb finely minced (ground)
    beef, lamb or veal
  1 egg, beaten
  30ml/2 tbsp plain (all-purpose) flour
  30ml/2 tbsp sunflower oil
  salt and ground black pepper
  tomato sauce, pickled vegetables and
    crispy fried onions, to serve

VARIATION
These burgers are quite plain. For extra
flavour, add freshly grated nutmeg to
the mixture, or a little chopped onion
fried in oil.

1 Cut the bread into chunks and crumb
in a food processor, or by using a metal
grater. Put the breadcrumbs in a bowl
and spoon over the milk. Leave to soak
for 3 minutes.

2 Add the minced meat, egg, salt and
pepper and mix all the ingredients
together thoroughly.

3 Divide the mixture into four equal
portions and shape into ovals, each
about 10cm/4in long and 5cm/2in wide.
Coat each with the flour.

4 Heat the oil in a frying pan and fry the
burgers for 6–7 minutes on each side.
Serve with a tomato sauce, pickled
vegetables and fried onions.

Energy 384kcal/1597kJ; Protein 26g; Carbohydrate 13g, of which sugars 1g; Fat 25.7g, of which saturates 9g; Cholesterol 116mg; Calcium 56mg; Fibre 0.4g; Sodium 183mg

BEEF STROGANOFF

THIS IS ONE OF THE MOST FAMOUS FAST MEAT DISHES, CONSISTING OF TENDER STRIPS OF STEAK IN A
TANGY SOUR CREAM SAUCE. SERVE IT WITH POTATO FRIES, AS HERE, OR WITH NOODLES.
Preparation: 3 minutes; Cooking: 12 minutes

SERVES FOUR

INGREDIENTS
  450g/1lb fillet steak (beef tenderloin)
    or rump steak, trimmed and
    tenderized with a rolling pin or
    meat mallet
  15ml/1 tbsp sunflower oil
  25g/1oz/2 tbsp butter
  1 onion, sliced
  15ml/1 tbsp plain (all-purpose) flour
  5ml/1 tsp tomato purée (paste)
  5ml/1 tsp Dijon mustard
  5ml/1 tsp lemon juice
  150ml/¼ pint/⅔ cup soured cream
  salt and ground black pepper
  fresh herbs, to garnish

1 Using a sharp cook's knife, cut the
tenderized steak into thin strips, about
5cm/2in long. Heat the oil and half the
butter in a frying pan and fry the beef
over a high heat for 2 minutes, or until
browned. Remove with a slotted spoon,
leaving any juices behind.

2 Melt the remaining butter in the pan
and gently fry the onion for 8 minutes,
until soft. Stir in the flour, tomato purée,
mustard, lemon juice and sour cream.
Return the beef to the pan and stir until
the sauce is bubbling. Season well and
garnish with fresh herbs.

Energy 308kcal/1282kJ; Protein 26.5g; Carbohydrate 5.8g, of which sugars 2.5g; Fat 20.1g, of which saturates 10.2g; Cholesterol 102mg; Calcium 50mg; Fibre 0.4g; Sodium 124mg

EASY
ENTERTAINING

One of the most frustrating things about entertaining is overhearing gales of laughter from the next room while you are slaving away in the kitchen. Missing some of the party is inevitable if you're the one wearing the apron, but the aim of this chapter is to make sure the cook spends as little time as possible missing the fun. So the dishes chosen for this section are quick, easy and exciting to eat. However, as distinct from the majority of recipes elsewhere in the collection, which are intended to take no more than 20 minutes from start to finish, some of these dishes demand a bit of advance preparation. This may mean marinating the meat, preparing a sauce or chilling a pâté, but since whatever you do early in the day saves stress later, this is a positive advantage. Where recipes need some advance preparation, this is clearly stated, so there is no excuse for getting it right on the night and serving sumptuous food with effortless ease.

TAPAS OF ALMONDS, OLIVES AND CHEESE

SERVING A FEW CHOICE NIBBLES WITH DRINKS IS THE PERFECT WAY TO GET AN EVENING OFF TO A GOOD START, AND WHEN YOU CAN GET EVERYTHING READY AHEAD OF TIME, LIFE'S EASIER ALL ROUND.

Preparation: 10–15 minutes; Cooking: 5 minutes; Make ahead

SERVES SIX TO EIGHT

INGREDIENTS

For the marinated olives
  2.5ml/½ tsp coriander seeds
  2.5ml/½ tsp fennel seeds
  2 garlic cloves, crushed
  5ml/1 tsp chopped fresh rosemary
  10ml/2 tsp chopped fresh parsley
  15ml/1 tbsp sherry vinegar
  30ml/2 tbsp olive oil
  115g/4oz/⅔ cup black olives
  115g/4oz/⅔ cup green olives
For the marinated cheese
  150g/5oz Manchego or other
    firm cheese
  90ml/6 tbsp olive oil
  15ml/1 tbsp white wine vinegar
  5ml/1 tsp black peppercorns
  1 garlic clove, sliced
  fresh thyme or tarragon sprigs
  fresh flat leaf parsley or tarragon
    sprigs, to garnish (optional)
For the salted almonds
  1.5ml/¼ tsp cayenne pepper
  30ml/2 tbsp sea salt
  25g/1oz/2 tbsp butter
  60ml/4 tbsp olive oil
  200g/7oz/1¾ cups blanched
    almonds
  extra salt for sprinkling (optional)

1 To make the marinated olives, crush the coriander and fennel seeds in a mortar with a pestle. Work in the garlic, then add the rosemary, parsley, vinegar and olive oil. Mix well. Put the olives in a small bowl and pour over the marinade. Cover with clear film (plastic wrap) and chill for up to 1 week.

2 To make the marinated cheese, cut the Manchego or other firm cheese into bitesize pieces, removing any rind, and put in a small bowl. Combine the oil, vinegar, peppercorns, garlic, thyme or tarragon and pour over the cheese. Cover with clear film and chill for up to 3 days.

3 To make the salted almonds, combine the cayenne pepper and salt in a bowl. Melt the butter with the oil in a frying pan. Add the almonds and fry them, stirring, for 5 minutes, or until golden.

4 Tip the almonds into the salt mixture and toss until the almonds are coated. Leave to cool, then store in an airtight container for up to 1 week.

5 To serve, arrange the almonds, olives and cheese in three separate small, shallow dishes. Garnish the cheese with fresh herbs if you like and sprinkle the almonds with a little more salt, to taste. Provide cocktail sticks (toothpicks) so that guests can pick up the cheese and olives easily.

COOK'S TIPS
• Whole olives, sold with the stone, invariably taste better than pitted ones. Don't serve them directly from the brine, but drain and rinse them, then pat dry with kitchen paper. Put the olives in a jar and pour over extra virgin olive oil to cover. Seal and store in the refrigerator for 1–2 months; the flavour of the olives will become richer. Serve the olives as a tapas dish, or add to salads. When the olives have been eaten, the fruity oil can be used as a dressing for hot food, or made into flavoursome salad dressings.
• A number of exotic stuffed olives are exported from Spain and are widely available in most large supermarkets. Popular varieties include pimiento-stuffed olives, which have been in existence for more than half a century; olives stuffed with salted anchovies; and olives filled with roast garlic.

Energy 383kcal/1580kJ; Protein 10.3g; Carbohydrate 1.8g, of which sugars 1.1g; Fat 36.8g, of which saturates 8.9g; Cholesterol 25mg; Calcium 217mg; Fibre 2.7g; Sodium 1051mg

ARTICHOKE <u>AND</u> CUMIN DIP

THIS DIP IS SO EASY TO MAKE AND IS UNBELIEVABLY TASTY. SERVE WITH OLIVES, HUMMUS AND WEDGES OF PITTA BREAD AS AN INFORMAL SUMMERY SNACK SELECTION.

Preparation: 2 minutes; Cooking: 0 minutes

SERVES FOUR

INGREDIENTS
  2 x 400g/14oz cans artichoke
    hearts, drained
  2 garlic cloves, peeled
  2.5ml/½ tsp ground cumin
  olive oil
  salt and ground black pepper

VARIATIONS
Grilled (broiled) artichokes bottled in oil have a fabulous flavour and can be used instead of canned artichokes. Try adding a handful of basil leaves to the artichokes before blending.

1 Put the artichoke hearts in a food processor with the garlic and ground cumin, and add a generous drizzle of olive oil. Process to a smooth purée and season with plenty of salt and ground black pepper to taste.

2 Spoon the purée into a serving bowl and serve with an extra drizzle of olive oil swirled on the top and slices of warm pitta bread or wholemeal (whole-wheat) toast fingers and carrot sticks for dipping.

Energy 76kcal/315kJ; Protein 1.6g; Carbohydrate 3.9g, of which sugars 3.5g; Fat 6.2g, of which saturates 1g; Cholesterol 0mg; Calcium 18mg; Fibre 3.5g; Sodium 4mg

CHICKEN LIVER AND BRANDY PATÉ

THIS PATÉ REALLY COULD NOT BE SIMPLER TO PUT TOGETHER, AND TASTES SO MUCH BETTER THAN ANYTHING YOU CAN BUY READY-MADE IN THE SUPERMARKETS. SERVE WITH CRISPY MELBA TOAST.

Preparation: 3 minutes; Cooking: 5–6 minutes; Make ahead

SERVES FOUR

INGREDIENTS

50g/2oz/¼ cup butter
350g/12oz chicken livers, trimmed
  and roughly chopped
30ml/2 tbsp brandy
30ml/2 tbsp double (heavy) cream
salt and ground black pepper

1 Heat the butter in a large frying pan. Add the chicken livers. Cook over a medium heat for 3–4 minutes, or until browned and cooked through.

2 Add the brandy and allow to bubble for a few minutes. Let the mixture cool slightly, then place in a food processor with the cream and some salt and pepper.

3 Process the mixture until smooth and spoon into ramekin dishes. Level the surface and chill overnight to set. If making more than 1 day ahead, seal the surface of each portion with a layer of melted butter. Serve garnished with sprigs of parsley to add a little colour.

Energy 227kcal/942kJ; Protein 15.7g; Carbohydrate 0.2g, of which sugars 0.2g; Fat 16.3g, of which saturates 9.6g; Cholesterol 369mg; Calcium 13mg; Fibre 0g; Sodium 144mg

GRILLED AUBERGINE IN HONEY AND SPICES

THE COMBINATION OF HOT, SPICY, SWEET AND FRUITY FLAVOURS IN THIS MOROCCAN DISH WILL HAVE EVERYONE ASKING FOR THE RECIPE. SERVE AS AN APPETIZER OR FOR A LIGHT SECOND COURSE.

Preparation: 2 minutes; Cooking: 15 minutes

SERVES FOUR

INGREDIENTS

2 aubergines (eggplants)
olive oil, for frying
2–3 garlic cloves, crushed
5cm/2in piece fresh root ginger,
 peeled and grated
5ml/1 tsp ground cumin
5ml/1 tsp harissa
75ml/5 tbsp clear honey
juice of 1 lemon
salt

COOK'S TIP
Grilled blood oranges make an excellent quick accompaniment to this dish. Dip the halves or quarters in icing sugar and grill until just about to blacken. Then thread on to metal skewers.

1 Preheat the grill (broiler) or a griddle pan. Cut the aubergines lengthways into thick slices.

2 Brush each aubergine slice with olive oil and cook in a pan under the grill or in a griddle pan. Turn the slices so that they are lightly browned on both sides.

3 Meanwhile, in a wide frying pan, fry the garlic in a little olive oil for a few seconds, then stir in the ginger, cumin, harissa, honey and lemon juice.

4 Add enough water to thin the mixture, then add the aubergine slices. Cook for about 10 minutes, or until they have absorbed all the sauce.

5 Add a little extra water, if necessary, season to taste with salt, and serve at room temperature, with chunks of fresh bread to mop up the juices.

Energy 168kcal/701kJ; Protein 1g; Carbohydrate 16.5g, of which sugars 16.3g; Fat 11.4g, of which saturates 1.7g; Cholesterol 0mg; Calcium 11mg; Fibre 2g; Sodium 4mg

SESAME-TOSSED ASPARAGUS WITH NOODLES

TENDER ASPARAGUS SPEARS TOSSED WITH SESAME SEEDS AND SERVED ON A BED OF CRISPY, DEEP-FRIED NOODLES MAKES A LOVELY DISH FOR CASUAL ENTERTAINING.

Preparation: 2–3 minutes; Cooking: 7–8 minutes

SERVES FOUR

INGREDIENTS
15ml/1 tbsp sunflower oil
350g/12oz thin asparagus
   spears, trimmed
5ml/1 tsp salt
5ml/1 tsp ground black pepper
5ml/1 tsp golden caster
   (superfine) sugar
30ml/2 tbsp Chinese cooking wine
   or sherry
45ml/3 tbsp light soy sauce
60ml/4 tbsp oyster sauce
10ml/2 tsp sesame oil
60ml/4 tbsp toasted sesame seeds
For the noodles
50g/2oz dried bean thread noodles
   or thin rice noodles
sunflower oil, for frying

2 Heat a clean wok over a high heat and add the sunflower oil. Add the asparagus and stir-fry for 3 minutes.

3 Put four bowls to warm so that they are ready for serving.

4 Add the salt, pepper, sugar and wine or sherry to the wok with the soy sauce and oyster sauce. Stir-fry for 2–3 minutes. Add the sesame oil, toss to combine and remove from the heat.

5 To serve, divide the crispy noodles between four warmed plates or bowls and top with the asparagus and juices. Sprinkle over the toasted sesame seeds and serve immediately.

1 First make the crispy noodles. Fill a wok one-third full of oil and heat to 180°C/350°F (or until a cube of bread, dropped into the oil, browns in 15 seconds). Add the noodles, small bunches at a time, to the oil; they will crisp and puff up in seconds. Using a slotted spoon, remove from the wok and drain on kitchen paper. Set aside.

COOK'S TIP
Thin asparagus spears, called sprue, are often cheaper than fat stalks. Look for them at farmer's markets.

Energy 131kcal/547kJ; Protein 4.6g; Carbohydrate 16.5g, of which sugars 6.9g; Fat 5.6g, of which saturates 0.6g; Cholesterol 0mg; Calcium 31mg; Fibre 2g; Sodium 1047mg

PEARS WITH BLUE CHEESE AND WALNUTS

SUCCULENT PEARS FILLED WITH BLUE CHEESE AND WALNUT CREAM LOOK PRETTY ON COLOURFUL LEAVES AND MAKE A GREAT APPETIZER. THEY ARE QUITE RICH, SO KEEP THE MAIN COURSE SIMPLE.

Preparation: 8–10 minutes; Cooking: 0 minutes

SERVES SIX

INGREDIENTS
  115g/4oz fresh cream cheese
  75g/3oz Stilton or other mature blue
    cheese, such as Roquefort
  30–45ml/2–3 tbsp single
    (light) cream
  115g/4oz/1 cup roughly
    chopped walnuts
  6 ripe pears
  15ml/1 tbsp lemon juice
  mixed salad leaves, such as frisée,
    oakleaf lettuce and radicchio
  6 cherry tomatoes
  sea salt and ground black pepper
  walnut halves and sprigs of fresh
    flat leaf parsley, to garnish
For the dressing
  juice of 1 lemon
  a little finely grated lemon rind
  a pinch of caster (superfine) sugar
  60ml/4 tbsp olive oil

1 Mash the cream cheese and blue cheese together in a mixing bowl with a good grinding of black pepper, then blend in the cream to make a smooth mixture. Add 25g/1oz/¼ cup of the chopped walnuts and mix to distribute evenly.

COOK'S TIP
You need small pears that are perfectly ripe for this recipe. Comice or Bartlett pears would be ideal.

2 Peel and halve the pears and scoop out the core from each. Put the pears into a bowl of water with the 15ml/ 1 tbsp lemon juice to prevent them from browning. Make the dressing by whisking the ingredients together with salt and pepper to taste.

3 Arrange a bed of salad leaves on six plates – shallow soup plates are ideal – add a cherry tomato to each and sprinkle over the remaining chopped walnuts.

4 Drain the pears well and pat dry with kitchen paper, then turn them in the prepared dressing and arrange, hollow side up, on the salad leaves.

5 Divide the blue cheese filling among the 12 pear halves and spoon the dressing over the top. Garnish each filled pear half with a walnut half and a sprig of flat leaf parsley before serving.

Energy 322kcal/1332kJ; Protein 5.1g; Carbohydrate 15.7g, of which sugars 15.7g; Fat 26.9g, of which saturates 10.2g; Cholesterol 30mg; Calcium 109mg; Fibre 3.7g; Sodium 218mg

WARM HALLOUMI AND FENNEL SALAD

HALLOUMI IS A ROBUST CHEESE THAT HOLDS ITS SHAPE WHEN COOKED ON A GRIDDLE OR BARBECUE.
DURING COOKING IT ACQUIRES THE DISTINCTIVE GRIDDLE MARKS THAT LOOK SO EFFECTIVE HERE.
Preparation: 13 minutes; Cooking: 6 minutes

SERVES FOUR

INGREDIENTS
  200g/7oz halloumi cheese,
    thickly sliced
  2 fennel bulbs, trimmed and
    thinly sliced
  30ml/2 tbsp roughly chopped
    fresh oregano
  45ml/3 tbsp lemon-infused olive oil
  salt and ground black pepper

COOK'S TIP
If you have time, chill the halloumi and
fennel mixture for about 2 hours before
cooking, so it becomes infused with
the dressing.

1 Put the halloumi, fennel and oregano
in a bowl and drizzle over the lemon-
infused oil. Season with salt and black
pepper to taste. (Halloumi is a fairly
salty cheese, so be very careful when
adding extra salt.)

2 Cover the bowl with clear film (plastic
wrap) and set aside for 10 minutes.

3 Place the halloumi and fennel on a
hot griddle pan or over the barbecue,
reserving the marinade, and cook
for about 3 minutes on each side,
until charred.

4 Divide the halloumi and fennel among
four serving plates and drizzle over the
reserved marinade. Serve immediately.

Energy 212kcal/876kJ; Protein 10g; Carbohydrate 1.4g, of which sugars 1.3g; Fat 18.6g, of which saturates 8.1g; Cholesterol 29mg; Calcium 199mg; Fibre 1.8g; Sodium 206mg

WARM CHORIZO AND SPINACH SALAD

SPANISH CHORIZO SAUSAGE CONTRIBUTES AN INTENSE SPICINESS TO ANY INGREDIENT WITH WHICH IT IS COOKED. IN THIS HEARTY WARM SALAD, SPINACH HAS SUFFICIENT FLAVOUR TO COMPETE.

Preparation: 2–3 minutes; Cooking: 5 minutes

SERVES FOUR

INGREDIENTS
225g/8oz baby spinach leaves
90ml/6 tbsp extra virgin olive oil
150g/5oz chorizo sausage, very
    thinly sliced
30ml/2 tbsp sherry vinegar

VARIATION
Watercress or rocket (arugula) could be used instead of the spinach. For an added dimension use an oil flavoured with rosemary, garlic or chilli.

1 Discard any tough stalks from the spinach. Pour the oil into a large frying pan and add the sausage. Cook gently for 3 minutes, until the sausage slices start to shrivel slightly and begin to change colour.

2 Add the spinach leaves and remove the pan from the heat. Toss the spinach in the warm oil until it just starts to wilt. Add the sherry vinegar and a little seasoning. Toss the ingredients briefly, then serve immediately, while still warm.

Energy 300kcal/1238kJ; Protein 5.6g; Carbohydrate 4.5g, of which sugars 1.4g; Fat 29g, of which saturates 7g; Cholesterol 18mg; Calcium 111mg; Fibre 1.4g; Sodium 364mg

FIGS WITH PROSCIUTTO AND ROQUEFORT

In this easy, stylish dish, figs and honey balance the richness of the ham and cheese.
Serve with warm bread for a simple appetizer before any rich main course.

Preparation: 2–3 minutes; Cooking: 4–5 minutes

SERVES FOUR

INGREDIENTS
  8 fresh figs
  75g/3oz prosciutto
  45ml/3 tbsp clear honey
  75g/3oz Roquefort cheese
  ground black pepper

COOK'S TIP
Fresh figs are a delicious treat, whether you choose dark purple, yellow green or green-skinned varieties. When they are ripe, you can split them open with your fingers to reveal the soft, sweet flesh full of edible seeds. They also taste great stuffed with goat's cheese.

1 Preheat the grill (broiler). Quarter the figs and place on a foil-lined grill rack. Tear each slice of prosciutto into two or three pieces. Crumple the pieces of prosciutto and place them on the foil beside the figs. Brush the figs with 15ml/1 tbsp of the clear honey and cook under the grill until lightly browned.

2 Crumble the Roquefort cheese and divide among four plates, setting it to one side. Add the honey-grilled figs and ham and pour over any cooking juices caught on the foil. Drizzle the remaining honey over the figs, ham and cheese, and serve seasoned with plenty of ground black pepper.

Energy 326kcal/1378kJ; Protein 10.7g; Carbohydrate 57.4g, of which sugars 57.4g; Fat 7.5g, of which saturates 3.8g; Cholesterol 25mg; Calcium 324mg; Fibre 6.9g; Sodium 512mg

GOAT'S CHEESE SALAD

YOU NEED A SOFT GOAT'S CHEESE WITH PLENTY OF FLAVOUR FOR THIS SALAD. IF YOU HAVE A GOOD CHEESE SHOP IN THE LOCALITY, MAKE A FRIEND OF THE OWNER AND ASK FOR SUGGESTIONS.

Preparation: 8–10 minutes; Cooking: 0 minutes

SERVES FOUR

INGREDIENTS

175g/6oz mixed salad leaves, such as
lamb's lettuce, rocket (arugula),
radicchio, frisée or cress
a few fresh large-leafed herbs, such
as chervil and flat leaf parsley
15ml/1 tbsp toasted hazelnuts,
roughly chopped
15–20 goat's cheese balls or cubes
For the dressing
30ml/2 tbsp hazelnut oil, olive oil
or sunflower oil
5–10ml/1–2 tsp sherry vinegar or
good wine vinegar, to taste
salt and ground black pepper

1 Tear up any large salad leaves. Put
all the leaves into a large salad bowl
with the fresh herbs and most of the
toasted, chopped nuts (reserve a few
for the garnish).

2 To make the dressing, whisk the
hazelnut, olive or sunflower oil and
vinegar together, and then season to
taste with salt and pepper.

VARIATIONS
Toasted flaked (sliced) almonds could
replace the hazelnuts (teamed with extra
virgin olive oil), while stronger flavoured
cheeses work well with walnuts and
walnut oil.

3 Just before serving, toss the salad in
the dressing and divide it among four
serving plates. Arrange the drained
goat's cheese balls or cubes over the
leaves, sprinkle over the remaining
chopped nuts and serve.

Energy 215kcal/893kJ; Protein 11.4g; Carbohydrate 1.5g, of which sugars 1.4g; Fat 18.3g, of which saturates 9.6g; Cholesterol 47mg; Calcium 84mg; Fibre 0.6g; Sodium 302mg

SIZZLING PRAWNS

WHEN YOU LASH OUT AND BUY A LUXURY ITEM LIKE THESE LARGE PRAWNS, YOU WANT TO BE SURE
THEY TASTE GREAT. THIS RECIPE IS SWIFT, SIMPLE AND ALWAYS A SURE-FIRE SUCCESS.
Preparation: 2–3 minutes; Cooking: 5 minutes

SERVES FOUR

INGREDIENTS
  1–2 dried chillies (to taste)
  60ml/4 tbsp olive oil
  3 garlic cloves, finely chopped
  16 large raw prawns (jumbo shrimp),
   in the shell
  salt and ground black pepper
  French bread, to serve

VARIATION
Another great way to serve the prawns
(shrimp) is in a warm lime and sweet
chilli dressing. Use garlic to flavour the
oil, but remove it before frying the
prawns. Let the oil for frying cool
slightly, then whisk in fresh lime juice
and a little sweet chilli sauce. Spoon
over the prawns.

1 Split the chillies lengthways and
discard the seeds. It is best to do this
with a knife and fork, because the
seeds, in particular, contain hot
capsaicin, which can be very irritating
to the eyes, nose and mouth.

2 Heat the oil in a large frying pan and
stir-fry the garlic and chilli for 1 minute,
until the garlic begins to turn brown.

3 Add the whole prawns and stir-fry
for 3–4 minutes, coating them well
with the flavoured oil.

4 Remove from the heat and divide the
prawns among four dishes. Spoon over
the flavoured oil and serve immediately.
(Remember to provide a plate for the
heads and shells, plus plenty of napkins
for messy fingers.)

Energy 124kcal/511kJ; Protein 5.7g; Carbohydrate 0g, of which sugars 0g; Fat 11.2g, of which saturates 1.6g; Cholesterol 63mg; Calcium 26mg; Fibre 0g; Sodium 62mg

THAI STEAMED MUSSELS IN COCONUT MILK

*AN IDEAL DISH FOR INFORMAL ENTERTAINING, MUSSELS STEAMED IN COCONUT MILK AND FRESH
AROMATIC HERBS ARE QUICK AND EASY TO PREPARE AND GREAT FOR A RELAXED DINNER WITH FRIENDS.*

Preparation: 10 minutes; Cooking: 6–7 minutes

SERVES FOUR

INGREDIENTS

1.6kg/3½lb mussels
15ml/1 tbsp sunflower oil
6 garlic cloves, roughly chopped
15ml/1 tbsp finely chopped fresh
  root ginger
2 large red chillies, seeded and
  finely sliced
6 spring onions (scallions),
  finely chopped
400ml/14fl oz/1⅔ cups coconut milk
45ml/3 tbsp light soy sauce
2 limes
5ml/1 tsp caster (superfine) sugar
a large handful of chopped
  coriander (cilantro)
salt and ground black pepper

3 Grate the rind of the limes into the
ginger mixture, then squeeze both fruit
and add the juice to the wok with the
coconut milk, soy sauce and sugar.
Stir to mix.

4 Bring the mixture to the boil, then
add the mussels. Return to the boil,
cover and cook briskly for 5–6 minutes,
or until all the mussels have opened.
Discard any unopened mussels.

5 Remove the wok from the heat and
stir in the chopped coriander. Season
the mussels well with salt and pepper.
Ladle into warmed bowls and serve
immediately.

COOK'S TIP
For an informal supper with friends, take
the wok straight to the table. There's
something utterly irresistible about
eating straight from the pan.

1 Scrub the mussels in cold water.
Scrape off any barnacles with a knife,
then pull out and discard the fibrous
"beard" visible between the hinge on
any of the shells. Discard any mussels
that are not tightly closed, or which fail
to close when tapped sharply.

2 Heat a wok over a high heat and then
add the oil. Stir in the garlic, ginger,
chillies and spring onions and stir-fry
for 30 seconds.

COOK'S TIP
The best-flavoured mussels are blue or
European mussels from cold British
waters. They are inexpensive, so don't be
afraid to buy more than you need!

Energy 160kcal/679kJ; Protein 21.5g; Carbohydrate 6.7g, of which sugars 6.7g; Fat 5.5g, of which saturates 1g; Cholesterol 48mg; Calcium 272mg; Fibre 0.2g; Sodium 630mg

SEARED TUNA ^{WITH} SPICY WATERCRESS SALAD

TUNA STEAKS ARE WONDERFUL SEARED AND SERVED SLIGHTLY RARE WITH A PUNCHY SAUCE. IN THIS RECIPE A WATERCRESS SALAD IS SERVED JUST WARM AS A BED FOR THE TENDER FISH.

Preparation: 6 minutes; Cooking: 10 minutes

SERVES FOUR

INGREDIENTS
  30ml/2 tbsp olive oil
  5ml/1 tsp harissa
  5ml/1 tsp clear honey
  4 x 200g/7oz tuna steaks
  salt and ground black pepper
  lemon wedges, to serve
For the salad
  30ml/2 tbsp olive oil
  a little butter
  25g/1oz fresh root ginger, peeled
    and thinly sliced
  2 garlic cloves, finely sliced
  2 fresh green chillies, seeded and
    thinly sliced
  6 spring onions (scallions), cut into
    bitesize pieces
  2 large handfuls watercress
  1 lemon, cut into 4 wedges

1 Mix the olive oil, harissa, honey and salt, and rub it over the tuna steaks.

VARIATION
Prawns (shrimp) and scallops can be cooked in the same way. The shellfish will just need to be cooked through briefly – too long and they will become rubbery.

2 Heat a frying pan, grease it with a little oil and sear the tuna steaks for about 2 minutes on each side. They should still be pink on the inside.

3 Keep the tuna warm while you quickly prepare the salad: heat the olive oil and butter in a heavy pan. Stir in the ginger, garlic, chillies and spring onions, cook until the mixture begins to colour, then add the watercress. As soon as the watercress begins to wilt, toss in the lemon juice and season well with salt and plenty of ground black pepper.

4 Tip the warm salad on to a serving dish or individual plates. Slice the tuna steaks and arrange on top of the salad. Serve immediately with lemon wedges for squeezing over.

COOK'S TIP
Harissa is a North African spice paste based on chillies, garlic, coriander and cumin seeds. It is sold in tubes, like tomato purée (paste), or jars, or can be made fresh.

WARM SWORDFISH AND ROCKET SALAD

SWORDFISH IS ROBUST ENOUGH TO TAKE THE SHARP FLAVOURS OF ROCKET AND PECORINO CHEESE.
THE FISH CAN BE DRY, SO DON'T SKIP THE MARINATING STAGE UNLESS YOU'RE REALLY PUSHED.

Preparation: 7 minutes; Cooking: 8–12 minutes

SERVES FOUR

INGREDIENTS
    4 swordfish steaks, about
        175g/6oz each
    75ml/5 tbsp extra virgin olive oil,
        plus extra for serving
    juice of 1 lemon
    30ml/2 tbsp finely chopped
        fresh parsley
    115g/4oz rocket (arugula) leaves,
        stalks removed
    115g/4oz Pecorino cheese
    salt and ground black pepper

1 Lay the swordfish steaks in a shallow dish. Mix 60ml/4 tbsp of the olive oil with the lemon juice. Pour over the fish. Season, sprinkle with parsley and turn the fish to coat. Cover the dish and leave to marinate for 5 minutes.

2 Heat a ridged griddle pan or the grill (broiler) until very hot. Take the fish out of the marinade and pat it dry with kitchen paper. Grill (broil) two steaks at a time for 2–3 minutes on each side until the swordfish is just cooked through, but still juicy.

3 Meanwhile, put the rocket leaves in a bowl and season with a little salt and plenty of pepper. Add the remaining 15ml/1 tbsp olive oil and toss well.

4 Place the swordfish steaks on four individual plates and arrange a little pile of salad on each steak. Shave the Pecorino over the top. Serve extra olive oil separately so it can be drizzled over the swordfish.

VARIATION
Tuna, shark or marlin steaks would be equally good in this recipe.

Energy 452kcal/1880kJ; Protein 43.6g; Carbohydrate 0.5g, of which sugars 0.4g; Fat 30.6g, of which saturates 9.5g; Cholesterol 101mg; Calcium 401mg; Fibre 0.6g; Sodium 581mg

GRIDDLED SWORDFISH WITH ROASTED TOMATOES

SLOW-ROASTING THE TOMATOES IS A GREAT TECHNIQUE WHEN YOU ARE ENTERTAINING AS THEY NEED NO LAST-MINUTE ATTENTION, BUT A MUCH QUICKER WAY IS SIMPLY TO GRILL THEM INSTEAD.

Preparation: 4 minutes; Cooking: 12 minutes, plus 3 hours if slow-roasting tomatoes

SERVES FOUR

INGREDIENTS

1kg/2¼lb large vine or plum
  tomatoes, peeled, halved
  and seeded
5–10ml/1–2 tsp ground cinnamon
a pinch of saffron threads
15ml/1 tbsp orange flower water
60ml/4 tbsp olive oil
45–60ml/3–4 tbsp sugar
4 x 225g/8oz swordfish steaks
rind of ½ preserved lemon,
  finely chopped
a small bunch of fresh coriander
  (cilantro), finely chopped
a handful of blanched almonds
a knob (pat) of butter
salt and ground black pepper

1 Preheat the oven to 110°C/225°F/ Gas ¼. Place the tomatoes on a baking sheet. Sprinkle with the cinnamon, saffron and orange flower water.

2 Trickle half the oil over, being sure to moisten every tomato half, and sprinkle with sugar. Place the tray in the bottom of the oven and cook the tomatoes for about 3 hours, then turn the oven off and leave them to cool. Alternatively, place under a medium grill (broiler) for 10 minutes.

VARIATION
If swordfish steaks are not available, use tuna or shark steaks.

3 Brush the remaining olive oil over the swordfish steaks and season with salt and pepper. Lightly oil a pre-heated cast-iron griddle and cook the steaks for 3–4 minutes on each side. Sprinkle the chopped preserved lemon and coriander over the steaks towards the end of the cooking time.

4 In a separate pan, fry the almonds in the butter until golden and sprinkle them over the tomatoes. Serve the steaks immediately with the tomatoes.

Energy 405kcal/1696kJ; Protein 42.3g; Carbohydrate 7.8g, of which sugars 7.8g; Fat 23g, of which saturates 5.2g; Cholesterol 98mg; Calcium 27mg; Fibre 2.5g; Sodium 330mg

GRILLED SOLE WITH CHIVE BUTTER

THE BEST WAY OF TRANSFORMING SIMPLE GRILLED FISH INTO A LUXURY DISH IS BY TOPPING IT WITH A FLAVOURED BUTTER. THIS ONE, FLAVOURED WITH LEMON GRASS AND LIME, IS A WINNER.

Preparation: 3–4 minutes; Cooking: 10 minutes

SERVES FOUR

INGREDIENTS

115g/4oz/½ cup unsalted (sweet)
   butter, softened, plus extra, melted
5ml/1 tsp diced lemon grass
pinch of finely grated lime rind
1 kaffir lime leaf, very finely
   shredded (optional)
45ml/3 tbsp chopped chives or
   chopped chive flowers, plus extra
   chives or chive flowers to garnish
2.5–5ml/½–1 tsp Thai fish sauce
4 sole, skinned
salt and ground black pepper
lemon or lime wedges, to serve

COOK'S TIP
Finer white fish fillets, such as plaice,
can be cooked in this way, but reduce
the cooking time slightly.

1 Cream the butter with the lemon grass, lime rind, lime leaf, if using, and chives or chive flowers. Season to taste with Thai fish sauce, salt and pepper.

2 Chill the butter mixture to firm it a little, then form it into a roll and wrap in foil or clear film (plastic wrap). Chill until firm. Preheat the grill (broiler).

3 Brush the fish with melted butter. Place it on the grill rack and season. Grill (broil) for about 5 minutes on each side, until firm and just cooked.

4 Meanwhile, cut the chilled butter into thin slices and put these on the fish. Garnish with chives and serve with lemon or lime wedges.

Energy 349kcal/1447kJ; Protein 27.4g; Carbohydrate 0.5g, of which sugars 0.5g; Fat 26.3g, of which saturates 15g; Cholesterol 136mg; Calcium 49mg; Fibre 0g; Sodium 591mg

STEAMED SALMON <u>WITH</u> CUCUMBER SAUCE

CUCUMBER AND FRESH DILL ARE A PERFECT COMBINATION IN THIS UNUSUAL HOT SAUCE, WHICH COMPLEMENTS THE STEAMED SALMON. THE GARNISH MAKES THIS A PARTICULARLY PRETTY DISH.

Preparation: 5 minutes; Cooking: 15 minutes

SERVES FOUR

INGREDIENTS
  ½ lemon, thickly sliced
  3 fresh dill sprigs
  675g/1½lb piece thick salmon fillet
  orange slices and salad leaves,
    to serve
For the cucumber sauce:
  1 large cucumber, peeled
  25g/1oz/2 tbsp butter
  120ml/4fl oz/½ cup dry white wine
  45ml/3 tbsp finely chopped
    fresh dill
  60ml/4 tbsp sour cream
  salt and ground black pepper

1 To make the sauce, cut the cucumber in half lengthways, scoop out the seeds, then dice the flesh into a colander. Toss lightly with salt and leave to stand.

2 Half-fill a metal steamer with boiling water, fit the insert, making sure it is clear of the water, and spread out the lemon slices and herb sprigs on top. Lay the salmon over the herbs.

3 Make sure there is enough space on either side of the fish for air to circulate freely. Lay a sheet of baking parchment loosely over the fish, cover the steamer tightly with the lid or foil and place over a medium heat. Steam the salmon for about 15 minutes or until it flakes easily when tested with the tip of a knife blade.

4 About halfway through the steaming time, prepare the sauce. Rinse and dry the cucumber. Melt the butter in a frying pan and cook the cucumber for 2 minutes. Add the wine and boil until it evaporates. Stir in the dill and sour cream and season lightly. Cut the fish into portions. Serve with the sauce, orange slices and salad leaves.

Energy 406kcal/1686kJ; Protein 35g; Carbohydrate 1.5g, of which sugars 1.5g; Fat 26.7g, of which saturates 8.3g; Cholesterol 107mg; Calcium 62mg; Fibre 0.3g; Sodium 123mg.

CHICKEN <u>WITH</u> LEMON <u>AND</u> GARLIC

CHICKEN STRIPS SPICED WITH PAPRIKA MAKE AN UNUSUAL COURSE FOR FOUR, AND ONLY NEED TO BE COOKED AT THE LAST MOMENT. SERVE THEM AS A MAIN COURSE WITH FRIED POTATOES.

Preparation: 3 minutes; Cooking: 3–5 minutes

SERVES TWO TO FOUR

INGREDIENTS

2 skinless chicken breast fillets
30ml/2 tbsp olive oil
1 shallot, finely chopped
4 garlic cloves, finely chopped
5ml/1 tsp paprika
juice of 1 lemon
30ml/2 tbsp chopped fresh parsley
salt and ground black pepper
fresh flat leaf parsley, to garnish
lemon wedges, to serve

VARIATION
For a variation on this dish, try using strips of turkey breast or pork fillet. They need slightly longer cooking. The whites of spring onions (scallions) can replace shallots, and the chopped green tops can be used instead of parsley.

1 Remove the little fillet from the back of each breast portion. If the breast still looks fatter than a finger, bat it with a rolling pin to make it thinner. Slice all the chicken meat into strips.

2 Heat the oil in a large frying pan. Stir-fry the chicken strips with the shallot, garlic and paprika over a high heat for about 3 minutes until cooked through.

3 Add the lemon juice and parsley and season with salt and pepper to taste. Serve hot with lemon wedges, garnished with flat leaf parsley.

COOK'S TIP
Chicken breasts have a little fillet strip that easily becomes detached. Collect these in a bag or container in the freezer for this dish.

Energy 139kcal/580kJ; Protein 18.6g; Carbohydrate 1.5g, of which sugars 1.1g; Fat 6.5g, of which saturates 1g; Cholesterol 53mg; Calcium 33mg; Fibre 0.8g; Sodium 50mg

SOY SAUCE AND STAR ANISE CHICKEN

ALTHOUGH THE CHICKEN COOKS QUICKLY, IT DOES BENEFIT FROM BEING MARINATED FIRST. THIS ONLY TAKES A MOMENT AND THERE'LL BE NO LAST-MINUTE WORK TO DO WHEN GUESTS ARRIVE.

Preparation: 3–4 minutes; Cooking: 16 minutes, plus marinating time (optional)

SERVES FOUR

INGREDIENTS
    4 skinless chicken breast fillets
    2 whole star anise
    45ml/3 tbsp olive oil
    30ml/2 tbsp soy sauce
    ground black pepper

1 Put the chicken breast fillets in a shallow, non-metallic dish and add the star anise.

2 In a small bowl, whisk together the oil and soy sauce and season with black pepper to make a marinade.

3 Pour the marinade over the chicken and stir to coat each breast fillet all over. Cover the dish with clear film (plastic wrap) and set aside for as much time as you have. If you are able to make it ahead, leave the chicken in the marinade for around 6–8 hours as the flavour will be improved. Place the covered dish in the refrigerator.

4 Cook the chicken under the grill (broiler), turning occasionally. It will need about 8 minutes on each side. Serve immediately.

VARIATION
If you prefer, cook on a barbecue. When the coals are dusted with ash, spread them out evenly. Remove the chicken breasts from the marinade and cook for 8 minutes on each side, spooning over the marinade from time to time, until the chicken is cooked through.

Energy 237kcal/992kJ; Protein 36.2g; Carbohydrate 0.6g, of which sugars 0.6g; Fat 9.9g, of which saturates 1.6g; Cholesterol 105mg; Calcium 9mg; Fibre 0g; Sodium 624mg

GINGERED DUCK WITH TAMARI AND MIRIN

DUCK TAKES VERY LITTLE TIME TO COOK ON A GRIDDLE AND TASTES GREAT WITH A TAMARI AND MIRIN GLAZE. IT LOOKS PRETTY ON ITS BED OF PANCAKES, WITH A DELICATE CUCUMBER GARNISH.

Preparation: 4–5 minutes; Cooking: 13 minutes

SERVES FOUR

INGREDIENTS
    4 large duck breast fillets, total
       weight about 675g/1½lb
    5cm/2in piece fresh root ginger,
       finely grated
    ½ large cucumber
    12 Chinese pancakes
    6 spring onions (scallions),
       finely shredded
For the sauce
    105ml/7 tbsp tamari
    105ml/7 tbsp mirin
    25g/1oz/2 tbsp sugar
    salt and ground black pepper

1 Make four slashes in the skin of each duck breast fillet, then lay them skin-side up on a plate. Squeeze the grated ginger over the duck to extract every drop of juice; discard the pulp. Generously rub the juice all over the duck, especially into the slashes.

2 Peel the cucumber in strips, then cut it in half, scoop out the seeds and chop the flesh. Set aside in a bowl.

3 To make the sauce, mix the tamari, mirin and sugar in a heavy pan and heat gently together until the sugar has dissolved. Increase the heat and simmer for 4–5 minutes, or until the sauce has reduced by about one-third and become syrupy.

4 Heat a griddle on the stove over a high heat until a few drops of water sprinkled on to the surface evaporate instantly. Sear the duck breasts, placing them skin-side down.

5 When the fat has been rendered, and the skin is nicely browned, remove the duck from the pan. Drain off the fat and wipe the pan clean with kitchen paper. Reheat it, return the duck flesh side down, and cook over a medium heat for about 3 minutes.

6 Brush on a little of the sauce, turn the duck over, brush the other side with sauce and turn again. This should take about 1 minute, by which time the duck should be cooked rare – you'll know because, when pressed, there should be some give in the flesh. Remove from the pan and let the duck rest for a few minutes before slicing each breast across at an angle.

7 Meanwhile, wrap the pancakes in foil and warm them in a steamer for about 3 minutes. Serve with the duck, sauce, spring onions and cucumber.

COOK'S TIP
To cook on the barbecue, position the duck on the grill rack over a large drip tray. Cook over hot coals, covered with a lid or tented heavy-duty foil.

Energy 436kcal/1829kJ; Protein 38g; Carbohydrate 23.3g, of which sugars 11g; Fat 21.6g, of which saturates 2.2g; Cholesterol 186mg; Calcium 113mg; Fibre 0.7g; Sodium 1615mg

CALF'S LIVER <u>WITH</u> CRISP ONIONS

SAUTÉED OR CREAMY MASHED POTATOES GO WELL WITH FRIED CALF'S LIVER. SERVE WITH A SALAD OF MIXED LEAVES AND FRESH HERBS, TO COMPLEMENT THE SIMPLE FLAVOURS OF THIS MAIN COURSE.

Preparation: 3–4 minutes; Cooking: 16 minutes

SERVES FOUR

INGREDIENTS

50g/2oz/¼ cup butter
4 onions, thinly sliced
5ml/1 tsp caster (superfine) sugar
4 slices calf's liver, each weighing about 115g/4oz
30ml/2 tbsp plain (all-purpose) flour
30ml/2 tbsp olive oil
salt and ground black pepper
parsley, to garnish

1 Melt the butter in a large, heavy-based pan with a lid. Add the onions and mix well to coat with butter. Cover the pan with a tight-fitting lid and cook gently for 10 minutes, stirring occasionally.

2 Stir in the sugar and cover the pan. Cook the onions for 8 minutes more, or until they are soft and golden. Increase the heat, remove the lid and stir the onions over a high heat until they are deep gold and crisp. Use a slotted spoon to remove the onions from the pan, draining off the fat.

3 Meanwhile, rinse the calf's liver in cold water and pat it dry on kitchen paper. Season the flour, put it on a plate and turn the slices of liver in it until they are lightly coated in flour.

COOK'S TIP

Take care not to cook the liver for too long as this may cause it to toughen.

4 Heat the oil in a large frying pan, add the liver and cook for about 2 minutes on each side, or until lightly browned and just firm. Arrange the liver on warmed plates, with the crisp onions. Garnish with parsley and serve with sautéed or mashed potatoes.

Energy 315kcal/1310kJ; Protein 22.7g; Carbohydrate 11.8g, of which sugars 4.4g; Fat 19.9g, of which saturates 8.5g; Cholesterol 452mg; Calcium 39mg; Fibre 1.3g; Sodium 160mg

CUMIN- AND CORIANDER-RUBBED LAMB

WHEN SUMMER SIZZLES, TURN UP THE HEAT A LITTLE MORE WITH THESE SPICY LAMB CHOPS.
IF YOU HAVE TIME, MARINATE THE CHOPS FOR AN HOUR OR MORE — THEY WILL TASTE EVEN BETTER.
Preparation: 3 minutes; Cooking: 10 minutes. I hour's marinating time recommended

SERVES FOUR

INGREDIENTS
  30ml/2 tbsp ground cumin
  30ml/2 tbsp ground coriander
  30ml/2 tbsp olive oil
  8 lamb chops
  salt and ground black pepper

VARIATION
To make ginger- and garlic-rubbed
pork, use pork chops instead of lamb
chops and substitute the cumin and
coriander with ground ginger and
crushed garlic. Increase the cooking time
to 7–8 minutes each side.

1 Prepare a barbecue or preheat the
grill (broiler). Mix the cumin, coriander
and oil in a bowl, beating with a spoon
until a smooth paste is formed. Season
with salt and pepper.

2 Rub the mixture all over the lamb
chops. Cook the chops for 5 minutes
on each side, until lightly charred on
the outside but still pink in the centre.
Serve immediately.

Energy 494kcal/2059kJ; Protein 55.6g; Carbohydrate 0g, of which sugars 0g; Fat 30.1g, of which saturates 12.6g; Cholesterol 220mg; Calcium 18mg; Fibre 0g; Sodium 150mg

THAI-STYLE RARE BEEF AND MANGO SALAD

RARE BEEF AND JUICY MANGOES — A MARRIAGE MADE IN HEAVEN. COME DOWN TO EARTH BY SERVING THE SALAD WITH A MIXTURE OF SLIGHTLY BITTER LEAVES IN A LEMON AND OIL DRESSING.

Preparation: 2 minutes; Cooking: 18 minutes; Marinating for 2 hours recommended

SERVES FOUR

INGREDIENTS
   450g/1lb sirloin steak
   45ml/3 tbsp garlic-infused olive oil
   45ml/3 tbsp soy sauce
   2 mangoes, peeled, stoned (pitted)
     and finely sliced
   ground black pepper

COOK'S TIP
This is a simplified version of the classic Thai beef salad which usually comes with a vast array of chopped vegetables. If you want to add a complement to this delicious no-fuss version, set out little bowls of fresh coriander (cilantro) leaves, chopped spring onions (scallions) and peanuts, for sprinkling.

1 Put the steak in a shallow, non-metallic dish and pour over the oil and soy sauce. Season with pepper and turn the steaks to coat them in the marinade. Marinate for at least 10 minutes; longer if you can spare the time. Two hours in a covered bowl in the refrigerator would be ideal.

2 Heat a griddle until hot. Remove the steak from the marinade and place on the griddle. Cook for 3–5 minutes on each side, moving the steak halfway through if you want a criss-cross pattern.

3 Transfer the steak to a board and leave to rest for 2 minutes. Meanwhile, heat the marinade in a pan. Cook for a few seconds, then remove from the heat. Slice the steak thinly and arrange on four serving plates with the mangoes. Drizzle over the pan juices to serve.

Energy 286kcal/1200kJ; Protein 27.4g; Carbohydrate 14.7g, of which sugars 14.4g; Fat 13.5g, of which saturates 3.5g; Cholesterol 57mg; Calcium 19mg; Fibre 2.6g; Sodium 615mg

VEAL ᵂᴵᵀᴴ ANCHOVIES ᴬᴺᴰ MOZZARELLA

SCALOPPINE ARE THIN ESCALOPES OF VEAL CUT ACROSS THE GRAIN. FOR THIS DISH, THEY ARE ROLLED AROUND A RICH ANCHOVY, TOMATO AND MOZZARELLA FILLING AND SERVED WITH A MARSALA SAUCE.

Preparation: 6 minutes; Cooking: 12 minutes

SERVES SIX

INGREDIENTS
50g/2oz/¼ cup unsalted
(sweet) butter
50g/2oz can anchovies
4 fresh tomatoes, peeled
and chopped
30ml/2 tbsp chopped fresh flat
leaf parsley
6 veal escalopes (scallops), about
100g/3¾oz each
200g/7oz mozzarella cheese, cut in
thin slices
30ml/2 tbsp olive oil
175ml/6fl oz/¾ cup Marsala or
medium dry sherry
30–45ml/2–3 tbsp whipping cream
salt and ground black pepper
fresh herbs, to garnish
cooked pasta, to serve

VARIATIONS
For a more defined flavour, try smoked mozzarella, Provolone or Bel Paese instead of regular mozzarella. If you prefer not to eat veal, substitute thinly sliced pork escalopes or turkey steaks. They will cook in roughly the same amount of time.

1 Melt half the butter in a small pan. Drain the anchovies and add them to the pan. Cook gently, stirring with a wooden spoon, until they break down to a pulp. Stir in the tomatoes and cook for about 3 minutes until they have softened and reduced. Transfer to a bowl, cool, then stir in the parsley.

2 Place each veal escalope in turn between two sheets of baking parchment and beat with a mallet or rolling pin until thin. Spread the escalopes out on a board and sprinkle with ground black pepper. Divide the anchovy and tomato mixture among them, leaving the edges free.

3 Top with the slices of cheese. Fold the long edges of each escalope towards the centre, then bring up the sides to form a neat parcel. Secure with kitchen string or cocktail sticks (toothpicks).

4 Heat the remaining butter with the oil in a large frying pan. Brown the rolled escalopes, then pour in the Marsala or sherry. Cook, uncovered, for 5 minutes or until the Marsala or sherry has reduced and thickened.

5 Transfer the rolls to a serving plate, stir the pan juices to incorporate any sediment, then pour in the cream. Reheat without boiling, then strain over the rolls. Garnish with fresh herbs and serve with tagliatelle, linguine or any other flat ribbon noodles.

Energy 367kcal/1529kJ; Protein 31.7g; Carbohydrate 4g, of which sugars 4g; Fat 22g, of which saturates 11.5g; Cholesterol 100mg; Calcium 161mg; Fibre 0.7g; Sodium 584mg

ESCALOPES OF VEAL WITH CREAM SAUCE

THIS QUICK, EASY DISH IS DELICIOUS SERVED WITH BUTTERED TAGLIATELLE AND LIGHTLY STEAMED GREEN VEGETABLES. IT WORKS JUST AS WELL WITH TURKEY ESCALOPES.

Preparation: 2–3 minutes; Cooking: 15–17 minutes

SERVES FOUR

INGREDIENTS

15ml/1 tbsp plain flour
4 veal escalopes (scallops),
 about 75–115g/3–4oz each
30ml/2 tbsp sunflower oil
1 shallot, chopped
150g/5oz/2 cups oyster
 mushrooms, sliced
30ml/2 tbsp Marsala or
 medium-dry sherry
200ml/7fl oz/scant 1 cup crème
 fraîche or sour cream
30ml/2 tbsp chopped fresh tarragon
salt and ground black pepper

COOK'S TIP
If they are too thick, flatten the escalopes (scallops) with a rolling pin. It'll help to cut down the cooking time.

1 Season the flour and use to dust the veal, then set the meat aside.

2 Heat the oil in a large frying pan and cook the shallot and mushrooms for 5 minutes. Add the escalopes and cook over a high heat for about 1½ minutes on each side. Pour in the Marsala or sherry and cook until reduced by half.

3 Use a spatula to remove the veal escalopes from the pan. Stir the crème fraîche, tarragon and seasoning into the juices remaining in the pan and simmer gently for 3–5 minutes, or until the sauce is thick and creamy.

4 Return the escalopes to the pan and heat through for 1 minute before serving.

Energy 377kcal/1567kJ; Protein 25.1g; Carbohydrate 5.9g, of which sugars 2.5g; Fat 27.5g, of which saturates 14.9g; Cholesterol 108mg; Calcium 45mg; Fibre 0.8g; Sodium 75mg

EATING
AL FRESCO

It's true what they say, food really does taste better out of doors. Fresh air hones the appetite, but

that's not the only reason we enjoy al fresco meals so much. It is also the relaxed atmosphere.

Schedules tend to slip as we sit in the sun, and if the fire burns a little more slowly than

expected, or someone has to go back to the kitchen to fetch a forgotten dressing, never mind. The

same laid-back approach applies to the recipes in this chapter. They still fulfil the "quick and

easy" brief, with the actual cooking kept to the shortest possible time, but someone will still have

to fire up the barbecue and put out the garden chairs. Unless, of course, you opt for food that

doesn't need cooking at all, like the divinely delicious Tortilla Cones with Smoked Salmon.

Alternatively, choose a dish that can be baked in the oven, while you serve an appetizer like

Summer Vegetable Kebabs with Harissa. In one or two of the recipes, some advance preparation

would be helpful, though not essential. A marinade might be suggested, or a spicy rub. Always

read recipes right through to see if this applies, but the recipes will work just as well without them.

SWEET PEPPERS STUFFED WITH TWO CHEESES

A DELICIOUS BARBECUE STARTER TO COOK BEFORE THE GRILL TASTES TOO STRONGLY OF MEAT.
ALTERNATIVELY, USE A DISPOSABLE BARBECUE FOR THESE TASTY PEPPERS.

Preparation: 5 minutes; Cooking: 12–14 minutes

SERVES FOUR

INGREDIENTS
    4 sweet romano peppers, preferably
      in mixed colours, total weight about
      350g/12oz
    90ml/6 tbsp extra virgin olive oil
    200g/7oz mozzarella cheese
    10 drained bottled sweet cherry
      peppers, finely chopped
    115g/4oz ricotta salata
    30ml/2 tbsp chopped fresh
      oregano leaves
    24 black olives
    2 garlic cloves, crushed
    salt and ground black pepper
    dressed mixed salad leaves and
      bread, to serve

1 Prepare a barbecue. Split the peppers lengthways and remove the seeds and membrane. Rub 15ml/1 tbsp of the oil all over the peppers. Place them hollow-side uppermost.

2 Slice the mozzarella and divide it equally among the pepper halves.

3 Sprinkle over the chopped cherry peppers, season lightly and crumble the ricotta salata over the top, followed by the oregano leaves and olives. Mix the garlic with the remaining oil and add a little salt and pepper. Spoon about half the mixture over the filling in the peppers.

4 Once the flames have died down, rake the coals to one side. Position a lightly oiled grill rack over the coals to heat. When the coals are medium-hot, or with a moderate coating of ash, place the filled peppers on the section of grill rack that is not over the coals.

5 Cover with a lid, or improvise with a wok lid or tented heavy-duty foil. Grill for 6 minutes, then spoon the remaining oil mixture over the filling, replace the lid and continue to grill for 6–8 minutes more, or until the peppers are lightly charred and the cheese has melted. Serve with a dressed green or leafy salad and bread.

VARIATION
The peppers can be cooked on a griddle if you prefer. It is a good idea to blanch them in boiling water before filling, to give them a head start.

Energy 371kcal/1532kJ; Protein 13.1g; Carbohydrate 6.6g, of which sugars 6.3g; Fat 32.6g, of which saturates 12.2g; Cholesterol 41mg; Calcium 203mg; Fibre 2g; Sodium 484mg

SUMMER VEGETABLE KEBABS WITH HARISSA

EATING IN THE GARDEN IS ONE OF THE PLEASURES OF SUMMER. THIS WOULD BE LOVELY FOR LUNCH OR AS AN APPETIZER FOR GUESTS TO NIBBLE WHILE WAITING FOR MORE FILLING BARBECUE FARE.

Preparation: 7 minutes; Cooking: 8–10 minutes

SERVES FOUR

INGREDIENTS
   60ml/4 tbsp olive oil
   juice of ½ lemon
   1 garlic clove, crushed
   5ml/1 tsp ground coriander
   5ml/1 tsp ground cinnamon
   10ml/2 tsp clear honey
   2 aubergines (eggplants), part peeled
      and cut into chunks
   2 courgettes (zucchini), cut
      into chunks
   2–3 red or green (bell) peppers,
      seeded and cut into chunks
   12–16 cherry tomatoes
   4 small red onions, quartered
   5ml/1 tsp salt
For the harissa and yogurt dip
   450g/1lb/2 cups Greek (US strained
      plain) yogurt
   30–60ml/2–4 tbsp harissa
   a small bunch of fresh coriander
      (cilantro), finely chopped
   a small bunch of mint, finely chopped
   salt and ground black pepper

1 Preheat the grill (broiler) or prepare a barbecue. Mix the olive oil, lemon juice and garlic in a bowl. Add ground coriander, cinnamon, honey and salt.

2 Add the aubergine and courgette chunks, with the peppers, cherry tomatoes and onion quarters. Stir to mix, then thread a generous number of vegetable pieces on to skewers, so that they are just touching each other.

3 Cook the kebabs under the grill or over the coals, turning occasionally until the vegetables are browned all over.

4 Meanwhile, make the dip. Put the yogurt in a bowl and beat in harissa to taste. Add most of the coriander and mint, reserving a little to garnish, and season well with salt and pepper.

5 As soon as the kebabs are cooked, serve on a bed of couscous and sprinkle with the remaining fresh coriander. Spoon a little of the yogurt dip on the side, and put the rest in a small serving bowl.

COOK'S TIP
As well as being a quick-cook aid, metal skewers enhance presentation tremendously.

Energy 305kcal/1267kJ; Protein 9.9g; Carbohydrate 24.8g, of which sugars 22.6g; Fat 19.1g, of which saturates 6.6g; Cholesterol 16mg; Calcium 230mg; Fibre 5.2g; Sodium 181mg

Mini Mozzarella Ciabatta Pizzas

IF EVER THERE'S AN ARGUMENT ABOUT WHOSE TURN IT IS TO MAKE LUNCH, VOLUNTEER TO COOK THESE DELICIOUS MINI CIABATTA PIZZAS. THEY'RE PERFECT FOR TAKING ON A PICNIC.

Preparation: 4 minutes; Cooking: 12–15 minutes

SERVES EIGHT

INGREDIENTS
2 red (bell) peppers
2 yellow (bell) peppers
1 loaf ciabatta bread
8 slices prosciutto or other
   thinly sliced ham, cut into
   thick strips
150g/5oz mozzarella cheese
ground black pepper
tiny basil leaves, to garnish

1 Preheat a grill (broiler). Grill (broil) the peppers, skin sides uppermost, until they are charred. Place them in a bowl, cover and leave for 5 minutes.

2 Cut the bread into eight thick slices and toast both sides until golden.

3 As soon as the roasted peppers are cool enough to touch, remove the skins, cut them into thick strips and arrange them on the toasted bread with the strips of ham.

4 Thinly slice the mozzarella cheese and arrange on top. Grind over plenty of black pepper. Place under the hot grill for 2–3 minutes until the cheese topping is bubbling and golden.

5 Arrange the fresh basil leaves on top and transfer to a serving dish or platter. Leave the cheese to cool for a few minutes, if serving the mini ciabatta pizzas to children.

Energy 154kcal/647kJ; Protein 8.6g; Carbohydrate 18.7g, of which sugars 6.2g; Fat 5.4g, of which saturates 2.9g; Cholesterol 16mg; Calcium 106mg; Fibre 2g; Sodium 325mg

TORTILLA CONES WITH SMOKED SALMON

SOPHISTICATED YET SIMPLE, THESE SALMON-FILLED TORTILLAS ALWAYS GO DOWN WELL. MAKE THEM SLIGHTLY AHEAD OF TIME, OR JUST SET OUT THE INGREDIENTS FOR A DIY PICNIC SNACK.

Preparation: 8 minutes; Cooking: 0 minutes

MAKES EIGHT

INGREDIENTS
   115g/4oz/½ cup soft white
     (farmer's) cheese
   30ml/2 tbsp roughly chopped
     fresh dill
   juice of 1 lemon
   1 small red onion
   15ml/1 tbsp drained bottled capers
   30ml/2 tbsp extra virgin olive oil
   30ml/2 tbsp roughly chopped fresh
     flat leaf parsley
   115g/4oz smoked salmon
   8 small wheat flour tortillas
   salt and ground black pepper
   lemon wedges, for squeezing

1 Place the soft cheese in a bowl and mix in half the chopped dill. Add a little salt and pepper and a dash of the lemon juice to taste. Reserve the remaining lemon juice in a separate mixing bowl.

2 Finely chop the red onion. Add the onion, capers and olive oil to the lemon juice in the mixing bowl. Add the chopped flat leaf parsley and the remaining dill and stir gently to mix the ingredients.

VARIATION
Tortilla cones can be filled with a variety of delicious ingredients. Try soft cheese with red pesto and chopped sun-dried tomatoes, or mackerel pâté with slices of cucumber.

3 Cut the smoked salmon into short, thin strips and add to the red onion mixture. Toss to mix. Season to taste with plenty of black pepper.

COOK'S TIP
If you use salted capers in this dish, rather than the unsalted variety, rinse them thoroughly before using.

4 Spread a little of the soft cheese mixture on each tortilla and top with the smoked salmon mixture.

5 Roll up the tortillas into cones and secure with wooden cocktail sticks (toothpicks). Arrange on a serving plate and add some lemon wedges, for squeezing. Serve immediately.

Energy 154kcal/645kJ; Protein 6.7g; Carbohydrate 14.5g, of which sugars 0.7g; Fat 8.1g, of which saturates 3.3g; Cholesterol 18mg; Calcium 50mg; Fibre 0.8g; Sodium 383mg

HOT SMOKED SALMON

THIS IS A FANTASTIC WAY OF SMOKING SALMON ON A BARBECUE IN NO TIME AT ALL. THE MOJO MAKES A MILDLY SPICY COMPANION.

Preparation: 5 minutes; Cooking: 11–13 minutes, plus soaking

SERVES 6

INGREDIENTS
    6 salmon fillets, each about
        175g/6oz, with skin
    15ml/1 tbsp sunflower oil
    salt and ground black pepper
    2 handfuls hickory wood chips,
        soaked in cold water for as much
        time as you have available,
        preferably 30 minutes
For the mojo
    1 ripe mango, diced
    4 drained canned pineapple
        slices, diced
    1 small red onion, finely chopped
    1 fresh long mild red chilli, seeded
        and finely chopped
    15ml/1 tbsp good quality sweet
        chilli sauce
    grated rind and juice of 1 lime
    leaves from 1 small lemon basil
        plant or 45ml/3 tbsp fresh
        coriander (cilantro) leaves,
        shredded or chopped

1 First, make the mojo by putting the mango, diced pineapple, chopped onion, and seeded and chopped chilli together in a bowl.

2 Add the chilli sauce, lime rind and juice, and the herb leaves. Stir to mix well. Cover tightly and leave in a cool place until needed.

3 Rinse the salmon fillets and pat dry, then brush each with a little oil.

4 Place the fillets skin side down on a lightly oiled grill rack over medium-hot coals. Cover the barbecue with a lid or tented heavy-duty foil and cook the fish for 3–5 minutes.

5 Drain the hickory chips into a colander and sprinkle about a third of them as evenly as possible over the coals. Carefully drop them through the slats in the grill racks, taking care not to scatter the ash as you do so.

6 Replace the barbecue cover and continue cooking for a further 8 minutes, adding a small handful of hickory chips twice more during this time. Serve the salmon hot or cold, with the mojo.

COOK'S TIP
When sweet pineapples are in season, you may prefer to use fresh ones in the mojo. You will need about half a medium pineapple. Slice off the skin, remove the core and cut the flesh into chunks.

Energy 364kcal/1519kJ; Protein 35.9g; Carbohydrate 7.8g, of which sugars 7.4g; Fat 21.2g, of which saturates 3.6g; Cholesterol 88mg; Calcium 58mg; Fibre 1.3g; Sodium 82mg

FIERY CHICKEN WINGS WITH BLOOD ORANGES

THIS IS A GREAT RECIPE FOR THE BARBECUE — IT IS QUICK AND EASY, AND BEST EATEN WITH THE FINGERS. THE ORANGES CAN BE COOKED SEPARATELY OR WITH THE WINGS.

Preparation: 3 minutes; Cooking: 10 minutes

SERVES FOUR

INGREDIENTS
  60ml/4 tbsp fiery harissa
  30ml/2 tbsp olive oil
  16–20 chicken wings
  4 blood oranges, quartered
  icing (confectioners') sugar
  a small bunch of fresh coriander
    (cilantro), chopped
  salt

COOK'S TIP
Try making your own harissa if you have a blender. You will need 6–8 dried red chillies, 2 crushed garlic cloves, 2.5ml/ ½ tsp salt, 5ml/1 tsp ground cumin, 2.5ml/½ tsp ground coriander and 120ml/ 4fl oz/1 cup olive oil. Blend to a paste. To store, spoon into a jar and cover with olive oil. It will keep for 1 month.

1 Mix the harissa with the olive oil in a small bowl, or, if using home-made harissa, simply measure the required amount into a bowl. Add a little salt and stir to combine. Brush this mixture over the chicken wings so that they are well coated. Cook the wings on a hot barbecue or under a hot grill (broiler) for 5 minutes on each side.

2 Once the wings begin to cook, dip the orange quarters lightly in icing sugar and grill (broil) them for a few minutes, until they are slightly burnt but not blackened. If you thread them on to skewers, it will be easier to turn them under the heat. Serve the chicken wings immediately with the oranges, sprinkled with a little chopped fresh coriander.

Energy 658kcal/2758kJ; Protein 61.9g; Carbohydrate 21.8g, of which sugars 20.7g; Fat 36.7g, of which saturates 10.1g; Cholesterol 264mg; Calcium 163mg; Fibre 2.6g; Sodium 866mg

PORK KEBABS WITH BBQ SAUCE

USE PORK FILLET FOR THESE KEBABS BECAUSE IT IS LEAN AND TENDER, AND COOKS VERY QUICKLY. THE KEBABS ARE GOOD SERVED WITH RICE, OR IN WARMED PITTA BREAD WITH LETTUCE.

Preparation: 3–4 minutes; Cooking: 10 minutes

SERVES FOUR

INGREDIENTS

    500g/1¼lb lean pork fillet
      (tenderloin)
    8 large, thick spring onions
      (scallions)
    120ml/4fl oz/½ cup barbecue sauce
    1 lemon

VARIATION

This is an unusual kebab recipe, in that the cubes of pork are only threaded on to the skewers after cooking. This is because the meat is regularly dipped in glaze, and it is easier to get an all-round coating if the cubes of pork are free. If you prefer to assemble the skewers first and cook them on the barbecue, do so. Use metal skewers that will not char, and baste frequently with the sauce.

1 Cut the pork into 2.5cm/1in cubes. Cut the spring onions into 2.5cm/1in-long sticks.

2 Preheat the grill (broiler) to high. Oil the wire rack and spread out the pork cubes on it. Grill (broil) the pork until the juices drip, then dip the pieces in the barbecue sauce and put back on the grill. Grill until cooked through, repeating the dipping process twice more. Set aside and keep warm.

3 Trim the spring onions and gently grill until soft and slightly brown on the outside. Do not dip in the barbecue sauce. Thread about four pieces of pork and three spring onion pieces on to each of eight bamboo skewers.

4 Arrange the skewers on a platter. Cut the lemon into wedges and squeeze a little lemon juice over each skewer. Serve immediately, offering the remaining lemon wedges separately.

Energy 192kcal/806kJ; Protein 27.6g; Carbohydrate 9.2g, of which sugars 8.8g; Fat 5.1g, of which saturates 1.8g; Cholesterol 79mg; Calcium 21mg; Fibre 0.6g; Sodium 578mg

PORK <u>ON</u> LEMON GRASS STICKS

THESE MAKE A SUBSTANTIAL SNACK, EITHER ON THEIR OWN OR AS PART OF A BARBECUE MENU. THE LEMON GRASS STICKS NOT ONLY ADD A SUBTLE FLAVOUR BUT ARE ALSO A GOOD TALKING POINT.

Preparation: 6 minutes; Cooking: 6–8 minutes

SERVES FOUR

INGREDIENTS
- 300g/11oz/1½ cups minced (ground) pork
- 4 garlic cloves, crushed
- 4 fresh coriander (cilantro) roots, finely chopped
- 2.5ml/½ tsp granulated sugar
- 15ml/1 tbsp soy sauce
- salt and ground black pepper
- 8 x 10cm/4in lengths lemon grass stalk
- sweet chilli sauce, to serve

VARIATION
Slimmer versions of these pork sticks are perfect for parties. The mixture will be enough for 12 lemon grass sticks if you use it sparingly.

1 Place the minced pork, crushed garlic, chopped coriander root, sugar and soy sauce in a large bowl. Season with salt and pepper to taste and mix well.

2 Divide into eight portions and mould each one into a ball. It may help to dampen your hands before shaping the mixture, to prevent it from sticking.

3 Stick a length of lemon grass halfway into each ball, then press the meat mixture around the lemon grass to make a shape like a chicken leg.

4 Cook the pork sticks under a hot grill (broiler) for 3–4 minutes on each side, until golden and cooked through. Serve with the chilli sauce for dipping.

Energy 132kcal/552kJ; Protein 14.7g; Carbohydrate 2g, of which sugars 1.6g; Fat 7.3g, of which saturates 2.7g; Cholesterol 50mg; Calcium 10mg; Fibre 0.2g; Sodium 317mg

BARBECUED LAMB <u>WITH</u> RED PEPPER SALSA

VIBRANT RED PEPPER SALSA BRINGS OUT THE BEST IN SUCCULENT LAMB STEAKS TO MAKE A DISH THAT LOOKS AS GOOD AS IT TASTES. SERVE A SELECTION OF SALADS AND CRUSTY BREAD WITH THE LAMB.

Preparation: 3 minutes; Cooking: 4–10 minutes; Marinating for 24 hours recommended

SERVES SIX

INGREDIENTS

6 lamb steaks
about 15g/½oz/½ cup fresh
  rosemary sprigs
2 garlic cloves, sliced
60ml/4 tbsp olive oil
30ml/2 tbsp maple syrup
salt and ground black pepper
For the salsa
200g/7oz red (bell) peppers,
  roasted, peeled, seeded
  and chopped
1 garlic clove, crushed
15ml/1 tbsp chopped chives
30ml/2 tbsp extra virgin olive oil
fresh flat leaf parsley, to garnish

1 Place the lamb steaks in a dish and season with salt and pepper. Pull the leaves off the rosemary and sprinkle them over the meat.

2 Add the slices of garlic, then drizzle the olive oil and maple syrup over the top. Cover and chill until ready to cook. If you have time, the lamb can be left to marinate in the fridge for up to 24 hours.

3 Make sure the steaks are liberally coated with the marinating ingredients, then cook them over a hot barbecue for 2–5 minutes on each side. The cooking time depends on the heat of the barbecue coals and the thickness of the steaks as well as the result required – rare, medium or well cooked.

4 While the lamb steaks are cooking, mix together all the ingredients for the salsa in a bowl. Serve the salsa spooned on to the plates with the meat or in a small serving dish on the side. Garnish the lamb with sprigs of flat leaf parsley and serve with a cool, crisp salad – iceberg lettuce would be ideal.

Energy 390kcal/1627kJ; Protein 44.1g; Carbohydrate 2.1g, of which sugars 2g; Fat 22.8g, of which saturates 6.8g; Cholesterol 158mg; Calcium 33mg; Fibre 0.5g; Sodium 106mg

PITTAS WITH SPICED LAMB KOFTAS

WHEN YOU ARE EATING AL FRESCO, A BITE IN THE HAND IS WORTH TWO ON THE PLATE. HARISSA GIVES THE LAMB KOFTAS A MILDLY FIERY FLAVOUR, EASILY TAMED BY A TRICKLE OF YOGURT.

Preparation: 10 minutes; Cooking: 10 minutes

SERVES FOUR

INGREDIENTS

 450g/1lb/2 cups minced
   (ground) lamb
 1 small onion, finely chopped
 10ml/2 tsp harissa paste
 8 pitta breads, salad vegetables,
   mint and yogurt, to serve
 salt and ground black pepper

1 Prepare a barbecue. Soak eight wooden skewers in cold water for 10 minutes.

2 Meanwhile, put the lamb in a large bowl and add the onion and harissa. Mix well to combine, and season with plenty of salt and pepper.

VARIATION
Instead of adding mint leaves and yogurt separately to the pittas, spoon in some tzatziki, made by mixing finely diced cucumber, spring onions (scallions) and crushed garlic with Greek (US strained plain) yogurt.

3 Divide the mixture into eight equal pieces and press on to the skewers in a sausage shape to make the koftas.

4 Cook the skewered koftas for about 10 minutes, turning occasionally, until cooked through.

5 Warm the pitta breads on the barbecue grill, then split. Place a kofta in each one, and remove the skewer. Add some cucumber and tomato slices, mint leaves and a drizzle of natural (plain) yogurt.

Energy 609kcal/2568kJ; Protein 35.3g; Carbohydrate 83.8g, of which sugars 5.4g; Fat 17g, of which saturates 7.3g; Cholesterol 87mg; Calcium 230mg; Fibre 3.8g; Sodium 737mg

STEAK CIABATTA WITH HUMMUS AND SALAD

PACKED WITH GARLICKY HUMMUS AND A MUSTARD-SEASONED DRESSING ON THE CRUNCHY SALAD,
THESE STEAK SANDWICHES ARE JUST RIGHT FOR LUNCH ON THE PATIO.
Preparation: 5 minutes; Cooking: 6−9 minutes

SERVES FOUR

INGREDIENTS
   3 garlic cloves, crushed to a
      paste with enough salt to season
      the steaks
   30ml/2 tbsp extra virgin olive oil
   4 sirloin steaks, 2.5cm/1in thick,
      total weight about 900g/2lb
   2 romaine lettuce hearts
   4 small ciabatta breads
   salt and ground black pepper
For the dressing
   10ml/2 tsp Dijon mustard
   5ml/1 tsp cider or white wine vinegar
   15ml/1 tbsp olive oil
For the hummus
   400g/14oz can chickpeas, drained
      and rinsed
   45ml/3 tbsp tahini
   2 garlic cloves, crushed
   juice of 1 lemon
   30ml/2 tbsp water

1 To make the hummus, place the chickpeas in a large bowl and mash to a paste. Add the tahini, garlic, lemon juice, salt and pepper. Stir in the water. Mash together well.

2 Make a dressing by mixing the mustard and vinegar in a jar. Add the oil and season to taste. Shake well.

3 Mix the garlic and oil in a dish. Add the steaks and rub the mixture into both surfaces.

4 Preheat the grill (broiler). Cook the steaks on a rack in a grill pan. For rare meat, allow 2 minutes on one side and 3 minutes on the second side. For medium steaks, allow 4 minutes on each side. Transfer to a plate, cover and rest for 2 minutes.

5 Dress the lettuce. Split each ciabatta and heat on the grill rack for a minute. Fill with hummus, the steaks and leaves. Cut each in half and serve immediately, just as they are.

Energy 765kcal/3210kJ; Protein 69.8g; Carbohydrate 55.2g, of which sugars 2.8g; Fat 30.8g, of which saturates 7.4g; Cholesterol 115mg; Calcium 222mg; Fibre 6.7g; Sodium 783mg

ON THE SIDE

Most vegetables benefit from being cooked in the shortest possible time, especially if they are

young and tender. Their glowing colours make any dish in which they feature look good, and

there are so many varieties of vegetable that you can cook a different dish every night and never

get bored. When you are in a hurry, it is better to cook just one vegetable accompaniment well,

than to get all steamed up — both literally and figuratively — by trying to offer a selection.

This chapter introduces some intriguing and innovative recipes, from Broccoli with Soy Sauce

and Sesame Seeds to Turnip Salad in Sour Cream. There are hot and cold dishes in a range of

textures, so you can choose whatever will best complement whatever else you are serving.

For freshness and great taste, buy vegetables that have been grown close to where you live,

from organic growers and farmer's markets if you can.

SAUTÉED HERB SALAD WITH CHILLI AND LEMON

FIRM-LEAFED FRESH HERBS, SUCH AS FLAT LEAF PARSLEY AND MINT TOSSED IN A LITTLE OLIVE OIL AND SEASONED WITH SALT, ARE FABULOUS WITH SPICY KEBABS OR STEAKS.

Preparation: 4–5 minutes; Cooking: 2 minutes

SERVES FOUR

INGREDIENTS
- a large bunch of flat leaf parsley
- a large bunch of mint
- a large bunch of fresh coriander (cilantro)
- a bunch of rocket (arugula)
- a large bunch of spinach leaves, about 115g/4oz
- 60–75ml/4–5 tbsp olive oil
- 2 garlic cloves, finely chopped
- 1 fresh green or red chilli, seeded and finely chopped
- ½ preserved lemon, finely chopped
- salt and ground black pepper
- 45–60ml/3–4 tbsp Greek (US strained plain) yogurt, to serve

1 Roughly chop the herbs and combine with the rocket and spinach. Heat the olive oil in a wide, heavy pan. Stir in the garlic and chilli, and fry until they begin to colour. Toss in the herbs and leaves and cook gently, until they begin to wilt.

2 Add the preserved lemon and season to taste. Serve warm with yogurt.

VARIATION
Flavour the yogurt with crushed garlic, if you like.

Energy 142kcal/585kJ; Protein 3.6g; Carbohydrate 3.1g, of which sugars 2.7g; Fat 12.9g, of which saturates 2.1g; Cholesterol 2mg; Calcium 216mg; Fibre 4.4g; Sodium 82mg

BROCCOLI WITH SOY SAUCE AND SESAME SEEDS

THE BEST WAY TO COOK BROCCOLI IS TO FRY IT QUICKLY IN A WOK, SO THAT THE RICH COLOUR AND CRUNCHY TEXTURE IS RETAINED. SOY SAUCE AND SESAME SEEDS ADD TO THE FLAVOUR.

Preparation: 2 minutes; Cooking: 3–4 minutes

SERVES TWO

INGREDIENTS
  225g/8oz purple sprouting broccoli
  15ml/1 tbsp sesame seeds
  15ml/1 tbsp olive oil
  15ml/1 tbsp soy sauce
  salt and ground black pepper

VARIATION
Purple sprouting broccoli has been used for this recipe. This vegetable is at its best when in season during early spring, so finding a good crop may not always be easy during the rest of the year. When it is not available, an ordinary variety of broccoli, such as calabrese, will also work very well. Or you could substitute the broccoli altogether for Chinese leaves, which offer just as much crunch.

1 Using a sharp knife, cut off and discard any thick stems from the broccoli and cut the broccoli into long, thin florets.

2 Spread out the sesame seeds in a small frying pan and dry-fry over a medium heat until toasted. Do not leave them unattended as they will readily burn if left just a fraction too long.

3 Heat the olive oil in a wok or large frying pan and add the broccoli. Stir-fry for 3–4 minutes, or until tender, adding a splash of water if the pan becomes too dry.

4 Add the soy sauce to the broccoli, then season with salt and ground black pepper to taste. Add sesame seeds, toss to combine and serve immediately.

Energy 135kcal/558kJ; Protein 6.6g; Carbohydrate 2.7g, of which sugars 2.3g; Fat 10.9g, of which saturates 1.7g; Cholesterol 0mg; Calcium 115mg; Fibre 3.5g; Sodium 545mg

WILTED SPINACH <u>WITH</u> RICE <u>AND</u> DILL

SPINACH AND RICE MAKES A VERY SUCCESSFUL COMBINATION. THIS IS A DELICIOUS DISH THAT CAN BE MADE IN VERY LITTLE TIME. SERVE IT SOLO OR WITH FRIED OR GRILLED FISH.

Preparation: 4 minutes; Cooking: 13 minutes

SERVES FOUR

INGREDIENTS

675g/1½lb fresh spinach, trimmed
  of any hard stalks
105ml/7 tbsp extra virgin olive oil
1 large onion, chopped
juice of ½ lemon
150ml/¼ pint/⅔ cup water
115g/4oz/generous ½ cup
  long grain rice
45ml/3 tbsp chopped fresh dill,
  plus extra sprigs to garnish
salt and ground black pepper

1 Thoroughly wash the spinach in several changes of cold water until clean, then drain it in a colander. Shake off the excess water and put the spinach leaves on a board. Shred them coarsely.

2 Heat the olive oil in a large pan and sauté the onion until translucent. Add the spinach and stir for a few minutes to coat it with the oil.

VARIATION
Baby broad (fava) beans go well with the rice and spinach. Add them to the rice for the final 5 minutes or so.

3 As soon as the spinach looks wilted, add the lemon juice and the measured water and bring to the boil. Add the rice and half of the dill, then cover and cook gently for about 10 minutes or until the rice is cooked to your taste.

4 Spoon into a serving dish and sprinkle the sprigs of dill over the top.

Energy 337kcal/1392kJ; Protein 7.5g; Carbohydrate 29.6g, of which sugars 5.3g; Fat 20.8g, of which saturates 2.9g; Cholesterol 0mg; Calcium 305mg; Fibre 4.3g; Sodium 238mg

CAULIFLOWER <u>WITH</u> EGG <u>AND</u> LEMON

ALTHOUGH CAULIFLOWER HAS SHRUGGED OFF ITS IMAGE AS THE VEGETABLE MOST PEOPLE LOVE TO HATE, IT STILL NEEDS A BIT OF A MAKEOVER NOW AND THEN.

Preparation: 2–3 minutes; Cooking: 12 minutes

SERVES FOUR

INGREDIENTS
75–90ml/5–6 tbsp extra virgin
   olive oil
1 medium cauliflower, divided into
   large florets
2 eggs
juice of 1 lemon
5ml/1 tsp cornflour (cornstarch),
   mixed to a cream with a little
   cold water
30ml/2 tbsp chopped fresh flat
   leaf parsley
salt

VARIATION
This delightful, summery style of
cooking cauliflower is popular in the
Mediterranean. It works equally well with
a close relative, broccoli. Divide the
broccoli into small florets and cook for
slightly less time than the cauliflower,
until just tender.

1 Heat the olive oil in a large heavy
pan, add the cauliflower florets and
sauté over a medium heat until they
start to brown.

2 Pour in enough hot water to almost
cover the cauliflower, add salt to taste,
then cover the pan and cook for
7–8 minutes until the florets are just
soft. Remove the pan from the heat
and leave to stand, covered, while you
make the sauce.

3 Beat the eggs in a bowl, add the
lemon juice and cornflour and beat until
mixed. Beat in a few tablespoons of the
hot liquid from the cauliflower.

4 Pour the egg mixture slowly over
the cauliflower, then stir gently.
Place the pan over a very gentle heat
for 2 minutes to thicken the sauce,
but do not allow to boil. Spoon into a
warmed serving bowl, sprinkle with
parsley and serve.

Energy 201kcal/833kJ; Protein 7g; Carbohydrate 4.4g, of which sugars 2.7g; Fat 17.5g, of which saturates 3g; Cholesterol 95mg; Calcium 51mg; Fibre 2.2g; Sodium 47mg

CRISPY CABBAGE

LIKE SO MANY BRASSICAS, CABBAGE IS LOVELY WHEN CRISP, HORRIBLE WHEN SOGGY. IN THIS RECIPE THE BALANCE IS JUST RIGHT, AND THE RESULT GOES VERY WELL WITH PORK OR HAM.

Preparation: 2–3 minutes; Cooking: 2–3 minutes

SERVES FOUR TO SIX

INGREDIENTS
1 medium green or
  small white cabbage
30–45ml/2–3 tbsp oil
salt and ground black pepper

VARIATION
For cabbage with a bacon dressing, fry 225g/8oz diced streaky (fatty) bacon in a pan. Set aside while cooking the cabbage. Remove the cabbage from the pan and keep warm with the bacon. Boil 15ml/1 tbsp wine or cider vinegar with the juices remaining in the pan. Bring to the boil and season with ground black pepper. Pour over the cabbage and bacon. This makes a versatile side dish, and is especially good with chicken.

1 Remove any coarse outside leaves from the cabbage and also the central rib from the larger remaining leaves. Place the cabbage on a board and use a sharp cook's knife to shred the leaves finely. Wash under cold running water, shake well and blot on kitchen paper to dry thoroughly.

2 Heat a wok or wide-based flameproof casserole over a fairly high heat. Heat the oil and add the cabbage. Stir-fry for 2–3 minutes, using one or two wooden spoons to keep the cabbage moving so that it cooks evenly but is still crunchy. Season with salt and pepper and serve immediately.

Energy 56kcal/230kJ; Protein 1.2g; Carbohydrate 4.2g, of which sugars 4.1g; Fat 3.8g, of which saturates 0.5g; Cholesterol 0mg; Calcium 41mg; Fibre 1.8g; Sodium 6mg

BRAISED LETTUCE AND PEAS

*THIS LIGHT VEGETABLE DISH IS BASED ON THE CLASSIC FRENCH METHOD OF BRAISING PEAS WITH
LETTUCE AND SPRING ONIONS IN BUTTER, AND IS DELICIOUS SERVED WITH GRILLED FISH OR DUCK.*

Preparation: 2–3 minutes; Cooking: 13 minutes

SERVES FOUR

INGREDIENTS

  50g/2oz/¼ cup butter
  4 Little Gem (Bibb) lettuces,
   halved lengthways
  2 bunches spring onions
   (scallions), trimmed
  400g/14oz shelled peas
   (about 1kg/2¼lb in pods)

VARIATIONS

• For a splash of extra colour, and to add
some crunch to the texture, braise about
250g/9oz baby carrots with the lettuce.
• Try a meatier alternative by cooking
115g/4oz chopped smoked bacon or
pancetta in the butter in step 1. Use
one bunch of spring onions (scallions)
and stir in some chopped parsley.

1 Melt half the butter in a wide, heavy
pan over a low heat. Add the lettuces
and spring onions.

2 Turn the vegetables in the butter, then
sprinkle with salt and plenty of ground
black pepper. Cover the pan with a
tight-fitting lid and cook the lettuces
and spring onions very gently for
5 minutes, stirring once.

3 Add the peas and turn them in the
buttery juices. Pour in 120ml/4fl oz/
½ cup water, then cover and cook over
a gentle heat for a further 5 minutes.
Uncover and increase the heat to
reduce the liquid to a few tablespoons.

4 Stir in the remaining butter and adjust
the seasoning. Transfer to a warmed
serving dish and serve immediately.

Energy 191kcal/790kJ; Protein 8g; Carbohydrate 13.3g, of which sugars 4.2g; Fat 12.3g, of which saturates 6.9g; Cholesterol 27mg; Calcium 52mg; Fibre 5.7g; Sodium 81mg

STIR-FRIED BRUSSELS SPROUTS WITH BACON

THIS IS A GREAT WAY OF COOKING BRUSSELS SPROUTS, HELPING TO RETAIN THEIR SWEET FLAVOUR AND CRUNCHY TEXTURE. STIR-FRYING GUARANTEES THAT THERE WILL NOT BE A SINGLE SOGGY SPROUT.

Preparation: 4 minutes; Cooking: 5 minutes

SERVES FOUR

INGREDIENTS
    450g/1lb Brussels sprouts, trimmed
      and washed
    30ml/2 tbsp sunflower oil
    2 streaky (fatty) bacon rashers
      (strips), finely chopped
    10ml/2 tsp caraway seeds,
      lightly crushed
    salt and ground black pepper

COOK'S TP
Save time on preparation by buying diced bacon or diced pancetta, available ready-packaged at the supermarket, which needs no further preparation. Just tip it straight into the pan.

1 Using a sharp knife, carefully cut all the Brussels sprouts into fine shreds.

2 Heat the oil in a wok or large frying pan. Add the shredded sprouts and turn quickly over the heat, season with salt and ground black pepper, then remove and set aside.

3 Use the the same wok or pan to cook the chopped bacon. Stir-fry for 1–2 minutes until golden.

4 Return the seasoned sprouts to the pan containing the bacon and stir in the caraway seeds. Cook for a further 1–2 minutes, then serve immediately.

Energy 131kcal/545kJ; Protein 5.9g; Carbohydrate 4.6g, of which sugars 3.5g; Fat 10g, of which saturates 2g; Cholesterol 8mg; Calcium 30mg; Fibre 4.6g; Sodium 164mg

STIR-FRIED CARROTS WITH MANGO AND GINGER

RIPE, SWEET MANGO TASTES WONDERFUL WITH CARROTS AND GINGER IN THIS SPICY VEGETABLE DISH,
WHICH IS GOOD ENOUGH TO SERVE ON ITS OWN WITH YOGURT AND A SALAD.

Preparation: 6 minutes; Cooking: 4–5 minutes

SERVES FOUR TO SIX

INGREDIENTS

   15–30ml/1–2 tbsp olive oil
   2–3 garlic cloves, chopped
   1 onion, chopped
   25g/1oz fresh root ginger, peeled
    and chopped
   5–6 carrots, sliced
   30–45ml/2–3 tbsp shelled pistachio
    nuts, roasted
   5ml/1 tsp ground cinnamon
   5–10ml/1–2 tsp ras el hanout
   1 small firm, ripe mango, peeled and
    coarsely diced
   a small bunch of fresh coriander
    (cilantro), finely chopped
   juice of ½ lemon
   salt

1 Heat the olive oil in a heavy frying pan or wok. Stir in the garlic, then the onion and ginger. Fry for 1 minute. Add the carrots, tossing them in the pan to make sure that they are mixed with the flavouring ingredients, and cook until they begin to brown.

2 Add the roasted pistachio nuts, ground cinnamon and ras el hanout, then gently mix in the diced mango. Sprinkle with the finely chopped fresh coriander, season with salt and pour over the lemon juice. Toss to mix and serve immediately.

Energy 89kcal/371kJ; Protein 1.7g; Carbohydrate 8.2g, of which sugars 7.5g; Fat 5.7g, of which saturates 0.8g; Cholesterol 0mg; Calcium 23mg; Fibre 2.2g; Sodium 47mg

CARROT AND PARSNIP PURÉE

PURÉED VEGETABLES AREN'T JUST FOR THE UNDER FIVES. THEIR CREAMINESS APPEALS TO ALL AGES, AND THEY ARE IDEAL PARTNERS FOR CRISP VEGETABLES SUCH AS LIGHTLY COOKED GREEN BEANS.

Preparation: 3 minutes; Cooking: 15–17 minutes

SERVES SIX TO EIGHT

INGREDIENTS
   350g/12oz carrots
   450g/1lb parsnips
   a pinch of freshly grated nutmeg
     or ground mace
   15g/½oz/1 tbsp butter
   about 15ml/1 tbsp single (light)
     cream or crème fraîche
   a small bunch of parsley, chopped,
     plus extra to garnish
   salt and ground black pepper

1 Peel the carrots and slice fairly thinly. Peel the parsnips and cut into bitesize chunks (they are softer and will cook more quickly than the carrots).

2 Boil the carrots and parsnips in separate pans of salted water until tender. Drain them well, then purée them together in a food processor, with the grated nutmeg or mace, a generous seasoning of salt and ground black pepper, and the butter. Whizz until smooth.

3 Transfer the purée to a bowl and beat in the cream or crème fraîche. Add the chopped parsley for extra flavour.

4 Transfer the carrot and parsnip purée to a warmed serving bowl, sprinkle with the remaining chopped parsley to garnish, and serve hot.

COOK'S TIP
• Any leftover purée can be thinned to taste with good quality chicken or vegetable stock and heated to make a quick home-made soup.
• The carrots can be substituted altogether for a small sweet potato. Peel and dice finely. As with the carrots, boil the sweet potato a little ahead of the parsnips if possible.

Energy 71kcal/298kJ; Protein 1.5g; Carbohydrate 10.7g, of which sugars 6.6g; Fat 2.7g, of which saturates 1.4g; Cholesterol 5mg; Calcium 49mg; Fibre 4g; Sodium 31mg

CARAMELIZED SHALLOTS

SWEET, GOLDEN SHALLOTS ARE GOOD WITH ALL SORTS OF MAIN DISHES, INCLUDING POULTRY OR MEAT. THEY ALSO TASTE GOOD WITH ROASTED CHUNKS OF BUTTERNUT SQUASH OR PUMPKIN.

Preparation: 3 minutes; Cooking: 17 minutes

SERVES FOUR TO SIX

INGREDIENTS

- 50g/2oz/¼ cup butter or 60ml/4 tbsp olive oil
- 500g/1¼lb shallots or small onions, peeled with root ends intact
- 15ml/1 tbsp golden caster (superfine) sugar
- 30ml/2 tbsp red or white wine, Madeira or port

1 Heat the butter or oil in a large frying pan and add the shallots or onions in a single layer. Cook gently, turning occasionally, for about 5 minutes, until they are lightly browned all over.

2 Sprinkle the sugar over the browned shallots and cook gently, turning the shallots in the juices, until the sugar begins to caramelize.

3 Pour the wine, Madeira or port over the caramelized shallots and increase the heat. Let the mixture bubble for 4–5 minutes.

4 Add 150ml/¼ pint/⅔ cup water and seasoning. Cover and cook for 5 minutes, then remove the lid and cook until the liquid evaporates and the shallots are tender and glazed. Adjust the seasoning before serving.

COOK'S TIP
Leaving the root ends of the shallots intact helps to ensure that they do not separate or unravel during cooking, but remain whole. They also look more presentable served in this way.

Energy 96kcal/399kJ; Protein 1.3g; Carbohydrate 5.4g, of which sugars 5.4g; Fat 7.5g, of which saturates 1.1g; Cholesterol 0mg; Calcium 22mg; Fibre 1.2g; Sodium 9mg

TURNIP SALAD IN SOUR CREAM

OFTEN NEGLECTED, TURNIPS MAKE AN UNUSUAL AND VERY TASTY ACCOMPANIMENT WHEN PREPARED IN THIS SIMPLE WAY. CHOOSE YOUNG, TENDER TURNIPS OF THE TYPE THE FRENCH CALL NAVETS.

Preparation: 5 minutes; Cooking: 0 minutes

SERVES FOUR

INGREDIENTS
2–4 young, tender turnips, peeled
¼–½ onion, finely chopped
2–3 drops white wine vinegar,
  or to taste
60–90ml/4–6 tbsp sour cream
salt and ground black pepper
chopped fresh parsley or paprika,
  to garnish

VARIATION
Crème fraîche or thick yogurt can be used instead of the sour cream, if you like.

1 Thinly slice or coarsely grate the turnips. Alternatively, thinly slice half the turnips and grate the ones that remain. Put in a bowl.

2 Add the onion, vinegar, salt and pepper, toss together then stir in the sour cream. Serve chilled, garnished with a sprinkling of parsley or paprika.

Energy 48kcal/198kJ; Protein 1.1g; Carbohydrate 4.1g, of which sugars 3.7g; Fat 3.2g, of which saturates 1.9g; Cholesterol 9mg; Calcium 42mg; Fibre 1.4g; Sodium 14mg

CREAMY LEEKS WITH CHEESE

THIS IS QUITE A RICH ACCOMPANIMENT THAT COULD EASILY BE SERVED AS A MEAL IN ITSELF WITH BROWN RICE OR COUSCOUS. FOR A VERY QUICK SNACK, JUST SERVE IT ON TOAST.

Preparation: 3–4 minutes; Cooking: 12 minutes

SERVES FOUR

INGREDIENTS

4 large leeks or 12 baby leeks,
  trimmed and washed
15ml/1 tbsp olive oil
150ml/¼ pint/⅔ cup double
  (heavy) cream
75g/3oz mature (sharp) Cheddar or
  Monterey Jack cheese, grated
salt and ground black pepper

1 If using large leeks, slice them lengthways. Heat the oil in a large frying pan and add the leeks. Season with salt and pepper and cook for about 4 minutes, stirring occasionally, until they become aromatic and the outsides start to turn golden.

2 Preheat the grill (broiler) to high. Pour the cream into the pan, drizzling it over the leeks, and stir until well combined. Lower the heat and allow to bubble gently for a few minutes, but do not over-boil as the cream may begin to curdle.

3 Transfer the creamy leeks to a shallow ovenproof dish and sprinkle with the cheese. Grill (broil) for 4–5 minutes, or until the cheese topping is golden brown and bubbling. Serve immediately.

VARIATIONS
• This recipe works well with all sorts of hard cheeses, from Parmesan and Gran Padano to Red Leicester, Double Gloucester and Caerphilly. Experiment with different flavours to suit your own tastes.
• For a more substantial dish, cook sliced button (white) mushroom with the leeks, or top the mixture with sliced cherry tomatoes before adding the cheese.
• To make the dish more appealing to meat lovers, add some diced smoky bacon or pancetta to the pan in step 1, after you have fried the leeks for a couple of minutes.

Energy 322kcal/1330kJ; Protein 7.8g; Carbohydrate 5g, of which sugars 4g; Fat 29.8g, of which saturates 17.1g; Cholesterol 70mg; Calcium 193mg; Fibre 3.3g; Sodium 147mg

SPICY POTATO <u>AND</u> OLIVE SALAD

DELICIOUS WARM OR CHILLED, THIS NEW POTATO SALAD IS ENLIVENED WITH CUMIN AND CORIANDER, THEN DRESSED IN OLIVE OIL AND A FRUITY VINEGAR. IT TASTES GOOD WITH COLD ROAST PORK OR HAM.

Preparation: 5 minutes; Cooking: 10 minutes

SERVES FOUR

INGREDIENTS

- 8 large new potatoes
- a large pinch of salt
- a large pinch of sugar
- 3 garlic cloves, chopped
- 15ml/1 tbsp vinegar of your choice, such as a fruit variety
- a large pinch of ground cumin or whole cumin seeds
- a pinch of cayenne pepper or hot paprika, to taste
- 30–45ml/2–3 tbsp extra virgin olive oil
- 30–45ml/2–3 tbsp chopped fresh coriander (cilantro) leaves
- 10–15 dry-fleshed black Mediterranean olives

1 Chop the new potatoes into chunks. Put them in a pan, pour in water to cover and add the salt and sugar. Bring to the boil, then reduce the heat and boil gently for about 10 minutes, or until the potatoes are just tender. Drain well and leave in a colander to cool.

2 When cool enough to handle, slice the potato chunks and put them in a bowl.

3 Sprinkle the garlic, vinegar, cumin and cayenne or paprika over the salad. Drizzle with olive oil and sprinkle over coriander and olives.

Energy 238kcal/998kJ; Protein 4g; Carbohydrate 32.6g, of which sugars 2.9g; Fat 11.1g, of which saturates 1.7g; Cholesterol 0mg; Calcium 49mg; Fibre 3.2g; Sodium 448mg

MASALA BEANS WITH FENUGREEK

THE SECRET OF THIS SUPER-FAST DISH IS THE SPICE MIXTURE THAT COATS THE VEGETABLES.
COOKING IS KEPT TO THE MINIMUM SO THAT INDIVIDUAL FLAVOURS ARE STILL DETECTABLE.
Preparation: 4–5 minutes; Cooking: 10–12 minutes

SERVES FOUR

INGREDIENTS
1 onion
5ml/1 tsp ground cumin
5ml/1 tsp ground coriander
5ml/1 tsp sesame seeds
5ml/1 tsp chilli powder
2.5ml/½ tsp crushed garlic
1.5ml/¼ tsp ground turmeric
5ml/1 tsp salt
30ml/2 tbsp vegetable oil
1 tomato, quartered
225g/8oz/1½ cups green
  beans, blanched
1 bunch fresh fenugreek leaves,
  stems discarded
60ml/4 tbsp chopped fresh
  coriander (cilantro)
15ml/1 tbsp lemon juice

1 Roughly chop the onion. Mix together the cumin and coriander, sesame seeds, chilli powder, garlic, turmeric and salt.

2 Put the chopped onion and spice mixture into a food processor or blender, and process for 30–45 seconds until you have a rough paste.

3 In a wok or large, heavy pan, heat the oil over a medium heat and fry the spice paste for about 5 minutes, stirring the mixture occasionally.

VARIATION
Instead of fresh fenugreek, substitute 15ml/1 tbsp dried fenugreek, which is available from Indian markets.

4 Add the tomato quarters, blanched green beans, fresh fenugreek and chopped coriander.

5 Stir-fry the contents of the pan for about 5 minutes, then sprinkle in the lemon juice and serve.

Energy 70kcal/289kJ; Protein 1.6g; Carbohydrate 2.7g, of which sugars 2.1g; Fat 6g, of which saturates 0.7g; Cholesterol 0mg; Calcium 47mg; Fibre 2g; Sodium 6mg

BEETROOT WITH FRESH MINT

THE LOVELY, BRIGHT COLOUR OF BEETROOT CONTRASTS BEAUTIFULLY WITH THE DEEP GREEN OF MINT. THE FLAVOURS WORK WELL TOGETHER, TOO, AND ARE ENHANCED BY THE SWEET BALSAMIC DRESSING.

Preparation: 3–4 minutes; Cooking: 0 minutes; Chilling recommended

SERVES FOUR

INGREDIENTS
4–6 cooked beetroot (beets)
5–10ml/1–2 tsp sugar
15–30ml/1–2 tbsp balsamic vinegar
juice of ½ lemon
30ml/2 tbsp extra virgin olive oil
1 bunch fresh mint, leaves stripped
   and thinly sliced
salt

VARIATIONS
• To make a spicy version, add harissa to taste and substitute fresh coriander (cilantro) for the mint.
• As an alternative, add a chopped onion and some fresh dill.

1 Slice the beetroot or cut it into even-size dice with a sharp knife. Put the beetroot in a bowl. Add the sugar, balsamic vinegar, lemon juice, olive oil and a pinch of salt and toss together to combine.

2 Add half the thinly sliced fresh mint to the salad and toss lightly until well combined. If you have time, chill the salad for about 1 hour. Serve garnished with the remaining thinly sliced mint leaves.

Energy 90kcal/376kJ; Protein 1.9g; Carbohydrate 7.8g, of which sugars 6.7g; Fat 5.9g, of which saturates 0.8g; Cholesterol 0mg; Calcium 45mg; Fibre 1.2g; Sodium 69mg

CURRIED RED CABBAGE SLAW

THREE SHADES OF RED COMBINE IN THIS FRESH, CRISP SLAW. EACH CONTRIBUTES A DIFFERENT TEXTURE AND FLAVOUR, FROM THE CRUNCH OF CABBAGE TO THE SATIN SMOOTHNESS OF PEPPER.

Preparation: 5 minutes; Cooking: 0 minutes; Chilling recommended

SERVES FOUR TO SIX

INGREDIENTS

½ red cabbage, thinly sliced
1 red (bell) pepper, chopped
  or very thinly sliced
½ red onion, chopped
60ml/4 tbsp red or white wine
  vinegar or cider vinegar
60ml/4 tbsp sugar, or to taste
120ml/4fl oz/½ cup Greek
  (US strained plain) yogurt or
  natural (plain) yogurt
120ml/4fl oz/½ cup mayonnaise,
  preferably home-made
1.5ml/¼ tsp curry powder
2–3 handfuls raisins
salt and ground black pepper

1 Put the cabbage, pepper and red onion in a bowl and toss to combine. In a small pan, heat the vinegar and sugar until the sugar has dissolved, then pour over the vegetables. Leave to cool slightly.

2 Combine the yogurt and mayonnaise, then mix into the cabbage mixture. Season to taste with curry powder, salt and ground black pepper, then mix in the raisins.

3 Chill the salad before serving, if you have time. Just before serving, drain off any excess liquid and briefly stir the slaw again.

VARIATION

If you prefer, ready-made low-fat mayonnaise can be used instead of the Greek yogurt and mayonnaise mixture. Stir the curry powder into the mayonnaise.

Energy 272kcal/1136kJ; Protein 3g; Carbohydrate 27.9g, of which sugars 27.5g; Fat 17.5g, of which saturates 3.4g; Cholesterol 15mg; Calcium 74mg; Fibre 2g; Sodium 120mg

FAST AND FABULOUS DESSERTS

You may not want to serve something sweet every day, but there are times when nothing

succeeds like a Chocolate Fudge Sundae. For a truly speedy dessert, whip up a Cool Chocolate

Float or a Blueberry Meringue Crumble. Both these treats are blitzed in the blender before

being served in tall glasses and are classy and cool. A more healthy choice might be Fresh Fruit

Salad or Summer Berries in Warm Sabayon Glaze, both of which are ideal for serving after a

rich or spicy main course. Some of the recipes in this chapter benefit from being made ahead

of time. Dried Fruit Salad falls into that category, as do the unashamedly indulgent

Chocolate and Prune Refrigerator Bars, but a few minutes in the kitchen

early in the day will mean instant satisfaction later.

RHUBARB AND GINGER TRIFLES

CHOOSE A GOOD QUALITY JAR OF RHUBARB COMPOTE FOR THIS RECIPE; TRY TO FIND ONE WITH LARGE, CHUNKY PIECES OF FRUIT. ALTERNATIVELY, USE WHOLE-FRUIT APRICOT JAM.

Preparation: 3–4 minutes; Cooking: 0 minutes

SERVES FOUR

INGREDIENTS
12 gingernut biscuits (gingersnaps)
50ml/2fl oz/¼ cup rhubarb compote
450ml/¾ pint/scant 2 cups extra
thick double (heavy) cream

1 Put the ginger biscuits in a plastic bag and seal. Bash the biscuits with a rolling pin until roughly crushed.

2 Set aside two tablespoons of crushed biscuits and divide the rest among four glasses.

3 Spoon the rhubarb compote on top of the crushed biscuits, then top with the cream. Place in the refrigerator and chill for about 30 minutes.

4 To serve, sprinkle the reserved crushed biscuits over the trifles and serve immediately.

Energy 695kcal/2874kJ; Protein 3.6g; Carbohydrate 27.1g, of which sugars 14.1g; Fat 64.3g, of which saturates 39.4g; Cholesterol 154mg; Calcium 98mg; Fibre 0.6g; Sodium 124mg

CHOCOLATE AND PRUNE REFRIGERATOR BARS

WICKEDLY SELF-INDULGENT AND VERY EASY TO MAKE, THESE FRUITY CHOCOLATE BARS WILL KEEP FOR 2–3 DAYS IN THE REFRIGERATOR – IF THEY DON'T ALL GET EATEN AS SOON AS THEY ARE READY.

Preparation: 4 minutes; Cooking: 0 minutes; Chilling recommended

MAKES TWELVE BARS

INGREDIENTS
   250g/9oz good quality
    milk chocolate
   50g/2oz/¼ cup unsalted
    (sweet) butter
   115g/4oz digestive biscuits
    (graham crackers)
   115g/4oz/½ cup ready-to-eat prunes

1 Break the chocolate into small pieces and place in a heatproof bowl. Add the butter and melt in the microwave on high for 1–2 minutes. Stir to mix and set aside. (Alternatively, place the chocolate pieces in a bowl over a pan of gently simmering water and leave until melted, stirring frequently.)

2 Put the biscuits in a plastic bag and seal, then bash into small pieces with a rolling pin. Alternatively, break up the biscuits in a food processor but do not let them become too fine. Use the pulse button. Roughly chop the prunes and stir into the melted chocolate with the biscuits.

3 Spoon the chocolate and prune mixture into a 20cm/8in square cake tin (pan) and smooth away any lumps and bumps with the back of the spoon. Chill for 1–2 hours until set. Remove the cake from the refrigerator and, using a sharp knife, cut into 12 bars of about 1.5cm/½ in thickness each.

Energy 197kcal/826kJ; Protein 2.5g; Carbohydrate 21.7g, of which sugars 16.4g; Fat 11.8g, of which saturates 6.8g; Cholesterol 18mg; Calcium 59mg; Fibre 0.9g; Sodium 102mg

BLUEBERRY MERINGUE CRUMBLE

IMAGINE THE MOST APPEALING FLAVOURS OF A BLUEBERRY MERINGUE DESSERT — FRESH TANGY FRUIT, CRISP SUGARY MERINGUE AND PLENTY OF VANILLA-SCENTED CREAM, ALL SERVED IN A TALL GLASS FOR EASY EATING.

Preparation: 4 minutes; Cooking: 0 minutes

SERVES THREE TO FOUR

INGREDIENTS

150g/5oz/1¼ cups fresh blueberries,
  plus extra to decorate
15ml/1 tbsp icing
  (confectioners') sugar
250ml/8fl oz/1 cup vanilla
  iced yogurt
200ml/7fl oz/scant 1 cup full cream
  (whole) milk
30ml/2 tbsp lime juice
75g/3oz meringues, lightly crushed

1 Put the blueberries and sugar in a blender or food processor with 60ml/4 tbsp water and blend until smooth, scraping the mixture down from the side once or twice, if necessary.

2 Transfer the purée to a small bowl and rinse out the blender or food processor bowl to get rid of any remaining blueberry juice.

4 Carefully pour alternate layers of the milkshake, blueberry syrup and the remaining crushed meringues into tall glasses, finishing with a few chunky pieces of meringue.

5 Drizzle any remaining blueberry syrup over the tops of the meringues and decorate with a few extra blueberries. Serve immediately.

COOK'S TIPS
• Buy good-quality meringues, not the brittle extra-sweet supermarket variety.
• The easiest way to crush the meringues is to put them in a plastic bag on a work surface and tap them gently with a rolling pin. Stop tapping the meringues as soon as they have crumbled into little bitesize pieces otherwise you'll just be left with tiny crumbs.

3 Put the iced yogurt, milk and lime juice in the blender and process until thoroughly combined. Add half of the crushed meringues and process again until smooth.

VARIATION
Iced yogurt is used to provide a slightly lighter note than ice cream, but there's nothing to stop you using ice cream instead.

Energy 164kcal/691kJ; Protein 6.2g; Carbohydrate 30.8g, of which sugars 30.8g; Fat 2.7g, of which saturates 1.6g; Cholesterol 8mg; Calcium 197mg; Fibre 1.2g; Sodium 96mg

COOL CHOCOLATE FLOAT

CHOCOLATE MILKSHAKE AND SCOOPS OF CHOCOLATE AND VANILLA ICE CREAM ARE COMBINED HERE TO MAKE THE MOST MELTINGLY DELICIOUS DESSERT DRINK EVER. IT'S CLASS IN A GLASS.

Preparation: 6 minutes; Cooking: 2 minutes

SERVES TWO

INGREDIENTS
 115g/4oz plain (semisweet)
  chocolate, broken into pieces
 250ml/8fl oz/1 cup milk
 15ml/1 tbsp caster (superfine) sugar
 4 large scoops classic vanilla
  ice cream
 4 large scoops dark (bittersweet)
  chocolate ice cream
 a little lightly whipped cream
 grated chocolate or chocolate curls,
  to decorate

4 Using a dessertspoon, drizzle the chocolate milk over and around the ice cream in each glass, so that it dribbles down in swirls.

5 Top with lightly whipped cream and sprinkle over a little grated chocolate or some chocolate curls to decorate. Serve immediately.

1 Put the chocolate in a heavy pan and add the milk and sugar. Heat gently, stirring with a wooden spoon until the chocolate has melted and the mixture is smooth. Pour into a bowl and set in a larger bowl of iced water to cool quickly.

2 Blend the cooled chocolate mixture with half of the ice cream in a blender or food processor until the mixture resembles chocolate milk.

3 Scoop the remaining ice cream alternately into two tall glasses: vanilla then chocolate.

COOK'S TIP
You can experiment with all kinds of flavours of ice cream. Try substituting banana, coconut or toffee flavours for the chocolate and vanilla ice cream if you prefer. The health-conscious cook might prefer to substitute frozen yogurt, but make sure it is a creamy variety.

Energy 990kcal/4149kJ; Protein 17.7g; Carbohydrate 115.4g, of which sugars 110.4g; Fat 52.3g, of which saturates 32g; Cholesterol 83mg; Calcium 518mg; Fibre 1.5g; Sodium 262mg

ZABAGLIONE

*LIGHT AS AIR AND HIGHLY ALCOHOLIC, THIS WARM CUSTARD IS A MUCH-LOVED ITALIAN PUDDING.
IT IS TRADITIONALLY MADE WITH MARSALA, BUT MADEIRA OR SWEET SHERRY CAN BE USED INSTEAD.*

Preparation: 8 minutes; Cooking: 5–7 minutes

2 Gradually add the Marsala, Madeira or sherry to the egg mixture, 15ml/ 1 tbsp at a time, whisking well after each addition.

3 Place the bowl over a pan of gently simmering water and continue to whisk for 5–7 minutes, until the mixture becomes thick; when the beaters are lifted they should leave a thick trail on the surface of the mixture. Do not be tempted to underbeat the mixture, as the zabaglione will be too runny and will be likely to separate.

4 Pour into four warmed, stemmed glasses and serve immediately with amaretti for dipping.

SERVES FOUR

INGREDIENTS
4 egg yolks
50g/2oz/¼ cup caster (superfine) sugar
60ml/4 tbsp Marsala, Madeira or sweet sherry
amaretti, to serve

VARIATION
To make a chocolate version of this dessert, whisk in 30ml/2 tbsp unsweetened cocoa powder with the wine or sherry and serve dusted with cocoa powder and icing (confectioners') sugar.

1 Place the egg yolks and sugar in a large heatproof bowl, and whisk with an electric beater until the mixture is pale and has thickened considerably.

COOK'S TIP
Zabaglione is also delicious served as a sauce with cooked fruit. Try serving it with poached pears, grilled (broiled) peaches or baked bananas to create a really special dessert.

Energy 131kcal/548kJ; Protein 3g; Carbohydrate 14.1g, of which sugars 14.1g; Fat 5.5g, of which saturates 1.6g; Cholesterol 202mg; Calcium 31mg; Fibre 0g; Sodium 12mg

PINEAPPLE AND RUM CREAM

WHEN PINEAPPLE IS HEATED, THE FLAVOUR INTENSIFIES AND THE GORGEOUS SWEET JUICES
CARAMELIZE. ADD RUM AND CREAM AND YOU HAVE A DREAM OF A DESSERT.

Preparation: 4 minutes; Cooking: 4 minutes

SERVES FOUR

INGREDIENTS
  25g/1oz/2 tbsp butter
  115g/4oz pineapple, roughly chopped
  45ml/3 tbsp dark rum
  300ml/½ pint/1¼ cups double
   (heavy) cream

VARIATIONS
Although a sumptuous dessert in its own right, this fruity alcoholic cream also works very well as a topping. Spoon over vanilla or rum-and-raisin ice cream for an extra special touch to a simple dessert. Peach slices, apple rings or halved bananas can also be used instead of pineapple pieces, if you prefer.

1 Heat the butter in a frying pan and add the pineapple. Cook over a moderate to high heat until the pineapple is starting to turn golden.

2 Add the rum and allow to bubble for 1–2 minutes, then remove and set aside. Pour the cream into a bowl and beat until soft. Fold the pineapple and rum mixture evenly through the cream, then spoon carefully into four glasses and serve immediately.

Energy 455kcal/1876kJ; Protein 1.4g; Carbohydrate 4.2g, of which sugars 4.2g; Fat 45.5g, of which saturates 28.3g; Cholesterol 116mg; Calcium 43mg; Fibre 0.4g; Sodium 55mg

CHOCOLATE AND BANANA FOOL

THIS DELICIOUS DESSERT HAS A LOVELY CITRUS FLAVOUR. IT IS QUITE RICH, SO IT IS A GOOD IDEA TO SERVE IT WITH SOME DESSERT COOKIES, SUCH AS SHORTBREAD OR BISCOTTI.

Preparation: 3 minutes; Cooking: 2 minutes; Chilling recommended

SERVES FOUR

INGREDIENTS
115g/4oz plain (semisweet)
  chocolate, broken into
  small pieces
300ml/½ pint/1¼ cups ready-made
  fresh custard
2 bananas

 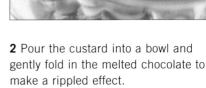

COOK'S TIPS
Good quality bought custard is ideal for this dessert. Don't be tempted to use anything but the best chocolate, though, or the flavour will be compromised. Look for a bar that contains at least 70 percent chocolate solids. A flavoured chocolate such as pistachio or orange takes the dessert into another dimension.

1 Put the chocolate pieces in a heat-proof bowl and melt in the microwave on high power for 1–2 minutes. Stir, then set aside. If you do not have a microwave, put the chocolate in a heatproof bowl and place it over a pan of gently simmering water and leave until melted, stirring frequently to remove any unmelted pieces.

2 Pour the custard into a bowl and gently fold in the melted chocolate to make a rippled effect.

3 Peel and slice the bananas and stir these into the chocolate and custard mixture. Spoon into four glasses. If you have time, chill for at least 30 minutes before serving.

Energy 268kcal/1127kJ; Protein 4.1g; Carbohydrate 42.1g, of which sugars 38.1g; Fat 9.6g, of which saturates 4.9g; Cholesterol 3mg; Calcium 81mg; Fibre 1.4g; Sodium 33mg

LEMON POSSET

THIS OLD-FASHIONED DESSERT WAS ONCE CONSIDERED A REMEDY FOR THE COMMON COLD. IT IS CERTAINLY WORTH SUFFERING A SNIFFLE IF IT MEANS YOU GET TO SAMPLE ITS SUPERB FLAVOUR.

Preparation: 2 minutes; Cooking: 8–10 minutes; Chilling recommended

SERVES FOUR

INGREDIENTS
600ml/1 pint/2½ cups double
  (heavy) cream
175g/6oz/scant 1 cup caster
  (superfine) sugar
grated rind and juice of
  2 unwaxed lemons

VARIATION
To intensify the lemon flavour of this lovely old dessert even more, swirl a spoonful of lemon curd or lemon cheese on the surface just before serving. Physalis make a suitable and very stylish accompaniment.

1 Pour the cream into a heavy pan. Add the sugar and heat gently until the sugar has dissolved, then bring to the boil, stirring constantly. Add the lemon juice and rind, reserving a little of the rind for decoration, and stir constantly over a medium heat until it thickens.

2 Pour the mixture into four heatproof serving glasses. Cool, then chill in the refrigerator until just set. Serve the posset decorated with a few strands of lemon rind, and with a selection of dessert biscuits (cookies), if you like. Rich, buttery shortbread is ideal.

Energy 917kcal/3801kJ; Protein 2.7g; Carbohydrate 48.5g, of which sugars 48.5g; Fat 80.6g, of which saturates 50.1g; Cholesterol 206mg; Calcium 98mg; Fibre 0g; Sodium 36mg

SYRUPY BRIOCHE SLICES WITH ICE CREAM

KEEP A FEW INDIVIDUAL BRIOCHE BUNS IN THE FREEZER TO MAKE THIS SUPER DESSERT. FOR A SLIGHTLY TARTER TASTE, USE FINELY GRATED LEMON RIND AND JUICE INSTEAD OF ORANGE RIND.

Preparation: 4 minutes; Cooking: 9–10 minutes

SERVES FOUR

INGREDIENTS
   butter, for greasing
   finely grated rind and juice of
      1 orange, such as Navelina or
      blood orange
   50g/2oz/¼ cup caster
      (superfine) sugar
   90ml/6 tbsp water
   1.5ml/¼ tsp ground cinnamon
   4 brioche buns
   15ml/1 tbsp icing
      (confectioners') sugar
   400ml/14fl oz/1⅔ cups vanilla
      ice cream

1 Lightly grease a gratin dish and set aside. Put the orange rind and juice, sugar, water and cinnamon in a heavy pan. Heat gently, stirring constantly, until the sugar has dissolved, then boil rapidly, without stirring, for 2 minutes, until thickened and syrupy.

2 Remove the orange syrup from the heat and pour it into a shallow heatproof dish. Preheat the grill (broiler). Cut each brioche vertically into three thick slices. Dip one side of each slice in the hot syrup and arrange in the gratin dish, syrupy sides down. Reserve the remaining syrup. Grill (broil) the brioche until lightly toasted.

VARIATION
Substitute the same amount of ground cardamom for the cinnamon.

3 Using tongs, turn the brioche slices over and dust well with icing sugar. Grill for about 3 minutes more, or until they are just beginning to caramelize around the edges.

4 Transfer the hot brioche to serving plates and top with scoops of vanilla ice cream. Spoon the remaining syrup over them and serve immediately.

COOK'S TIP
You could also use slices of a larger brioche, rather than buns, or madeleines, sliced horizontally in half. These are traditionally flavoured with lemon or orange flower water, making them especially tasty.

Energy 399kcal/1681kJ; Protein 8.5g; Carbohydrate 65.5g, of which sugars 42.5g; Fat 12g, of which saturates 7.2g; Cholesterol 25mg; Calcium 174mg; Fibre 1.3g; Sodium 252mg

HONEY BAKED FIGS <u>WITH</u> HAZELNUT ICE CREAM

FIGS BAKED IN A LEMON-GRASS SCENTED HONEY SYRUP HAVE THE MOST WONDERFUL FLAVOUR, ESPECIALLY WHEN SERVED WITH A GOOD-QUALITY ICE CREAM DOTTED WITH ROASTED HAZELNUTS.

Preparation: 4 minutes; Cooking: 16 minutes

SERVES FOUR

INGREDIENTS

1 lemon grass stalk, finely chopped
1 cinnamon stick, roughly broken
60ml/4 tbsp clear honey
200ml/7fl oz/scant 1 cup water
75g/3oz/¾ cup hazelnuts
8 large ripe dessert figs
400ml/14fl oz/1⅔ cups good-quality
   vanilla ice cream
30ml/2 tbsp hazelnut liqueur
   (optional)

1 Preheat the oven to 190°C/375°F/ Gas 5. Make the syrup by mixing the lemon grass, cinnamon stick, honey and measured water in a small pan. Heat gently, stirring until the honey has dissolved, then bring to the boil. Simmer for 2 minutes.

2 Meanwhile spread out the hazelnuts on a baking sheet and grill (broil) under a medium heat until golden brown. Shake the sheet occasionally, so that they are evenly toasted.

3 Cut the figs into quarters, leaving them intact at the bases. Stand in a baking dish, pour the syrup over and cover tightly with foil and bake for 13–15 minutes until the figs are tender.

4 While the figs are baking, remove the ice cream from the freezer and let soften slightly. Chop the hazelnuts roughly and beat the softened ice cream briefly with an electric beater, then beat in the nuts.

5 To serve, puddle a little of the syrup from the figs on to each dessert plate. Arrange the figs on top and add a spoonful of ice cream. Spoon a little hazelnut liqueur over the ice cream if you like.

COOK'S TIP
If the hazelnut skins need to be removed, tip the nuts into a clean dish towel and rub them off.

Energy 433kcal/1816kJ; Protein 7.8g; Carbohydrate 53.6g, of which sugars 52.1g; Fat 21.2g, of which saturates 7g; Cholesterol 24mg; Calcium 227mg; Fibre 4.2g; Sodium 88mg

SUMMER BERRIES IN WARM SABAYON GLAZE

THIS LUXURIOUS COMBINATION CONSISTS OF SUMMER BERRIES UNDER A LIGHT AND FLUFFY SAUCE FLAVOURED WITH LIQUEUR. THE TOPPING IS LIGHTLY GRILLED TO FORM A CRISP, CARAMELIZED CRUST.

Preparation: 9 minutes; Cooking: 2 minutes

SERVES FOUR

INGREDIENTS

450g/1lb/4 cups mixed summer berries, or soft fruit

4 egg yolks

50g/2oz/¼ cup vanilla sugar or caster (superfine) sugar

120ml/4fl oz/½ cup liqueur, such as Cointreau, kirsch or Grand Marnier, or a white dessert wine

a little icing (confectioners') sugar, sifted, and mint leaves, to decorate (optional)

COOK'S TIP

If you prefer to omit the alcohol, use grape, mango or apricot juice.

1 Arrange the fruit in four heatproof ramekins. Preheat the grill (broiler).

2 Whisk the yolks in a large bowl with the sugar and liqueur or wine. Place over a pan of hot water and whisk constantly until thick, fluffy and pale.

3 Pour equal quantities of the sauce into each dish. Place under the grill for 1–2 minutes until just turning brown. Dust the fruit with icing sugar and sprinkle with mint leaves just before serving, if you like. You could also add an extra splash of liqueur.

Energy 235kcal/984kJ; Protein 3.9g; Carbohydrate 27.1g, of which sugars 27.1g; Fat 5.6g, of which saturates 1.6g; Cholesterol 202mg; Calcium 48mg; Fibre 1.3g; Sodium 18mg

GRAPEFRUIT IN HONEY AND WHISKY

CREATE A SIMPLE YET ELEGANT DESSERT BY ARRANGING A COLOURFUL FAN OF PINK, RED AND WHITE GRAPEFRUIT SEGMENTS IN A SWEET WHISKY SAUCE. THIS DESSERT IS PERFECT AFTER A RICH MEAL.

Preparation: 4 minutes; Cooking: 14 minutes; Chilling recommended

SERVES FOUR

INGREDIENTS
  1 pink grapefruit
  1 red grapefruit
  1 white grapefruit
  50g/2oz/¼ cup sugar
  60ml/4 tbsp clear honey
  45ml/3 tbsp whisky
  mint leaves, to decorate

1 Cut a thin slice of peel and pith from each end of the grapefruit. Place the cut side down on a plate and cut off the peel and pith in strips. Remove any remaining pith. Cut out each segment leaving the membrane behind. Put the segments into a shallow bowl.

2 Put the sugar and 150ml/¼ pint/ ⅔ cup water into a heavy pan. Bring to the boil, stirring constantly, until the sugar has completely dissolved, then simmer, without stirring, for 10 minutes, until thickened and syrupy.

3 Heat the honey in a pan and boil until it becomes a slightly deeper colour and begins to caramelize. Remove the pan from the heat, add the whisky and, using a match or taper, carefully ignite, if you like, then pour the mixture into the sugar syrup.

VARIATION
The whisky can be replaced with brandy, Cointreau or Grand Marnier.

4 Bring to the boil, and pour over the grapefruit segments. Cover and leave until cold. To serve, put the grapefruit segments on to four serving plates, alternating the colours, pour over some of the syrup and decorate with the mint leaves.

Energy 154kcal/649kJ; Protein 1.1g; Carbohydrate 32.7g, of which sugars 32.7g; Fat 0.1g, of which saturates 0g; Cholesterol 0mg; Calcium 35mg; Fibre 1.6g; Sodium 6mg

FRESH FRUIT SALAD

ORANGES ARE AN ESSENTIAL INGREDIENT FOR A SUCCESSFUL AND REFRESHING FRUIT SALAD, WHICH CAN INCLUDE ANY FRUIT IN SEASON. A COLOURFUL COMBINATION TAKES JUST MINUTES TO MAKE.

Preparation: 6 minutes; Cooking: 0 minutes

SERVES SIX

INGREDIENTS
2 apples
2 oranges
2 peaches
16–20 strawberries
30ml/2 tbsp lemon juice
15–30ml/1–2 tbsp orange
   flower water
icing (confectioners') sugar,
   to taste (optional)

COOK'S TIP
The easiest way to remove the pith and peel from an orange is to cut a thin slice from each end of the orange first, using a sharp knife. It will then be easier to cut off the remaining peel and pith.

1 Peel and core the apples and cut into thin slices. Remove the pith and peel from the oranges and cut each one into segments. Squeeze the juice from the membrane and retain.

2 Blanch the peaches for 1 minute in boiling water. Peel and slice thickly.

3 Hull and halve the strawberries, and place all the fruit in a large bowl.

4 Blend together the lemon juice, orange flower water and any reserved orange juice. Taste and add a little icing sugar to sweeten, if you like. Pour the fruit juice over the salad and serve.

Energy 42kcal/180kJ; Protein 1.1g; Carbohydrate 9.8g, of which sugars 9.8g; Fat 0.1g, of which saturates 0g; Cholesterol 0mg; Calcium 28mg; Fibre 1.9g; Sodium 5mg

DRIED FRUIT SALAD

THIS DESSERT DOESN'T TAKE LONG TO PREPARE, BUT MUST BE MADE AHEAD OF TIME, TO ALLOW THE DRIED FRUIT TO PLUMP UP AND FLAVOURS TO BLEND. IT IS ALSO GOOD FOR BREAKFAST.

Preparation: 6 minutes; Cooking: 12 minutes; Make ahead

SERVES FOUR

INGREDIENTS
115g/4oz/½ cup ready-to-eat dried
   apricots, halved
115g/4oz/½ cup ready-to-eat dried
   peaches, halved
1 pear
1 apple
1 orange
115g/4oz/1 cup mixed raspberries
   and blackberries
1 cinnamon stick
50g/2oz/¼ cup caster
   (superfine) sugar
15ml/1 tbsp clear honey
30ml/2 tbsp lemon juice

1 Place the dried fruit in a large pan and add 600ml/1 pint/2½ cups water.

2 Peel and core the pear and apple, then dice. Remove peel and pith from the orange and cut into wedges. Add all the cut fruit to the pan with the raspberries and blackberries.

3 Pour in a further 150ml/¼ pint/⅔ cup water, the cinnamon, sugar and honey, and bring to the boil. Cover and simmer for 10 minutes, then remove the pan from the heat. Stir in the lemon juice. Leave to cool completely, then transfer the fruit and syrup to a bowl and chill for 1–2 hours before serving.

Energy 190kcal/811kJ; Protein 3.3g; Carbohydrate 46g, of which sugars 46g; Fat 0.5g, of which saturates 0g; Cholesterol 0mg; Calcium 75mg; Fibre 6g; Sodium 13mg

CLEMENTINES WITH STAR ANISE

LOOKING DRAMATIC, WITH THE DARK STARS OF ANISE AGAINST THE SUNSHINE ORANGE CLEMENTINES, THIS IS A SIMPLY DELICIOUS DESSERT. IT TASTES BEST CHILLED, SO ALLOW TIME FOR THAT.

Preparation: 6–8 minutes; Cooking: 12 minutes; Chilling recommended

SERVES SIX

INGREDIENTS
    1 lime
    350ml/12fl oz/1½ cups sweet
      dessert wine, such as Sauternes
    75g/3oz/6 tbsp caster
      (superfine) sugar
    6 star anise
    1 cinnamon stick
    1 vanilla pod (bean)
    30ml/2 tbsp Cointreau or other
      orange liqueur
    12 clementines

VARIATION
Tangerines or seedless oranges can be used instead of clementines.

1 Thinly pare 1 or 2 strips of rind from the lime. Put them in a pan, with the wine, sugar, star anise and cinnamon. Split the vanilla pod and add it to the pan. Bring to the boil, then lower the heat and simmer for 10 minutes.

2 Remove the pan from the heat and leave to cool, then stir in the liqueur.

3 Peel the clementines. Cut some of them in half and place them all in a dish. Pour over the wine and chill.

Energy 149kcal/632kJ; Protein 0.9g; Carbohydrate 24.7g, of which sugars 24.7g; Fat 0.1g, of which saturates 0g; Cholesterol 0mg; Calcium 40mg; Fibre 1g; Sodium 12mg

FRUIT-FILLED SOUFFLÉ OMELETTE

THIS IMPRESSIVE DISH IS SURPRISINGLY QUICK AND EASY TO MAKE. THE CREAMY OMELETTE FLUFFS UP IN THE PAN, FLOPS OVER TO ENVELOP ITS FRUIT FILLING AND THEN SLIDES ON TO THE PLATE.

Preparation: 5 minutes; Cooking: 4–5 minutes

SERVES TWO

INGREDIENTS
  75g/3oz/¾ cup strawberries, hulled
  45ml/3 tbsp kirsch, brandy
    or Cointreau
  3 eggs, separated
  30ml/2 tbsp caster (superfine) sugar
  45ml/3 tbsp double (heavy)
    cream, whipped
  a few drops of vanilla extract
  25g/1oz/2 tbsp butter
  icing (confectioners') sugar, sifted

3 Melt the butter in an omelette pan. When sizzling, pour in the egg mixture and cook until set underneath, shaking occasionally. Spoon on the strawberries and liqueur and, tilting the pan, slide the omelette so that it folds over.

4 Carefully slide the omelette on to a warm serving plate, spoon over the remaining liqueur, and serve dredged with icing sugar. Cut the omelette in half, transfer to two warmed plates and eat immediately.

1 Cut the strawberries in half and place in a bowl. Pour over 30ml/2 tbsp of the liqueur and set aside to macerate.

2 Beat the egg yolks and sugar together until pale and fluffy, then fold in the whipped cream and vanilla extract. Whisk the egg whites until stiff, then carefully fold in the yolks.

COOK'S TIP
You can give your omelette a professional look by marking sizzling grill lines on top. Protecting your hand with an oven glove, hold a long, wooden-handled skewer directly over a gas flame until it becomes very hot and changes colour. Sprinkle the top of the omelette with icing sugar, then place the hot skewer on the sugar, which will caramelize very quickly. Working quickly, before the skewer becomes too cold to caramelize the sugar, make as many lines as you like.

Energy 434kcal/1802kJ; Protein 10.2g; Carbohydrate 18.4g, of which sugars 18.4g; Fat 30.7g, of which saturates 16.4g; Cholesterol 343mg; Calcium 70mg; Fibre 0.4g; Sodium 189mg

PASSION FRUIT SOUFFLÉS

IF YOU SHUN SOUFFLÉS BECAUSE YOU IMAGINE THEM TO BE DIFFICULT, TRY THESE DELIGHTFULLY EASY DESSERTS BASED ON BOUGHT CUSTARD. THEY ARE GUARANTEED TO RISE TO THE OCCASION.

Preparation: 3–4 minutes; Cooking: 8–10 minutes

SERVES FOUR

INGREDIENTS
   200ml/7fl oz/scant 1 cup ready-made
      fresh custard
   3 passion fruits
   2 egg whites
   softened butter, for greasing

1 Preheat the oven to 200°C/400°F/
Gas 6. Grease four 200ml/7fl oz/scant
1 cup ramekin dishes with the butter.

COOK'S TIP
Run the tip of the spoon handle around
the inner rim of the soufflé mixture in
each ramekin before baking to ensure
even rising.

2 Pour the custard into a large mixing
bowl. Cut the passion fruits in half.
Using a teaspoon, carefully scrape out
the seeds and juice from the halved
passion fruit so that they drop straight
on to the custard. Beat the mixture with
a metal spoon until well combined, and
set aside.

3 Whisk the egg whites until stiff, and
fold a quarter of them into the custard.
Carefully fold in the remaining egg
whites, then spoon the mixture into
the ramekin dishes. Place the dishes
on a baking sheet and bake for 8–10
minutes, or until the soufflés are well
risen. Serve immediately.

Energy 59kcal/249kJ; Protein 3.1g; Carbohydrate 8.8g, of which sugars 7.1g; Fat 1g, of which saturates 0g; Cholesterol 1mg; Calcium 48mg; Fibre 0.4g; Sodium 53mg

CHOCOLATE HAZELNUT GALETTES

THIS STUNNING DESSERT DOESN'T REQUIRE ANY COOKING, BUT YOU DO NEED TO ALLOW TIME FOR THE CHOCOLATE TO SET. IT MAKES AN IMPRESSIVE FINALE FOR A SOPHISTICATED DINNER PARTY.

Preparation: 10–12 minutes; Cooking: 0 minutes; Chilling recommended

SERVES FOUR

INGREDIENTS
175g/6oz plain (semisweet)
  chocolate, broken into squares
45ml/3 tbsp single (light) cream
30ml/2 tbsp flaked (sliced) hazelnuts
115g/4oz white chocolate, broken
  into squares
175g/6oz/¾ cup fromage frais
  or mascarpone
15ml/1 tbsp dry sherry
60ml/4 tbsp finely chopped
  hazelnuts, toasted
physalis, dipped in white chocolate,
  to decorate

1 Melt the chocolate in a small heatproof bowl over a pan of just-boiled water, then remove from the heat and stir in the cream.

2 Draw 12 x 7.5cm/3in circles on sheets of baking parchment. Turn the paper over and spread the chocolate and cream mixture over each marked circle, covering in a thin, even layer. Sprinkle flaked hazelnuts over four of the circles, then leave to set.

3 Melt the white chocolate in a heatproof bowl over just-boiled water, then stir in the fromage frais or mascarpone and dry sherry. Fold in the chopped, toasted hazelnuts. Leave to cool until the mixture holds its shape.

4 Remove the chocolate rounds carefully from the paper and sandwich them together in stacks of three, spooning the hazelnut cream between each layer and using the hazelnut-covered rounds on top. Chill for around half an hour before serving, if possible.

5 To serve, place the galettes on individual plates and decorate with chocolate-dipped physalis.

VARIATION
Use almonds instead of hazelnuts if you prefer, and add a drop or two of almond extract to the fromage frais or mascarpone mixture.

COOK'S TIP
The chocolate could be spread over heart shapes instead, for a special Valentine's Day dessert.

Energy 597kcal/2489kJ; Protein 10.7g; Carbohydrate 48.1g, of which sugars 47.2g; Fat 41.1g, of which saturates 17.5g; Cholesterol 13mg; Calcium 182mg; Fibre 2.6g; Sodium 55mg

CHOCOLATE FUDGE SUNDAES

YOU COULD PUT ON WEIGHT JUST READING THE INGREDIENTS LIST, BUT WHAT A LOVELY WAY TO DO IT. ICE CREAM, BANANAS, ALMONDS AND RICH MOCHA SYRUP MAKE FOR SHEER INDULGENCE.

Preparation: 10 minutes; Cooking: 6 minutes

SERVES FOUR

INGREDIENTS

    4 scoops each vanilla and coffee
      ice cream
    2 small ripe bananas, sliced
    whipped cream
    toasted flaked (sliced) almonds
For the sauce
    50g/2oz/¼ cup soft light brown sugar
    120ml/4fl oz/½ cup golden (light
      corn) syrup
    45ml/3 tbsp strong black coffee
    5ml/1 tsp ground cinnamon
    150g/5oz plain (semisweet)
      chocolate, chopped
    75ml/3fl oz/⅓ cup whipping cream
    45ml/3 tbsp coffee liqueur (optional)

1 To make the sauce, place the sugar, syrup, coffee and cinnamon in a heavy pan. Simmer for around 5 minutes, stirring constantly with a spoon.

2 Turn off the heat and stir in the chocolate. When melted and smooth, stir in the cream and liqueur.

3 Fill four glasses with one scoop of vanilla and another of coffee ice cream.

4 Arrange the sliced bananas over the ice cream. Pour the warm fudge sauce over the bananas, then top each sundae with a generous swirl of whipped cream. Sprinkle toasted almonds over the cream and serve at once.

VARIATION
This is a great dessert for special occasions, and you can ring the changes through the year by choosing other flavours of ice cream such as strawberry, toffee or chocolate. In the summer, substitute raspberries or strawberries for the bananas, and sprinkle chopped roasted hazelnuts on top in place of the flaked (sliced) almonds.

Energy 595kcal/2498kJ; Protein 6.3g; Carbohydrate 88.1g, of which sugars 85.3g; Fat 26.5g, of which saturates 14.1g; Cholesterol 26mg; Calcium 139mg; Fibre 1.8g; Sodium 144mg

PINEAPPLE BAKED ALASKA

NO MATTER HOW MANY TIMES YOU MAKE THIS CLASSIC PUDDING, YOU'LL ALWAYS MARVEL AT HOW THE ICE CREAM STAYS COLD UNDER ITS MERINGUE JACKET, EVEN AFTER ITS ENCOUNTER WITH A HOT OVEN.

Preparation: 5 minutes; Cooking: 5–7 minutes

SERVES THREE TO FOUR

INGREDIENTS
   3 large egg whites
   150g/5oz/¾ cup caster
   (superfine) sugar
   25g/1oz/⅓ cup desiccated (dry
   unsweetened shredded) coconut
   175–225g/6–8oz piece ready-made
   cake, such as ginger or chocolate
   6 slices ripe, peeled pineapple
   500ml/17fl oz/2 cups vanilla ice
   cream, in a brick
   a few cherries or figs, to decorate

1 Preheat the oven to 230°C/450°F/
Gas 8. Whisk the egg whites in a
grease-free bowl until stiff, then whisk
in the sugar until the mixture is stiff and
glossy. Fold in the coconut.

2 Slice the cake into two thick layers
the same rectangular shape as the ice
cream. Cut the pineapple into triangles
or quarters, cutting it over the cake to
catch any drips. On a baking sheet,
arrange the fruit on top of one slice of
cake. Top with the ice cream and then
the second layer of cake.

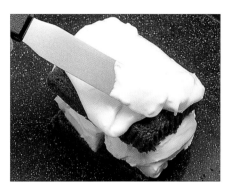

3 Spread the meringue over the cake
and ice cream, and bake in the oven for
5–7 minutes, or until turning golden.
Serve immediately, topped with fruit.

COOK'S TIP
Do not use soft-scoop ice cream for this
dessert as it will soften too quickly.

Energy 667kcal/2808kJ; Protein 10.8g; Carbohydrate 104.6g, of which sugars 93.9g; Fat 25.7g, of which saturates 9.9g; Cholesterol 33mg; Calcium 215mg; Fibre 2.3g; Sodium 317mg

INDEX